250 *Treasured* COUNTRY DESSERTS

MOUTHWATERING, TIME-HONORED,

250 *Treasured*

TRIED & TRUE, SOUL-SATISFYING,

COUNTRY

HANDED-DOWN SWEET COMFORTS

DESSERTS

Andrea Chesman & Fran Raboff

Storey Publishing

The mission of Storey Publishing is to serve our customers by
publishing practical information that encourages
personal independence in harmony with the environment.

Edited by Margaret Sutherland and Nancy D. Wood
Art direction and book design by Mary Winkelman Velgos
Cover design by Alethea Morrison
Text production by Jennifer Jepson Smith

Cover and interior illustration by © Julia Rothman

Indexed by Andrea Chesman

Some recipes previously appeared in *Mom's Best Desserts* (Storey Publishing, 2002). *Mom's Best Desserts* was originally published as *The Great American Dessert Cookbook* (The Crossing Press, 1990).

Printed in the United States by Versa Press
10 9 8 7 6 5 4 3 2 1

LIBRARY OF CONGRESS CATALOGING-IN-PUBLICATION DATA
Chesman, Andrea.
  250 treasured country desserts / by Andrea Chesman & Fran Raboff.
    p. cm.
  Includes index.
  Based on the author's Mom's best desserts, 100 classic treats
  that taste as good now as they did.
  ISBN 978-1-60342-152-2 (pbk. : alk. paper)
  1. Desserts. 2. Cookery, American. I. Raboff, Fran. II. Title.
  III. Title: Two hundred and fifty country desserts.
TX773.C521975 2009
641.8′6—dc22
                    2009013731

Contents

ACKNOWLEDGMENTS

This book has been a project that grew and grew and grew. My thanks go to Elaine Gill, who saw this book through in its earliest incarnation (*The Great American Dessert Cookbook*), to Dianne Cutillo who supported its growth and evolution into *Mom's Best Desserts,* and to Margaret Sutherland, who has helped it blossom into the book it is today. My thanks go to all of the folks at Storey who have contributed to the look and feel and reach of the book.

Everyone loves dessert, so it was not hard to solicit tasters. Still, I thank all of my tasters — witting and unwitting — at the Ripton Community Coffee House, who gave me reason to bake batch after batch of muffins and cookies. My thanks, as ever, go to Richard, Rory, Sam, and Sara for being critical tasters, appreciative eaters, and thoughtful responders.

Most of all, I'd like to thank Fran Raboff, whose drive to perfectionism and tireless testing has inspired and humbled me. I have been greatly enriched by our collaboration.

— A. C.

Baking has been one of the great pleasures of my life, more so because the results are always shared. This book is yet another way to share those pleasures with others.

I particularly enjoy the processes and changes that go into the making of a recipe. It's an ongoing adventure, always in flux, from concept to final resolution. Many people have supported me throughout this process. The first was Al Raboff, whose engineering expertise and inventive spirit frequently found its way into my kitchen as he devised new tools and materials to fuel my culinary explorations. He and our daughters, Ellen Badgley and Laura Raboff, continually encouraged me to follow my instincts and to keep challenging myself to do more.

Warmest thanks to my grandchildren, Allegra Gordon, Danielle Roth, and Jeremy Gordon for being reliable and supportive (and very willing) taste testers.

Many of the recipes in *250 Treasured Country Desserts* were tested in the cooking classes that I've taught. It has been very rewarding to prepare these recipes with my students, and a pleasure to spend time eating together and sharing in lively conversations.

I also thank Andrea Chesman, whose intelligence and insight are always valued. I have greatly appreciated the clarity and honesty in the way we've worked together as this book (and our relationship) has grown over the years.

Final thanks to Storey Publishing, particularly Pam Art, Margaret Sutherland, and their staff, for their support.

— F. R.

INTRODUCTION

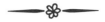

Here is a collection of truly great desserts — chocolate cake and blueberry pie, cherry cobblers and apple pandowdy, lemon meringue and chocolate cream pies, chocolate chip cookies and gingerbread men, butterscotch pudding and baked apple dumplings. The classics, the originals, the best.

When you want a birthday cake, nothing but Mom's tall devil's food cake will do. And when strawberries are finally available locally, your first impulse is to make strawberry shortcake. Likewise, gingerbread brings a smile to a friend laid up with a broken leg, and a creamy rice pudding soothes the soul after a hard week at work. We all have eaten and enjoyed the elaborate restaurant desserts created by trained pastry chefs, but we love the good old, old-fashioned desserts best — the ones our mothers and grandmothers made. That is what this book is about.

One of the heirloom recipes we tested for this book was an old "receipt" for chocolate cake that came from a Hershey's cocoa tin. At one time or another, probably half the households in the United States ate that cake. The saying may be "as American as apple pie," but the truth is that the apple pie was invented in England. What America can proudly claim as her own is the layer cake, and the chocolate layer cake may be its best example.

Baking powder, the leavening agent in layer cakes, was an American invention. Before the days of baking powder, cakes were leavened with eggs, sometimes with yeast. The egg cakes required a phenomenal amount of beating. Old recipes can be found that begin with "Separate your eggs and beat for five hours . . ." Tall cakes were layers of baked sponge cake, sandwiched with sweetened creams and jellies.

As early as the Middle Ages, professional bakers knew that baked goods could be leavened with alkaline salts. They made something called pearl ash from refined wood ash and from a type of Spanish seaweed. In northern Europe, bakers used refined salts from the ash of deer antlers.

Native Americans added wood ash to their cornmeal cakes to sweeten the batter. (The wood ash also added essential amino acids to the corn, making it a complete protein.) American colonists took the innovation a step further by using sour milk to moisten the corn cakes. When the acid of the sour milk reacted with the alkaline wood ash, bubbles of carbon dioxide were formed, which made the cakes lighter. The colonists called the wood ash *potash*, and later changed the name to *pearl ash*. By the 1790s, America was shipping tons of pearl ash to Europe.

Pearl ash was eventually replaced by *saleratus* (an early version of baking soda), which was chemically similar. Both required an acid — sour milk, buttermilk, chocolate, or molasses — to work. Saleratus was sold in little envelopes with recipes printed on the back. Imagine what a vast improvement in the housewife's life saleratus represented! She could make bread without long rising times, cakes without hours of beating eggs.

The development of the iron cooking range made the ready adoption of saleratus possible. The cookstove provided the intense heat needed for the chemical activation of saleratus, something that open fireplaces couldn't provide. Besides freeing the housewife from the slow methods of hearth cookery, the iron cookstove enabled her to utilize timesaving ingredients — including saleratus and, later, baking soda — in her baking.

Then it was discovered that baking soda plus cream of tartar could be used in a batter made with fresh milk, rather than sour milk or buttermilk. This signaled the start of the baking powder industry — and the American fascination with layer cakes. It also gave rise to the development of countless recipes for quick breads and muffins.

Pies were ever a standard in the American colonies. What better way to use fresh summer berries and cold-stored apples than to encase them in a crust made of flour and lard?

From the South come some of our most beloved pies. Sure, apple pie is a favorite, but southern states gave us pecan pie, chess pie, black bottom pie, and Key lime pie, to name a few. The South was the center of pastry innovations in part because granulated sugar was plentiful there while the rest of the country still relied on the more heavily flavored molasses and maple syrup. Skillful slave cooks contributed significantly to this period of culinary development. Also, after the Civil War, a shortage of dairy cows led to the introduction of canned condensed milk — the creamy base for Key lime pies and countless other chiffon pies. Pie, at any time of the day, even for breakfast, became the rage in the 1800s.

The history of American desserts, indeed American cooking, is a rich one. Following the Native Americans, who sweetened corn cakes, came the stern Puritans of New England, the industrious Quakers of Pennsylvania, and the prosperous colonists of Virginia. In the far North and again in the South, French colonists also exerted a profound influence. From these beginnings come our deep-dish fruit pies and cobblers, whimsically named fools, and sweet and creamy puddings.

A second wave of immigration brought Scottish-Irish, German, and Dutch cooking. Meanwhile, the African slaves can be credited with bringing both new foods and new techniques to what was to become American cooking. Into this melting pot of international cookery traditions, American foods — cornmeal, maple syrup, and an abundance of fruits and nuts — were stirred.

The very first American cookbook, Eliza Smith's *The Compleat Housewife*, was printed in Williamsburg, Virginia, in 1742 and in New York in 1764. American by imprint only, the book was a best seller in England. A few more books followed, but until 1796, these cookbooks reflected the culinary arts of England.

We know, however, from diaries and handwritten "receipt" books that a distinctive American cuisine was emerging prior to 1796, but it wasn't until that year that these new foods and dishes were committed to print — in Amelia Simmons's *American Cookery*, which was published in Hartford, Connecticut.

Simmons described herself as an American orphan, suggesting that those who aren't fortunate enough to be privy to the cooking secrets of mother and grandmother must rely on the printed word. And so began, perhaps, the whole tradition of American self-help books.

Mothers and grandmothers would have been a help in those days, even when the aid of a cookbook was available. Recipes in early cookbooks disdained measures and timing. All was approximate because ingredients and temperatures in fireplaces and woodstove ovens were hardly standardized.

Our culinary forebears invented recipes that fit the larder; they had no choice but to bake with what was at hand — flour, sugar, butter, eggs, and fresh and preserved fruit. To make things more interesting, they gave their creations whimsical names, including snickerdoodles, grunts, slumps, buckles, and dowdies. Not all the names can be explained, but all of these desserts can be enjoyed as much now as they were when Grandmother and Great-grandmother made them.

Basic Baking Tips

Experience is the best teacher when it comes to baking. Some of us were lucky enough to learn how to bake by watching our moms and grandmothers as they went about their busy days at home. Others of us have learned in classes and from books. For the book learners, here is a list of distilled baking wisdom we have gathered over the years. For further tips, see the introductions to each chapter.

Ingredients

○ **Bring ingredients to room temperature.** Soften butter by removing it from the refrigerator and letting it stand at room temperature for 30 to 45 minutes. You can speed this up by about 15 minutes by cutting the butter into chunks. When time is limited, grate the cold butter and let it stand for 10 minutes in a bowl set over (not in) hot water. A microwave will warm butter unevenly, but you can try it at 30 percent power for 30 seconds. Bring chilled eggs to room temperature quickly by placing them in a pan of very warm water for 10 to 15 minutes. Cream cheese takes about 20 minutes to soften at room temperature.

○ **Don't use imitation ingredients.** Vanilla extract, high-quality chocolate, and butter (not margarine) do make a difference.

○ **Buy ground spices in small quantities.** They lose their pungency and aroma quickly, so label the date of purchase and discard them after 6 months. For instance, freshly grated nutmeg is incomparable in flavor to ground nutmeg, which is why we recommend purchasing and grating whole nutmegs.

○ **Recipes often specify whether light or dark brown sugar will yield the better results.** Dark brown sugar has more flavor, but feel free to use whichever type you have on hand. Brown sugar is usually pressed down firmly in a cup for measuring.

○ **Although many baking books insist on using unsalted butter in all recipes, we do not.** Whether you prefer salted or unsalted butter is a matter of regional and personal taste. The salt acts as a preservative and sometimes masks off flavors. So the choice is yours.

If using salted butter, you do not have to adjust the amount of salt the recipe requires.

✪ **Toast nuts before adding them to the batter, to maximize flavor.** Nuts should be toasted whole, then chopped. (It is a good idea to taste them before using to make sure they haven't gone rancid.) To toast nuts, preheat the oven to 300°F. Spread out the nuts in a single layer on a baking sheet and toast for 6 to 8 minutes, stirring once, until the nuts are slightly colored and fragrant. Let cool, then chop as needed.

Equipment

✪ **The first step in most recipes is preheating the oven and preparing the baking pans.** Unless otherwise specified, the oven rack should be put in the middle of the oven. It takes 10 to 15 minutes to preheat most ovens.

✪ **Glass bakeware conducts and retains heat better than metal,** so your dessert may bake more quickly in glass pans than in metal ones. If your baked good seems to be browning too quickly, reduce the oven temperature by 25 degrees.

✪ **To figure out if you have the correct-size baking dish for a specific recipe** (if it's not marked on the pan), use a ruler to check the dimensions from inside edge to inside edge. Measure the depth from the inside. Measure the volume of a pan (for example, a 1½-quart baking dish) by filling it with water and then pouring off the water into a measuring cup.

✪ **Use nesting dry measuring cups to measure most dry ingredients** (such as flour and sugar) accurately. A set usually contains ¼-, ⅓-, ½-, and 1-cup sizes. Spoon the ingredient into a dry measuring cup, then level off the top with the straight edge of a knife. Don't tap the cup or press down on the ingredients.

✪ **Use clear, spouted measuring cups when measuring liquids.** Hold the cup at eye level and fill to the appropriate line. To measure maple syrup, honey, oil, or other sticky liquids, rinse the measuring cup in hot water first. The liquid will pour out more cleanly. If you can, measure oil first, then sweeteners.

Techniques

✪ **Planning ahead is key.** Read your recipe and line up the ingredients on the counter, preferably in the order called for in the recipe. As each ingredient is used, set it aside. When the phone rings or the kids shout from another room, you can come back to the mixing bowl knowing whether the salt has already been added.

✪ **To grease a pan, put a little butter or solid shortening in the pan.** Use a piece of butter wrapping, waxed paper, or paper towel to spread the butter over the bottom and up the sides of the pan.

✪ **Measure shortening or softened butter by packing it into a measuring cup, then leveling it off with a knife.** The wrapping on sticks of butter shows where to cut for tablespoon measures. One stick of butter equals ½ cup or 8 tablespoons. Do not use whipped butter in baking; it contains 30 to 45 percent air and won't measure accurately.

✪ **Before beating egg whites, make sure that your bowl and beaters are clean** by rinsing with vinegar, then clean water. Dry carefully.

○ **You can use either a flour sifter or any fine-mesh sieve to sift flour.**

○ **When you are baking in more than one pan at a time, leave space between the pans** and make sure there is at least 6 inches of space between oven racks. Rotate the pans from front to back and top to bottom when halfway through baking.

○ **If your baked goods are baking too fast or too slowly, check to make sure the oven temperature is accurate.** Oven thermometers are available at kitchen supply stores.

○ **Always cool baked goods completely, on a wire rack, before storing.** This includes cakes filled or frosted with whipped cream, cheesecakes, cream pies, and puddings. Perishable desserts should be stored, well wrapped, in the refrigerator and eaten within 3 days.

○ **Generally speaking, most baked goods, well wrapped in aluminum foil and placed in an airtight bag, can be frozen for 2 to 3 months.** Unfrosted cakes freeze more successfully than do frosted cakes.

Basic Equipment

Having a well-equipped kitchen makes baking easier. For the majority of recipes in this book, all you will need are the standard assortment of baking pans, mixing bowls, and utensils that most kitchens have. Here are the ones we use most frequently.

○ **Measuring cups for liquid** (these are see-through and have pouring spouts)

○ **Measuring cups for dry measures** (these have flat tops for leveling the ingredients)

○ **Measuring spoons** (two or more sets will be handy)

○ **Mixing bowls in assorted sizes** (a heat-proof metal bowl can double as the top of a double boiler)

○ **Rubber spatulas, for scraping bowls**

○ **Flour sifter**

○ **Rolling pin**

○ **Pastry brush, for applying glazes**

○ **Handheld electric beater or standing mixer**

○ **Baking sheets**

○ **8-inch square baking pan**

○ **8-inch round baking pans**

○ **9- by 13-inch rectangular baking pan**

○ **9- by 5-inch loaf pan**

○ **9-inch pie pans**

○ **9-inch square baking pan**

○ **9-inch round cake pans**

○ **10-inch Bundt pan**

○ **10-inch tube pan with removable bottom**

○ **Standard 12-cup muffin pan**

○ **Kitchen timer**

○ **Wire cooling racks**

Baker's Wish List

If you love to bake and have the space, here are additional tools you might want to acquire.

○ **Pastry wheel**

○ **Pastry cutter**

○ **Assorted cookie cutters**

○ **Pastry bag and tips**

○ **Pie weights or bakers beans, for baking unfilled pie shells**

○ **Pastry scraper, to lift dough**

○ **Offset spatula or palette knife, for spreading frosting**

○ **8- or 9-inch springform pan**

○ **Angel food cake pan**

- Half sheet cake pan (11 by 17 inches)
- Scissors, for cutting dried fruit
- Metal microplane, for grating chocolate and citrus zest
- Small (1½-ounce) trigger-style ice cream scoop, for measuring cookie dough or scooping up small ice cream balls
- Flour shaker, for sprinkling work surface or baking sheet
- Confectioners' sugar shaker
- Oven thermometer
- Candy thermometer

Every Day Is a Holiday

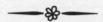

EVERY DAY IS A REASON FOR A DESSERT, but some days are official days to celebrate specific desserts. Some are declared by presidential proclamation or by Congress or other federal government organizations, such as the USDA and the FDA, or by state or even city governments. Other sources are industry groups, such as the National Confectioners' Association (National Chocolate Day) and the American Egg Board. Some are declared by individual companies.

January 2	National Cream Puff Day	February 1	National Baked Alaska Day
January 5	National Whipped Cream Day	February 3	National Carrot Cake Day
January 6	National Shortbread Day	February 10	National Cream Cheese Brownie Day
January 9	National Apricot Day	February 11	National Peppermint Patty Day
January 10	National Bittersweet Chocolate Day	February 16	National Almond Day
January 13	National Peach Melba Day	February 17	National Indian Pudding Day
January 15	National Strawberry Ice Cream Day	February 19	National Chocolate Mint Day
January 16	National Fig Newton Day	February 20	National Cherry Pie Day
January 20	National Buttercrunch Day	February 27	National Chocolate Cake Day
January 22	National Blonde Brownie Day	February 27	National Strawberry Day
January 23	National Pie Day	March 1	National Peanut Butter Lovers' Day
January 23	National Rhubarb Pie Day	March 1	National Fruit Compote Day
January 24	National Peanut Butter Day	March 2	National Banana Cream Pie Day

March 4	National Poundcake Day	July 20	National Ice Cream Day
March 15	National Peanut Lovers' Day	July 23	National Vanilla Ice Cream Day
March 29	National Lemon Chiffon Cake Day	July 25	National Hot Fudge Sundae Day
April 3	National Chocolate Mousse Day	July 30	National Cheesecake Day
April 7	National Coffee Cake Day	August 2	National Ice Cream Sandwich Day
April 13	National Peach Cobbler Day	August 4	National Chocolate Chip Day
April 14	National Pecan Day	August 9	National Rice Pudding Day
April 20	National Pineapple Upside-Down Cake Day	August 15	National Lemon Meringue Pie Day
		August 17	National Vanilla Custard Day
April 28	National Blueberry Pie Day	August 18	National Ice Cream Pie Day
April 30	National Oatmeal Cookie Day	August 20	National Chocolate Pecan Pie Day
May 1–7	National Raisin Week	August 23	National Spongecake Day
May 8	National Coconut Cream Pie Day	August 24	National Peach Pie Day
May 13	National Apple Pie Day	September 17	National Apple Dumpling Day
May 17	National Cherry Cobbler Day	September 19	National Butterscotch Pudding Day
May 19	National Devil's Food Cake Day	October 5	National Apple Betty Day
May 22	National Vanilla Pudding Day	October 9	National Dessert Day
May 31	National Macaroon Day	October 10	National Angel Food Cake Day
June 5	National Gingerbread Day	October 18	National Chocolate Cupcake Day
June 6	National Applesauce Cake Day	October 22	National Nut Day
June 7	National Chocolate Ice Cream Day	October 23	National Boston Cream Pie Day
June 9	National Strawberry-Rhubarb Pie Day	October 28	National Chocolate Day
June 11	National German Chocolate Cake Day	November 10	National Vanilla Cupcake Day
June 12	National Peanut Butter Cookie Day	November 13	National Indian Pudding Day
June 14	National Strawberry Shortcake Day	November 26	National Cake Day
June 17	National Apple Strudel Day	December 1	National Pie Day
June 23	National Pecan Sandies Day	December 2	National Fritters Day
June 26	National Chocolate Pudding Day	December 4	National Cookie Day
July 1	National Gingersnap Day	December 8	National Brownie Day
July 5	National Apple Turnover Day	December 12	National Ambrosia Day
July 9	National Sugar Cookie Day	December 25	National Pumpkin Pie Day
July 12	National Pecan Pie Day	December 27	National Fruitcake Day
July 17	National Peach Ice Cream Day		

Cookies

Most of us begin our dessert-making apprentice-ship with cookies. Many recipes, especially ones for drop cookies (no rolling pin required), are so simple to make that even kids can tackle them, with a little parental supervision. Most cookie doughs are forgiving and can be handled by unskilled hands and still result in beautiful and tasty treats.

Whether you are a kid or a grown-up, whether your tastes run to chocolate or nuts, spice or vanilla, crisp or chewy, there is bound to be a cookie favorite in this chapter. Home-baked cook-ies still warm from the oven are one of life's simple pleasures.

Ingredients

○ **Don't use imitation ingredients.** Use vanilla extract, high-quality chocolate, and butter (not margarine). Avoid artificial ingredients.

○ **Butter should always be used at room temperature to ensure that it is fully blended with the sugar.** Lumps of cold, hard butter in the dough will cause flat cookies.

○ **Chocolate should be melted over low heat to avoid scorching.** The easiest way to do this is in a double boiler set over a pan of barely simmering water. If you don't have a double boiler, you can fashion one by placing a metal mixing bowl over, not in, a saucepan of barely simmering water.

○ **Toast nuts before adding them to the batter, to maximize flavor.** Nuts should be toasted whole, then chopped. (It is a good idea to taste them before using, to make sure they haven't gone rancid.) To toast, preheat the oven to 300°F. Spread out the nuts in a single layer on a baking sheet and toast for 7 to 10 minutes, stirring once, until the nuts are slightly colored and fragrant. Let them cool, then chop.

○ **Raisins that are hard and shriveled going into the cookie dough will be hard and shriveled in the baked cookie.** To reconstitute, pour boiling water over them and let them sit for 10 minutes. Then drain off the water and proceed as the recipe directs. For additional flavor, soak raisins in wine, brandy, or fruit juice.

Equipment

○ **Always start by preheating the oven with an oven rack in the middle of the oven, unless the recipe specifies otherwise.**

○ **Do not grease the baking sheets unless the recipe requires it.**

○ **Parchment paper is the baker's best friend;** it prevents cookies from sticking to the pan and makes cleanup very simple. There is no need to grease parchment paper when baking cookies. Also, when baking multiple batches of cookies, you can place unbaked cookies on parchment paper and slide the whole thing onto a baking sheet after it has been used for the first batch of cookies. Pop the pan into the oven, and then start your third batch on another piece of parchment paper.

○ **If your cookies are browning too much on the bottom, your pan may be the problem.** Shiny, light-colored baking sheets do a better job of evenly browning the bottoms than dark sheets do. Next time, cover the pan with parchment paper or aluminum foil.

○ **If your baking sheets are thin and the cookie bottoms burn, try stacking two pans together to create an insulated cookie pan.** You may have to increase the baking time slightly.

Techniques

○ **Carefully measure out the batter to keep cookie size consistent.** Cookies that are the same size will bake in the same amount of time. A small (1½-ounce), trigger-style ice cream scoop makes portioning cookie dough easy.

✪ **You can shape dropped cookies by forming them into balls.** If you flatten the balls of dough before they bake, they will be more uniform in shape than they will be if you let them spread naturally. To flatten them, use the bottom of a glass dipped in sugar.

✪ **The most difficult part of making rolled cookies is keeping the dough from sticking to the work surface.** If too much flour is used, the dough becomes tough. Instead of simply flouring your work surface, try using a mix of equal parts flour and confectioners' sugar.

✪ **When making rolled cookies, gather together all the scraps of dough, form them into a ball, and roll out the dough again.** If the dough is too soft to handle easily or is sticking to the work surface, chill it in the freezer for 5 to 10 minutes before rolling.

✪ **Don't crowd the cookies on a pan.** Generally leave 1 to 2 inches of space between cookies.

✪ **Unless a recipe specifies otherwise, cookies can be baked on two baking sheets at a time.** If the baking sheets don't fit on the oven rack side by side, place them on the middle and bottom racks. Halfway through the baking time, switch the trays and rotate them 180 degrees for even baking. When baking only one sheet at a time, place it on the oven rack in the middle of the oven.

✪ **Do not overbake cookies.** If a recipe specifies baking for 10 minutes, check for doneness after 8 minutes. Generally, cookies are done when they are lightly colored around the edges and appear dry on top.

✪ **The most common reason why cookies burn is that the baker was distracted.** The very best way to avoid overbaking cookies is to set a timer each time a batch goes in.

✪ **Remove cookies from the pan when they are firm enough to handle.** If the cookies are very delicate and threaten to break as you slide a spatula under them, you can bake them on a parchment paper–lined pan and then remove the entire sheet of parchment paper with the cookies still on it. Set the sheet on wire racks to cool.

✪ **Store completely cooled cookies in an airtight container at room temperature.** Cookies are at their best within a few days of baking. If cookies soften, they can be made crisp by putting them on a baking sheet in a 300°F oven for 5 to 8 minutes.

Chocolate Chip Cookies

Does anyone ever outgrow the childhood pleasure of biting into a chewy chocolate chip cookie, still warm from the oven? This is a classic recipe for America's favorite cookie, at its best when served with a glass of cold milk.

Makes about 100 small cookies

2¼ cups sifted unbleached all-purpose flour
1 teaspoon salt
1 cup (2 sticks) butter, at room temperature
¾ cup firmly packed light brown sugar

¾ cup granulated sugar
2 large eggs, beaten
1 teaspoon baking soda
1 teaspoon hot water
2 cups chocolate chips
1 cup chopped walnuts or pecans
1 teaspoon vanilla extract

1. Preheat the oven to 375°F. Lightly grease two baking sheets.

2. Sift together the flour and salt.

3. Cream together the butter, brown sugar, and granulated sugar in a large bowl. Beat in the eggs. Combine the baking soda and hot water and add to the creamed mixture. Stir in the flour mixture, and then stir in the chocolate chips, nuts, and vanilla.

4. Drop rounded teaspoons of the dough onto the prepared baking sheets about 1 inch apart.

5. Bake for 8 to 10 minutes, until the cookies are golden.

6. Transfer the cookies to wire racks to cool.

Birth of the
Chocolate Chip Cookie

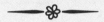

THERE WAS A TIME, NOT SO LONG AGO, when chocolate came in great slabs; there were no chips, bits, or morsels. In 1933, Mrs. Ruth Wakefield was making a batch of butter dewdrop cookies (or butter dropdos; accounts vary) for the guests at the Toll House Inn in Whitman, Massachusetts, and she was in a rush. Instead of melting the chocolate as her recipe required, she decided to chop up the chocolate and let it melt into the cookies as they baked. The chocolate bits retained their shape, and the chocolate chip cookie was born.

At first Mrs. Wakefield called them chocolate crunch cookies (or chocolate crispies, again depending on whose account you read), but soon she changed the name to Toll House cookies. Before long, the recipe was published in a newspaper, and sales of Nestlé chocolate began to rise. Recognizing a good thing when it saw the sales charts, Nestlé began printing the recipe (with Mrs. Wakefield's permission) on packages of specially scored chocolate bars that broke easily into bits. A few years later, Nestlé bought the legal rights to use the Toll House trade name and began marketing chocolate chips. In 1997, the Massachusetts State Legislature declared the chocolate chip the official state cookie.

Chocolate Chocolate-Chip Cookies

Chocolate chip cookies are a perfect cookie, but the chocolate quotient is limited. This cookie is for chocolate lovers who aren't satisfied with a brown-sugar cookie dotted here and there with chocolate.

Makes about 36 cookies

- 4 ounces unsweetened chocolate, coarsely chopped
- 4 ounces dark or bittersweet chocolate, coarsely chopped
- ½ cup (1 stick) butter, cut into pieces
- 1 cup unbleached all-purpose flour
- ½ teaspoon baking powder
- ½ teaspoon salt

- 3 large eggs
- 1¼ cups firmly packed light or dark brown sugar
- 2 teaspoons vanilla extract
- 1 cup chocolate chips
- 1 cup walnut or pecan pieces
- ½ cup granulated sugar

1. Melt the unsweetened chocolate, dark chocolate, and butter in the top of a double boiler set over simmering water. Stir until completely smooth and glossy. Remove the top of the double boiler from the heat and let cool slightly.

2. Whisk the flour, baking powder, and salt in a medium bowl.

3. Beat the eggs and brown sugar in a large bowl with an electric mixer set at medium-high speed until very thick, about 4 minutes. Beat in the vanilla until well mixed. Reduce the speed to low and add the chocolate mixture. Beat until well mixed.

4. Fold in the flour mixture with a spatula. Fold in the chocolate chips and nuts. Cover the bowl and let stand at room temperature for 30 minutes to stiffen the batter.

5. Preheat the oven to 350°F. Line three baking sheets with parchment paper.

6. Using a small, trigger-style ice cream or cookie scoop or a tablespoon, form the cookie dough into walnut-size balls and roll in the sugar. Place about 2 inches apart on the prepared baking sheets.

7. Bake, one sheet at a time, on the middle rack of the oven for 12 to 14 minutes, until the cookies spread out and look dry.

8. Transfer the parchment paper to racks and cool the cookies before removing them from the paper.

Chocolate Chip Brownie Drop Cookies

These quick and delicious cookies have the taste and texture of brownies, which makes them simply irresistible to the average chocoholic, whose numbers are legion.

Makes 30 to 40 cookies

½ cup unbleached all-purpose flour
¼ teaspoon baking soda
   Pinch of salt
1½ cups chocolate chips
4 tablespoons butter, at room temperature

¾ cup sugar
1 large egg
1½ teaspoons vanilla extract
½ cup chopped toasted walnuts, optional

1. Preheat the oven to 350°F. Butter two large baking sheets.

2. Whisk the flour, baking soda, and salt in a small bowl.

3. Melt 1 cup of the chocolate chips in the top of a double boiler set over simmering water. Stir until completely smooth. Remove the top of the double boiler from the heat and let cool slightly.

4. Beat together the butter and sugar in a large bowl until creamy. Add the egg and vanilla and beat until fluffy. Mix in the melted chocolate. Stir in the flour mixture, blending thoroughly. Add the remaining ½ cup chocolate chips and the walnuts, (if using), stirring until combined.

5. Drop rounded teaspoons of the dough onto the prepared baking sheets about 2 inches apart.

6. Bake the cookies, one sheet at a time, for 8 minutes. Do not overbake; the tops will be soft, but will firm up as they cool.

7. Transfer the cookies to wire racks to cool.

Oatmeal Chocolate Chip Cookies

These cookies are the best of the best: a cross between chocolate chip cookies and oatmeal raisin cookies. It is the combination of cinnamon and chocolate that proves utterly irresistible.

Makes 30 to 40 cookies

1½ cups unbleached all-purpose flour
1½ teaspoons ground cinnamon
¾ teaspoon baking powder
¾ teaspoon baking soda
½ teaspoon salt
¾ cup (1½ sticks) butter, at room temperature
¾ cup firmly packed light brown sugar

¾ cup granulated sugar
2 large eggs
2 teaspoons vanilla extract
2 cups rolled oats (not quick-cooking)
1½ cups chocolate chips
1 cup chopped walnuts or pecans

1. Preheat the oven to 375°F.

2. Sift the flour, cinnamon, baking powder, baking soda, and salt into a medium bowl.

3. Combine the butter, brown sugar, granulated sugar, eggs, and vanilla in a large bowl. Beat until creamy. Add the flour mixture and beat until blended. Beat in the oats, chocolate chips, and nuts.

4. Drop rounded tablespoons of the dough 2 inches apart on ungreased baking sheets.

5. Bake for 12 to 15 minutes, until the cookies are golden.

6. Let the cookies cool on the baking sheets for a few minutes. Then use a spatula to carefully transfer the cookies to wire racks to cool completely.

Oatmeal Cookies

Studded with raisins and nuts, these are satisfying, homey cookies. A bite conjures up images of *Leave-It-to-Beaver* moms and after-school snacks of cookies and milk.

Makes about 60 cookies

1½ cups unbleached all-purpose flour
1 teaspoon baking soda
1 teaspoon ground cinnamon
½ teaspoon salt
1 cup (2 sticks) butter, at room temperature
1 cup firmly packed dark brown sugar
½ cup granulated sugar

2 large eggs
2 tablespoons molasses
¼ cup hot water
1 teaspoon vanilla extract
3 cups rolled oats (not quick-cooking)
1½ cups raisins
1 cup chopped walnuts (optional)

1. Preheat the oven to 375°F.

2. Sift the flour, baking soda, cinnamon, and salt into a medium bowl.

3. Beat together the butter, brown sugar, and granulated sugar in a large bowl until creamy. Add the eggs, one at a time, beating well after each addition. Mix in the molasses, hot water, and vanilla, beating until fluffy. Stir in the flour mixture, blending thoroughly. Add the oats, raisins, and walnuts (if using), stirring until combined.

4. Drop rounded tablespoons of the dough 2 inches apart on ungreased baking sheets. Press with a wet spoon or spatula to flatten.

5. Bake for 12 to 15 minutes, until the cookies are golden.

6. Let the cookies cool on the baking sheets for a few minutes. Then use a spatula to carefully transfer the cookies to wire racks to cool completely.

Crispy Oatmeal Raisin Cookies

Some people prefer their oatmeal cookies soft and chewy; others like them crisp. These are for the crispy-crunchy fans. But no one likes a crunchy raisin; if your raisins are not soft, soak them in hot water for 10 minutes, then drain and pat dry before starting.

Makes about 36 cookies

¾ cup raisins
½ cup (1 stick) butter
¼ cup water
1 teaspoon vanilla extract
1 cup firmly packed light or dark
    brown sugar
¾ cup sifted unbleached all-purpose
    flour

½ teaspoon baking soda
½ teaspoon ground cinnamon
½ teaspoon salt
¼ teaspoon ground ginger
¼ teaspoon freshly grated nutmeg
⅛ teaspoon ground cloves
1½ cups rolled oats (not quick-
    cooking)

1. Preheat the oven to 350°F. Line two baking sheets with parchment paper.

2. Combine the raisins, butter, and water in a medium saucepan over medium heat. Cook, stirring, until the butter melts. Remove from the heat and stir in the vanilla and the brown sugar. Let cool.

3. Mix together the flour, baking soda, cinnamon, salt, ginger, nutmeg, and cloves in a medium bowl until thoroughly combined, and then blend into the raisin mixture in the saucepan. Stir in the oats. The mixture will be quite dense.

4. Drop rounded teaspoons of the dough onto the prepared baking sheets about 2 inches apart. Flatten slightly with the back of a wet tablespoon.

5. Bake, one sheet at a time, on the middle rack of the oven for 12 to 15 minutes, until the cookies are golden brown.

6. Transfer the sheets to racks and cool the cookies before removing them from the baking sheets.

Soft and Chewy Oatmeal Cookies

These cookies are a wonderful choice for making any type of cookie sandwich. Chocolate ganache and marshmallow filling are both delicious, and a small scoop of ice cream works well too.

Makes 24 to 30 cookies

1½ cups unbleached all-purpose flour	¾ cup firmly packed light brown sugar
1 teaspoon baking soda	¾ cup granulated sugar
½ teaspoon ground cinnamon	2 large eggs, at room temperature
¼ teaspoon freshly grated nutmeg	⅓ cup applesauce
½ teaspoon salt	1½ teaspoons vanilla extract
1½ cups rolled oats (not quick-cooking)	1 cup raisins, chocolate chips, or chopped toasted walnuts or a combination (optional)
½ cup (1 stick) butter, at room temperature	

1. Preheat the oven to 375°F. Line two baking sheets with parchment paper.

2. Whisk the flour, baking soda, cinnamon, nutmeg, and salt in a medium bowl. Add the oats and mix until combined.

3. Combine the butter, brown sugar, and granulated sugar in a large bowl; beat until creamy. Beat in the eggs, one at a time, and then mix in the applesauce and vanilla. Add the flour mixture and mix until blended. Stir in the raisins (if using).

4. For each cookie, drop 1 small, trigger-style ice cream scoop of dough (about 2 rounded tablespoons) onto the parchment paper, placing them about 3 inches apart to allow the cookies to spread. Press down on the dough with wet fingers to spread the dough mixture into a circle about 2½ inches in diameter and a little less than ¼ inch thick.

5. Bake, one sheet at a time, for 10 to 13 minutes, until the cookies are light brown at the edges and dry to the touch but still soft in the middle.

6. Let the cookies cool on the sheet for a few minutes, then transfer with a spatula to a wire rack to cool completely.

Vanilla Cookies

These are rather plain cookies, waiting to be dressed up for a special occasion — perhaps made into a sandwich cookie (see page 13) or an ice cream sandwich. If you aren't planning to embellish this cookie with a filling, consider spicing it up with ¼ teaspoon each of freshly grated nutmeg and ground cinnamon.

Makes about 36 cookies

- 2¾ cups unbleached all-purpose flour
- 1 teaspoon baking powder
- ½ teaspoon baking soda
- ½ teaspoon salt
- 1 cup (2 sticks) butter, at room temperature
- 1¼ cups plus ⅛ cup granulated sugar
- ¼ cup firmly packed light brown sugar
- 1 large egg
- 1 tablespoon plain yogurt or sour cream
- 1½ teaspoons vanilla extract

1. Whisk the flour, baking powder, baking soda, and salt in a medium bowl.

2. Combine the butter, the 1¼ cups granulated sugar, and the brown sugar in a large bowl. Beat until light and creamy. Beat in the egg, yogurt, and vanilla. Add the flour mixture and mix until blended. Cover the bowl and refrigerate for 45 minutes, until the dough is chilled enough to handle.

3. Preheat the oven to 375°F. Line two baking sheets with parchment paper.

4. Put the ⅛ cup granulated sugar in a small dish. Shape the dough into balls the size of large walnuts and roll them in the sugar. Place the balls 3 inches apart on the prepared baking sheets. With a small glass, press down on each dough ball until it flattens to a 2½-inch circle about ¼ inch thick.

5. Bake for 8 to 10 minutes, just until the cookies start to turn light brown at the edges and are dry to the touch but still soft in the middle.

6. Let the cookies cool on the baking sheets for a minute or two. Lift off the parchment paper with the cookies still on it and place on a countertop to cool quickly. When the cookies are firm, remove with a spatula. The cookies are best if used as soon as possible after baking.

Oatmeal Sandwich Cookies

What's better than a rich, chewy oatmeal cookie? A cookie that is sandwiched with chocolate. Or, if chocolate is not your ideal, try the filling for Whoopie Pies, on page 48.

Makes 12 to 15 cookies

....

24–30 Soft and Chewy Oatmeal Cookies
(page 11)
Chocolate Ganache (page 145)

....

1. To make sandwich cookies, lay half of the cookies bottom-side up. Spread the ganache on the bottom-side-up cookies. Sandwich the other cookies on top, with the bottom-side down on the ganache.

2. Serve immediately. Or store in an airtight container and freeze for up to 1 week. Or wrap individually and freeze.

Vanilla Sandwich Cookies

Sandwich cookies are double the pleasure. The only trick is to make the cookies as identically shaped as possible. Using a small, trigger-style ice cream scoop (the 1½-inch size) will help with this.

Makes 15 to 18 cookies

....

Vanilla Cookies (page 12)
Chocolate Ganache (page 145)

....

1. To make sandwich cookies, lay half of the cookies bottom-side up. Spread the ganache on the bottom-side-up cookies. Layer the other cookies on top, with the bottom-side down on the ganache.

2. Serve immediately. Or store in an airtight container and freeze for up to 1 week. Or wrap individually and freeze.

Peanut Butter Cookies

Peanuts are thought to have originated in Brazil and found their way to Europe with Portuguese explorers. From Europe, peanuts spread throughout the world, making the journey from Africa to North America via African slaves. Since the Civil War, peanuts have been an important agricultural crop in the South, where the little ground nut is also known as a ground-pea and as a goober.

In 1890, peanut butter was invented by a St. Louis doctor who promoted it as a health food. It was an instant hit in the United States. But to most of the world, peanuts are valued primarily as a source of oil and as cattle feed. What a shame!

Makes about 36 cookies

....

1¾ cups unbleached all-purpose flour
½ teaspoon baking powder
½ teaspoon baking soda
½ teaspoon salt
½ cup (1 stick) butter, at room
    temperature
½ cup crunchy peanut butter
½ cup firmly packed dark brown
    sugar

½ cup granulated sugar
1 large egg
2 tablespoons freshly squeezed
    orange juice
1 teaspoon vanilla extract
½ cup chopped peanuts, to garnish

....

1. Sift the flour, baking powder, baking soda, and salt into a medium bowl.

2. Beat together the butter, peanut butter, brown sugar, and granulated sugar in a large bowl until creamy. Beat in the egg. Mix in the orange juice and vanilla, beating until fluffy. Stir in the flour mixture, blending thoroughly. Wrap in plastic wrap and refrigerate the dough for 1 hour, until firm.

3. Preheat the oven to 350°F.

4. Shape the dough into 1-inch balls. Arrange them 2 inches apart on ungreased baking sheets. Flatten the balls with a wet fork, pressing a crisscross pattern into each top. Sprinkle with the chopped peanuts.

5. Bake for 8 to 10 minutes, until the cookies are golden.

6. Let the cookies cool on the baking sheets for a few minutes. Use a spatula to carefully transfer them to wire racks to cool completely.

Why the Crisscross?

COOKIES THAT ARE FORMED AS BALLS and then flattened will be more uniform in size than cookies that are left to spread naturally. Peanut butter cookie dough is pretty dense, so it is easier to flatten them with a fork than with your hands. A peanut butter cookie recipe in a 1931 Pillsbury cookbook recommended the crisscross pattern, and bakers have followed that advice ever since.

Peanut Butter Blossoms

These cookies were originally a Pillsbury Bake-Off–winning recipe, which will come as no surprise once you taste this delicious combination of chocolate and peanut butter. Then they were made with Hersey's milk chocolate kisses, but I think a superior cookie is made with dark chocolate kisses. See what you think.

Makes about 36 cookies

¾ cup smooth peanut butter
½ cup (1 stick) butter, at room temperature
½ cup firmly packed dark or light brown sugar
½ cup granulated sugar
1 large egg

1 teaspoon vanilla extract
1½ cups unbleached all-purpose flour
1 teaspoon baking powder
½ teaspoon baking soda
½ teaspoon ground cinnamon
Approximately 36 dark chocolate kisses, unwrapped

1. Preheat the oven to 350°F.

2. Combine the peanut butter, butter, brown sugar, and granulated sugar in a food processor and process until well blended. Add the egg and vanilla, and process until well blended. Add the flour, baking powder, baking soda, and cinnamon. Process until the dough comes together. The dough should be soft enough to hold together in a ball.

3. Pinch off bits of dough the size of walnuts and roll them in your hands to form smooth balls. Place about 2 inches apart on ungreased baking sheets.

4. Bake, one sheet at a time, for 8 to 9 minutes, until the cookies are just barely done. Remove from the oven and immediately position a chocolate kiss in the center of each cookie, pressing gently. The cookies will crack but not break. Return to the oven to bake for 1 minute longer.

5. Let the cookies cool on the baking sheet for at least 5 minutes before removing them to finish cooling on wire racks.

Snickerdoodles

Like many American cookies, these are probably the invention of the Pennsylvania Dutch. We're not sure what the name conjures up (it's probably a nonsense word), but snickerdoodles emerge from the oven as round little pillows delicately flavored with a cinnamon-and-sugar coating.

Makes about 60 cookies

2¾ cups unbleached all-purpose flour
1 teaspoon baking soda
1 teaspoon cream of tartar
½ teaspoon salt
¼ teaspoon freshly grated nutmeg
1⅛ cups plus 3 tablespoons sugar

1 cup (2 sticks) butter or vegetable shortening, at room temperature
2 large eggs
1 teaspoon vanilla extract
1 tablespoon ground cinnamon

1. Sift the flour, baking soda, cream of tartar, salt, and nutmeg into a medium bowl.

2. Beat together the 1⅛ cups sugar and the butter in a large bowl until creamy. Add the eggs, one at a time, beating well after each addition. Add the vanilla. Stir in the flour mixture, blending thoroughly.

3. Wrap the dough in plastic wrap and refrigerate for 1 hour.

4. Preheat the oven to 375°F.

5. Combine the cinnamon and the 3 tablespoons sugar in a small bowl. Shape the dough into 1-inch balls. Roll the balls in the cinnamon-sugar mixture. Arrange the cookies 2 inches apart on ungreased baking sheets.

6. Bake for 12 minutes, until the cookies are golden.

7. Transfer the cookies to wire racks to cool completely.

Jam Thumbprints

Considering how pretty they look sitting on a plate, these cookies are surprisingly easy to make. Though kids love them, Jam Thumbprints aren't your basic after-school treat; they are special-occasion cookies, worthy of the good china. If you can, use two types of jam, perhaps apricot and raspberry, and the cookies will sparkle.

Makes about 5 dozen cookies

2¼ cups all-purpose flour
1 cup confectioners' sugar
½ teaspoon baking soda
¼ teaspoon salt
½ cup finely ground almonds
1 (8-ounce) package cream cheese,
    at room temperature

¾ cup (1½ sticks) butter, at room
    temperature
½ teaspoon vanilla extract
⅓–½ cup jam

1. Sift the flour, confectioners' sugar, baking soda, and salt into a medium bowl. Stir in the ground almonds.

2. Combine the cream cheese and butter in a food processor and process until smooth. Add the vanilla and process until combined. Add the flour mixture and process until well blended.

3. Form the dough into a ball, wrap it in plastic wrap, and refrigerate for at least 30 minutes.

4. Preheat the oven to 350°F. Line three baking sheets with parchment paper.

5. Shape the dough into 1-inch balls. Place 1½ inches apart on the prepared baking sheets. Using the handle of a wooden spoon, make a generous indentation in the center of each cookie, twisting the handle to spread the opening. (You can use your thumb, but a spoon makes a neater hole.) Using the tip of a pointed teaspoon (not a measuring spoon), fill with ¼ to ½ teaspoon jam. You want a generous amount of jam, but don't overfill; make the holes bigger if necessary.

6. Bake for 14 to 16 minutes, until the cookies are light golden brown.

7. Transfer the cookies to wire racks to cool.

Russian Tea Cakes

You might know these melt-in-your-mouth cookies as Mexican wedding cakes, snow balls, moldy mice, sandies, sand tarts, or butterballs. The recipe is one and the same. Outside of the United States, you might encounter these cookies as *biscochitos* (in Mexico), tea cakes (in Sweden), *dandulas kiflik* (in Bulgaria), *biscochos* (in Cuba), *des kourabi* (in Greece), *polvorones* (in Italy and Spain), and *rohlichky* (in Ukraine).

Makes about 36 cookies

1 *cup pecans, walnuts, or hazelnuts, toasted*
2 *cups confectioners' sugar*
1 *cup (2 sticks) butter, at room temperature*
½ *teaspoon vanilla extract*
2 *cups unbleached all-purpose flour*
½ *teaspoon salt*

1. Put the nuts and 1 cup of the confectioners' sugar in a food processor. Process until the nuts are finely ground. Add the butter and vanilla and beat until light and fluffy. Beat in the flour and salt until combined. Cover and refrigerate the dough for about 1 hour, until firm.

2. Preheat the oven to 350°F. Line two baking sheets with parchment paper.

3. Form the dough into 1-inch balls and place them 2 inches apart on the prepared baking sheets.

4. Bake for 15 to 20 minutes, until the cookies are lightly browned.

5. While the cookies are baking, put the remaining 1 cup confectioners' sugar in a shallow bowl.

6. Cool the cookies on the parchment sheets for a few minutes. While the cookies are still warm, roll them in half the remaining confectioners' sugar. Place on a wire rack to cool.

7. When the cookies have cooled, roll them in the rest of the confectioners' sugar to give them an even coating. Store in an airtight container between sheets of parchment or waxed paper. They will keep well for at least 1 week.

Molasses Cookies

M olasses wasn't exactly the sweetener of choice in early American cooking; it was just about the only affordable sweetener (honey and maple syrup were available in limited quantities, depending on where you lived). In the early days of the republic, molasses played an important role in the slave trade. Slavers would capture Africans to fill their ships bound for the West Indies. There, the slaves would be sold and the empty ships loaded with barrels of molasses bound for the States, where much of the molasses was distilled into rum. Then the ships would carry timber and other New World products back to Europe. Abolitionists in New England called for a boycott of molasses and exhorted people to use maple syrup instead. "Make your own sugar" was the advice of the *Farmer's Almanac* in 1803, "and send not to the Indies for it. Feast not on the toil, pain, and misery of the wretched."

Eventually, the cane sugar and sugar beet industries made granulated sugar affordable, and this sugar replaced molasses in most recipes.

Makes about 48 cookies

2¼ cups unbleached all-purpose flour	1 cup firmly packed dark brown sugar
2 teaspoons baking soda	
1 teaspoon ground cinnamon	¾ cup (1½ sticks) butter, at room temperature
½ teaspoon ground ginger	
¼ teaspoon ground allspice	1 large egg
¼ teaspoon ground cloves	⅓ cup dark molasses
¼ teaspoon salt	Granulated sugar

1. Preheat the oven to 375°F. Lightly grease two baking sheets.

2. Sift the flour, baking soda, cinnamon, ginger, allspice, cloves, and salt into a medium bowl.

3. Beat together the brown sugar and butter in a large bowl until creamy. Beat in the egg and molasses. Stir in the flour mixture, blending thoroughly. (If the dough is too soft to handle, chill in the refrigerator for 1 hour.)

4. Shape the cookie dough into balls the size of walnuts. Dip the tops of each ball into granulated sugar. Place them sugar-side up, 2 inches apart, on the prepared baking sheets.

5. Bake for 10 to 12 minutes, until the cookies are lightly browned.

6. Transfer the cookies to wire racks to cool.

Joe Froggers

IN ANOTHER TIME AND PLACE, molasses cookies were also called Joe Froggers. It seems that in Marblehead, Massachusetts, there lived an elderly African American gentleman who was known as Uncle Joe. Uncle Joe lived on the edge of a frog pond and enjoyed a certain reputation for making the best cookies in town, as large as lily pads and as dark as the frogs in the pond. Seamen stocked up on Joe Froggers because they kept well in sea chests. The fame of these cookies spread when they were traded for rum.

Hermits

Looking for a spice cookie with good keeping qualities? Look no further. These are great cookies to make when you have the time to do a little baking in advance of a potluck or bake sale. Hermits will keep in an airtight container for at least 1 week.

Makes about 48 cookies

1⅓ cups unbleached all-purpose flour	½ cup (1 stick) butter, at room temperature
1 teaspoon ground cinnamon	1 large egg
½ teaspoon baking soda	½ cup sour cream
½ teaspoon freshly grated nutmeg	1 teaspoon vanilla extract
¼ teaspoon ground allspice	1 cup chopped raisins or dried currants
¼ teaspoon ground cloves	
¼ teaspoon salt	¾ cup chopped walnuts or hickory nuts
1 cup firmly packed dark brown sugar	

1. Preheat the oven to 350°F. Lightly grease several baking sheets.

2. Sift the flour, cinnamon, baking soda, nutmeg, allspice, cloves, and salt into a medium bowl.

3. Beat together the sugar and butter in a large bowl until creamy. Add the egg and beat until fluffy. Mix in the sour cream and vanilla. Stir in the flour mixture, blending thoroughly. Add the raisins and nuts, stirring until combined.

4. Arrange rounded teaspoons of the cookie dough 2 inches apart on the prepared baking sheets.

5. Bake for 12 to 15 minutes, until the cookies are golden.

6. Transfer the cookies to wire racks to cool completely.

Hermit History

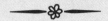

THE OLDER THE RECIPE, the more likely it is that there will be some fanciful stories behind its origins. In the case of the hermit, we know that the first printed reference dates back to only 1896, but the cookie seems to be much older. Sometimes hermits were called Harwich hermits, suggesting that they originated in Harwich, Massachusetts. The theory goes that seamen took these cookies with them on trading ships because the dried fruits kept the cookies soft and fresh-tasting for a while. Some writers have speculated that the name refers to the cookies' long-keeping nature — they're best when hidden away like a hermit for several days. Others say that the name refers to their brown, lumpy appearance, which resembles a hermit's robe.

There is no dispute about what makes a hermit. It is a spicy, chewy cookie studded with raisins or currants. But is it a bar cookie or a drop cookie? That is another important question. Miss Fanny Farmer made her hermits as drop cookies in the 1896 edition of her famous cookbook. Round or square, they are delicious and great to pack in sea chests or lunch boxes.

Gingery Gingersnaps

Gingersnaps most likely have their origin with the Pennsylvania Dutch, and their name probably comes from the word *snappen*, which means "easy." The cookies are rolled in sugar before baking, giving them a lovely, crinkly top.

Makes about 40 cookies

1⅛ cups unbleached all-purpose flour
½ teaspoon baking soda
⅛ teaspoon salt
2 tablespoons dark molasses
1 tablespoon warm brewed coffee
6 tablespoons butter, at room temperature
¾ cup plus 3 tablespoons granulated sugar

¼ cup firmly packed brown sugar
1 teaspoon ground ginger
½ teaspoon ground cinnamon
¼ teaspoon ground cloves
½ cup finely chopped crystallized ginger

1. Sift the flour, baking soda, and salt into a medium bowl.

2. Combine the molasses and coffee in a small bowl.

3. Cream together the butter, the ¼ cup granulated sugar, and the brown sugar, ginger, cinnamon, and cloves in a large bowl. Add the molasses mixture and the flour mixture, beating until well blended. Stir in the crystallized ginger. Gather together the dough in a ball, wrap in plastic wrap, and chill for at least 1 hour, until firm.

4. Preheat the oven to 350°F. Lightly grease two baking sheets.

5. Shape the dough into 1-inch balls. Roll the balls in 2 tablespoons of the granulated sugar. Place them on the prepared baking sheets about 2 inches apart. Press down each cookie with the bottom of a glass dipped in the remaining 1 tablespoon granulated sugar until the cookies are nice and thin.

6. Bake, one sheet at a time, for about 10 minutes. Remove the cookies from the oven before their edges start to brown; they will be soft in the center but will harden when cool. Watch the cookies carefully and do not allow them to scorch.

7. Transfer the cookies to wire racks to cool.

Rich Chocolate Crinkles

Intensely chocolaty, these cookies will stay fresh for a week or more in an airtight container, making them the perfect treat to send in a care package to an unhappy camper or lonely college student.

Makes about 36 cookies

- 4 ounces unsweetened chocolate, coarsely chopped
- 4 ounces dark or bittersweet chocolate, coarsely chopped
- ½ cup (1 stick) butter, cut into pieces
- 1 cup unbleached all-purpose flour
- ½ teaspoon baking powder
- ½ teaspoon salt
- 3 large eggs
- 1¼ cups firmly packed light or dark brown sugar
- 2 teaspoons vanilla extract
- ½ cup granulated sugar

1. Melt the unsweetened chocolate, dark chocolate, and butter in the top of a double boiler set over simmering water. Stir until completely smooth and glossy. Remove the top of the double boiler from the heat and let cool slightly.

2. Whisk the flour, baking powder, and salt in a medium bowl.

3. Beat the eggs and brown sugar in a large bowl with an electric mixer set at medium-high speed until very thick, about 4 minutes. Beat in the vanilla until well mixed. Reduce the speed to low and add the chocolate mixture. Beat until well blended.

4. Fold in the flour with a large rubber spatula. Cover the bowl and let stand at room temperature for 30 minutes to stiffen the dough.

5. Preheat the oven to 350°F. Line three baking sheets with parchment paper.

6. Using a small, trigger-style ice cream scoop or a tablespoon, form the cookie dough into walnut-size balls and roll them in the granulated sugar. Place about 2 inches apart on the baking sheets. Flatten slightly with the back of a spoon.

7. Bake, one sheet at a time, for 12 to 14 minutes, until the tops of the cookies appear dry.

8. Transfer the sheets to racks and cool the cookies before removing them from the baking sheets.

Chocolate Almond Crinkles

Crinkles have a crackly surface, achieved by dusting the cookies with sugar before baking. The sugar draws moisture from the batter, leaving the surface of the cookies cracked.

Makes about 36 cookies

4 ounces unsweetened chocolate, coarsely chopped
2 ounces dark or bittersweet chocolate, coarsely chopped
½ cup (1 stick) butter, cut into pieces
1 cup unbleached all-purpose flour
½ teaspoon baking powder
½ teaspoon salt

3 large eggs
1¼ cups firmly packed light or dark brown sugar
1 teaspoon vanilla extract
½ teaspoon almond extract
1 cup blanched slivered almonds
½ cup granulated sugar
36 whole almonds

1. Melt the unsweetened chocolate, dark chocolate, and butter in the top of a double boiler set over simmering water. Stir until completely smooth and glossy. Remove the top of the double boiler from the heat and let cool slightly.

2. Whisk the flour, baking powder, and salt into a medium bowl.

3. Beat the eggs and brown sugar in a large bowl with an electric mixer set at medium-high speed until very thick, about 4 minutes. Beat in the vanilla and almond extracts until well mixed. Reduce the speed to low and add the chocolate mixture. Beat until well mixed.

4. Fold in the flour mixture with a rubber spatula. Fold in the slivered almonds. Cover the bowl and let stand at room temperature for 30 minutes to stiffen the dough.

5. Preheat the oven to 350°F. Line three baking sheets with parchment paper.

6. Using a small, trigger-style ice cream scoop or a tablespoon, form the cookie dough into walnut-size balls and roll in the granulated sugar. Place about 2 inches apart on the baking sheets. Firmly press one almond into the center of each cookie.

7. Bake, one sheet at a time, for 12 to 14 minutes, until the tops of the cookies appear dry.

8. Transfer the parchment paper to racks and cool the cookies before removing them from the paper.

Frosted Cream Cheese Lemon Drops

I f all the raindrops were lemon drops and gum drops, oh what a rain that would be!"
Maybe the song doesn't refer to these bite-size, slightly soft cookies that are both sweet
and tart, but oh, what a rain *that* would be.

Makes 2½ to 4 dozen cookies

½ cup (1 stick) butter, at room
    temperature
4 ounces cream cheese, at room
    temperature
¾ cup granulated sugar
1 large egg yolk
2 teaspoons finely grated lemon zest
1½ teaspoons fresh lemon juice
1 cup unbleached all-purpose flour

FROSTING

1 cup sifted confectioners' sugar
1 teaspoon finely grated lemon
    zest
1½–2½ tablespoons fresh lemon juice

1. Preheat the oven to 350°F. Position one oven rack in bottom third of the oven and one rack in top third. Line two baking sheets with parchment paper.

2. Combine the butter, cream cheese, and sugar in a medium bowl and beat until light and creamy. Add the egg yolk, lemon zest, and lemon juice and beat until well blended. Gradually add the flour, blending until thoroughly combined.

3. Drop rounded teaspoons of the dough 2 inches apart on the baking sheets.

4. Bake for 13 to 15 minutes, rotating the sheets halfway through baking, until the cookies are golden around the edge.

5. Transfer the cookies to a wire rack to cool while you make the frosting.

6. To prepare the frosting, combine the confectioners' sugar, lemon zest, and 1½ tablespoons of lemon juice and beat until smooth. Add the extra lemon juice if needed to make a smooth, slightly stiff frosting.

7. While the cookies are still warm, use a teaspoon to spread the frosting over the tops of the cookies. Let the cookies remain on the rack to cool completely for several hours before storing. As they cool, they will firm up.

Scottish Shortbread

There's no question about the origin of these buttery morsels. There was a significant wave of Scottish immigration to the South in the early 1700s, and with the immigrants came shortbread (*short*, or shortening, in the form of butter, and *bread* because these cookies aren't particularly sweet). This recipe makes very buttery, very crisp shortbreads, as close to the traditional old-time Scottish shortbread flavor as possible.

Makes 36 square or 12 wedge-shaped cookies

1½ cups sifted unbleached all-purpose flour	¼ teaspoon salt
1 cup sifted confectioners' sugar	1 cup (2 sticks) butter, cut into small pieces
½ cup cornstarch	1 teaspoon vanilla extract

1. Preheat the oven to 325°F. Line an 8- or 9-inch square baking pan, a 9-inch pie pan, or a 9-inch tart pan with parchment paper.

2. Combine the flour, sugar, cornstarch, and salt in a large bowl.

3. Using your fingers, blend the butter and vanilla into the flour mixture until fully absorbed. Shape the dough into a pancake, then knead or mix well for 10 minutes. (If using an electric mixer, beat for 5 minutes.)

4. Transfer the dough to the prepared pan. Flatten the dough into an even layer. (If the dough is too sticky to spread, refrigerate it for a few minutes first.) With a knife, score the dough partway through and mark into squares or wedges. Prick the surface of the shortbread with a fork.

5. Bake for 30 minutes, until the shortbread is light golden. Do not overbake.

6. Cut into squares or wedges while still hot. Cool on a rack before removing from the pan.

Cinnamon-Sugar Icebox Cookies

Iceboxes were invented in 1802 by Maryland farmer Thomas Moore, who designed an insulated "ice box" for keeping food cold. By the 1830s, these iceboxes were found in most kitchens, giving rise to the "ice man," who came with 100-pound blocks of ice that were harvested from frozen northern lakes. It wasn't too long before enterprising bakers discovered they could keep logs of cookie dough in the icebox, ready to be baked whenever freshly baked cookies were desired.

Makes about 120 small cookies

3 cups unbleached all-purpose flour
1 teaspoon baking powder
½ teaspoon baking soda
½ teaspoon salt
1 cup (2 sticks) butter, at room
    temperature
1 cup plus 2 tablespoons granulated
    sugar
¼ cup firmly packed light brown
    sugar
½ cup sour cream, at room
    temperature
1 tablespoon vanilla extract
½ teaspoon ground cinnamon

1. Sift the flour, baking powder, baking soda, and salt into a large bowl.

2. Beat the butter with the 1 cup granulated sugar and the brown sugar in a large bowl until creamy. Mix in the sour cream and the vanilla. Stir in the flour mixture, blending thoroughly.

3. Divide the dough into four portions. Using a doubled sheet of waxed paper as a guide, roll each portion into a tight smooth log about 6 inches long and 2 inches in diameter. Wrap in waxed paper and aluminum foil. Freeze until firm but not frozen solid, 1 to 2 hours.

4. Preheat the oven to 350°F. Lightly grease several baking sheets or line with parchment paper. Combine the 2 tablespoons granulated sugar with the cinnamon.

5. With a sharp, thin knife, slice the cookies about 3/16 inch thick. Place the cookies 1 inch apart on the prepared baking sheets. Sprinkle with the cinnamon-sugar.

6. Bake for 10 to 12 minutes, until the cookies are lightly golden around the edges.

7. Use a spatula to carefully transfer the cookies to wire racks to cool completely.

Mocha-Glazed Chocolate Icebox Cookies

A chocolate cookie for grown-ups. Try a few of these not-too-sweet cookies with coffee; they are even better with vanilla ice cream.

Makes about 60 small cookies

1¼ cups unbleached all-purpose flour
1 teaspoon baking powder
1 teaspoon instant coffee powder
¼ teaspoon salt
¾ cup granulated sugar
½ cup (1 stick) butter, at room temperature

3 ounces unsweetened chocolate, melted
1 large egg
1 teaspoon vanilla extract

Mocha Glaze

1 cup confectioners' sugar
3 tablespoons unsweetened cocoa powder
2 tablespoons hot brewed coffee (plus 1 teaspoon, if needed)

1 tablespoon butter at room temperature
½ teaspoon vanilla extract

1. Sift the flour, baking powder, instant coffee powder, and salt into a medium bowl.

2. Beat the sugar and butter in a large bowl until creamy. Stir in the chocolate. Add the egg and vanilla and beat until well combined. Stir in the flour mixture, blending thoroughly.

3. Divide the dough into two portions. Using a doubled sheet of waxed paper as a guide, roll each portion into a tight smooth log about 6 inches long and 2 inches in diameter. Wrap in waxed paper and aluminum foil. Refrigerate until firm, about 2 hours. (These logs slice better when refrigerated, not frozen.)

4. While the dough chills, prepare the glaze. Sift the confectioners' sugar and cocoa into a small bowl. Mix together the hot coffee, butter, and vanilla. Gradually add to the confectioners' sugar mixture and stir until smooth. If the glaze is too thick to spread, stir in another teaspoon of coffee. Cover and set aside.

5. Preheat the oven to 350°F. Lightly grease several baking sheets or line with parchment paper.

6. With a very sharp thin knife, slice the cookies about 3⁄16 inch thick. Place the cookies 1 inch apart on the prepared baking sheets.

7. Bake for 8 to 10 minutes, until the cookies are almost firm to the touch and just beginning to get slightly darker around the edges. Watch carefully because they burn easily.

8. Use a spatula to carefully transfer the cookies to wire racks. While the cookies are still warm, brush them with the glaze. Cool until set.

Florentines

With a name like "Florentines," you'd think these would be Italian cookies, but Austria is the home of these chewy delights. The cookies are chock-full of nuts and candied orange peel and are dipped in chocolate, resulting in cookies that almost cross the line into candy.

Makes 42 to 48 cookies

3 tablespoons butter	⅛ teaspoon salt
½ cup whipping cream	½ cup finely chopped almonds
½ cup sugar	½ cup sliced almonds
2 tablespoons honey	¾ cup very finely chopped candied
3 tablespoons unbleached	orange peel (about 4 ounces)
all-purpose flour	

CHOCOLATE FROSTING

8 ounces semisweet chocolate
4 teaspoons butter

1. Preheat the oven to 350°F. Line two baking sheets with parchment paper.

2. Combine the butter, cream, sugar, and honey in a heavy saucepan over low heat. Bring to a boil, stirring until the sugar dissolves. Continue cooking, stirring gently over low heat, for 2 minutes. Remove from the heat. Stir in the flour, salt, chopped and sliced almonds, and orange peel.

3. Drop small teaspoons of the batter onto the prepared baking sheets about 3 inches apart. Dip the tines of a fork into water and press gently on each cookie to slightly flatten it.

4. Bake, one sheet at a time, for 8 to 10 minutes, until the edges of the cookies are lightly browned and the centers bubbling. Watch the cookies carefully, so they don't get too dark brown or burnt.

5. Let the cookies cool on the baking sheet for about 2 minutes, just until they become slightly firm. Use the tip of a very thin metal spatula to help you lift off the cookies and transfer to a rack to cool completely. (If the cookies stick to the baking sheet, reheat the pan for 1 minute, then finish removing them from the pan.)

6. To frost the bottoms, turn the cold cookies upside down on a piece of waxed paper placed on a baking sheet. Combine the chocolate and butter in the top of a double boiler set over simmering water. Stir until completely melted and smooth. With a small, wide spreading knife or soft pastry brush, spread or paint a thin coating of chocolate over the bottom of each cookie. To speed up the cooling time, place the cookies in the refrigerator until the chocolate sets. Store in an airtight container with sheets of waxed paper placed between each layer.

All you need is love. But a little chocolate now and then doesn't hurt.

— Charles M. Schulz, cartoonist (1922–2000)

Rolled Sugar Cookies

George Washington would be surprised to learn that cherry pies are associated with his name. His own favorite dessert was said to be Martha's "sugar cakes," which she rolled thin and cut rather large. These sugar cookies would probably delight old George.

Makes 24 to 30 cookies

2 cups unbleached all-purpose flour
1 teaspoon baking powder
½ teaspoon salt
1 cup sugar
½ cup (1 stick) butter, at room temperature

1 large egg
1 tablespoon milk
1½ teaspoons vanilla extract
   Granulated sugar or colored sugar crystals, to garnish

1. Sift the flour, baking powder, and salt into a medium bowl.

2. Beat together the sugar and butter in a large bowl until creamy. Beat in the egg. Mix in the milk and vanilla, beating until fluffy. Stir in the flour mixture, blending thoroughly.

3. Divide the dough in half and wrap each portion in plastic wrap. Refrigerate for 2 hours, until firm enough to handle.

4. Preheat the oven to 375°F. Lightly grease several baking sheets or line with parchment paper.

5. Working with one portion of the dough at a time, roll out the dough to a thickness of ⅛ inch on a lightly floured work surface. Cut out individual cookies with a 3-inch round cookie cutter or the cutter of your choice. Carefully lift the cookies with a large spatula and transfer to the prepared baking sheets, setting them 1 inch apart. Sprinkle the tops with sugar.

6. Bake for 8 to 10 minutes, until the edges of the cookies are lightly browned.

7. Let the cookies cool on the baking sheets for a few minutes. Then use a spatula to carefully transfer them to wire racks to cool completely.

Gingerbread Men

Traditionally eaten at Christmastime, these cookies are welcome any time of the year. Legend has it that Queen Elizabeth I of England invented gingerbread men.

Makes 12 to 16 cookies

2½ cups unbleached all-purpose flour
2 teaspoons ground ginger
½ teaspoon baking soda
½ teaspoon ground cinnamon
¼ teaspoon ground allspice
¼ teaspoon salt
4 tablespoons butter, at room temperature

¼ cup solid vegetable shortening, at room temperature
½ cup firmly packed light brown sugar
½ cup dark molasses
2 tablespoons water
Currants or raisins and cinnamon candies

1. Sift the flour, ginger, baking soda, cinnamon, allspice, and salt into a medium bowl.

2. Beat the butter and shortening in a large bowl until creamy. Add the brown sugar gradually and beat until fluffy. Stir in the molasses and water. Add the flour mixture, mixing until well blended.

3. Wrap the dough in plastic wrap and refrigerate until chilled, 1 to 2 hours.

4. Preheat the oven to 375°F. Lightly grease two baking sheets or line with parchment paper.

5. On a lightly floured work surface, roll out the dough to a thickness of about ³⁄₁₆ inch. Cut with gingerbread cookie cutters. Carefully lift the cookies with a large spatula and transfer them to the prepared baking sheets. Decorate with currants or raisins and cinnamon candies.

6. Bake for 8 to 10 minutes, until the cookies are set.

7. Let the cookies cool on the baking sheets for a few minutes. Then use a spatula to carefully transfer them to wire racks to cool completely.

Almond Crescents

In the 1600s, the Turks invaded Vienna, but were soon driven out. The Viennese, so legend goes, then made crescent-shaped pastries (symbolizing the Turkish flag) to celebrate. The Viennese, in effect, swallowed the enemy by eating the crescent-shaped pastry. Something to think about as you enjoy these delicious little cookies.

Makes 36 to 48 cookies

1 cup toasted almonds	1 cup (2 sticks) butter, chilled and
1¾ cups unbleached all-purpose flour	diced
¼ teaspoon salt	1 teaspoon almond extract
2¼ cups sifted confectioners' sugar	1 teaspoon vanilla extract

1. Finely chop the almonds in a food processor, but do not grind to a flour. Remove from the processor and set aside.

2. Combine the flour and salt in a small bowl.

3. Put ¾ cup of the confectioners' sugar in a food processor. With the motor running, add the butter and process for a few seconds, until creamy. Add the almond and vanilla extracts and process just to mix in. Add the flour mixture and process for 30 seconds. With the motor running, add the almonds and process until the dough forms a ball.

4. Cut the dough into thirds, then shape each portion into a rectangle about 1 inch thick and wrap in plastic wrap. Chill for several hours or overnight.

5. Preheat the oven to 325°F. Line three baking sheets with parchment paper.

6. Remove one portion of the dough from the refrigerator. The dough will be firm and should not be overworked. For each cookie, pull off about a tablespoon of dough and roll it between the palms of your hands into a ⅜-inch cylinder. Taper the ends, then place each cookie on a baking sheet, turning down the ends to form a crescent. Place the cookies about 1½ inches apart on the prepared baking sheets. Chill the cookies on the baking sheets in the freezer for 5 to 10 minutes before baking.

7. Bake for 20 to 25 minutes, until the bottoms and edges of the cookies are golden and the tops almost white.

8. Transfer the cookies to a rack to cool for a few minutes. Put 1 cup of the confectioners' sugar in a lunch-size paper bag. While the cookies are still hot, drop a dozen or so into the bag and shake gently. When the cookies are coated with sugar, remove to a wire rack to cool completely. Add the remaining ½ cup confectioners' sugar to the paper bag. Repeat with the remaining cookies. Store in an airtight container with waxed paper separating the layers.

Variations

Cinnamon-Walnut Crescents. Use walnuts instead of almonds. Add ½ teaspoon ground cinnamon and ⅛ teaspoon freshly grated nutmeg to the dough. Omit the almond extract.

Chocolate Horseshoes. For each cookie, use 2 tablespoons of dough. Form into ½-inch cylinders and make into horseshoe shapes without pointed ends. Reduce the confectioners' sugar to ¾ cup. When the cookies are cool, instead of coating in confectioners' sugar, dip the ends of each cookie into melted semisweet chocolate.

Oh, weary mothers, rolling dough

Don't you wish that food would grow?

How happy all the world would be,

With a cookie bush, and a doughnut tree.

— Mrs. Harold J. Wells,
from The 20th Century Bride's Cook Book, 1929

Linzer Cookies

Linzer cookies are an inspired remake of the classic linzertorte, a rich raspberry jam tart first made in Linz, Austria. These are elegant cookies, suitable for a holiday dessert table. The top cookie, dusted with confectioners' sugar, has a cutout so the preserves are visible. When cut into a round shape with a round cutout, they are known as "Linzer Eyes" (*Linzer Augen*).

Makes about 36 cookies

1¾ cups unbleached all-purpose flour
1 tablespoon unsweetened cocoa powder
1 teaspoon ground cinnamon
⅛ teaspoon ground cloves
⅛ teaspoon salt
¾ cup ground almonds
¾ cup (1½ sticks) butter, at room temperature

¾ cup granulated sugar
1 teaspoon finely grated lemon zest
1 large egg
1 teaspoon vanilla extract
Confectioners' sugar
⅔ cup seedless raspberry jam

1. Line two large baking sheets with parchment paper.

2. Whisk the flour, cocoa, cinnamon, cloves, and salt in a medium bowl. Stir in the almonds, mixing until thoroughly combined.

3. Beat together the butter, granulated sugar, and lemon zest in a large bowl until creamy. Beat in the egg and the vanilla. Stir in the flour mixture, blending thoroughly.

4. Divide the dough in half and form each half into a rectangle about ½ inch thick. Wrap each portion in plastic wrap. Refrigerate for 2 hours.

5. Preheat the oven to 350°F.

6. Working with one portion of dough at a time (keep the other in the refrigerator), roll out the dough between two pieces of waxed paper to a thickness of about ³⁄₁₆ inch. Remove the top sheet of waxed paper. Cut out the dough, using a 2- to 2½-inch round cookie cutter, and transfer to the baking sheet, spacing the cookies about 1 inch apart. Cut out the center of all the cookies with a small heart- or

star-shaped cutter. Use the tip of a knife to lift out the center heart or star. (The round cookies with cutouts will become the tops of the linzer cookies.) Reroll the removed centers to make a few more cookies, again making a cutout in each one. Place the baking sheet in the freezer to chill for a few minutes while preparing the rest of the dough.

7. Roll out the second half of the dough between two pieces of waxed paper to a thickness of about 3/16 inch. Remove the top sheet of waxed paper. Cut out the dough, using a 2- to 2½-inch round cookie cutter, and transfer to the prepared baking sheet, spacing the cookies about 1 inch apart. Do not cut out the centers of these cookies; they will form the bottom half of the cookie sandwiches.

8. Bake, one sheet at a time, for 12 to 14 minutes, until the cookies are light golden brown.

9. Transfer the cookies to a rack and cool completely. Sift confectioners' sugar over the tops of the cookies with cutouts. Turn over the uncut cookies to expose the cookie bottoms and spread the bottoms with raspberry jam. Place a sugar-topped cut-out cookie on each jam-topped cookie to form a sandwich. If desired, use a small spoon to fill the center holes with an additional drop of jam. It's best to fill the cookies with jam shortly before serving them.

Baker's Tips

❋ It's important to keep dough chilled at every stage of preparation.

❋ If you don't have small cookie cutters, cut out ½-inch circles by using the cap of an extract bottle or a pastry bag tip.

Apricot Rugelach

These cookies aren't hard to make, but they do require attention to the details. Be sure to roll up the dough tightly, and remove the cookies from the baking sheet as soon as they come out of the oven in order to leave behind any filling that has leaked.

Makes about 60 cookies

1 (8-ounce) package cream cheese, at room temperature
1 cup (2 sticks) butter, at room temperature
½ cup confectioners' sugar
    Pinch of salt
½ teaspoon fresh lemon juice or cider vinegar
½ teaspoon vanilla extract
2 cups unbleached all-purpose flour
¾ cup apricot jam
⅓ cup finely chopped walnuts
1 large egg, beaten
    About 1 tablespoon milk
    About 1 tablespoon granulated sugar

1. Mix together the cream cheese, butter, confectioners' sugar, salt, lemon juice, and vanilla in a food processor. Add the flour and pulse until a very soft dough results. Form into a ball and refrigerate for at least 1 hour.

2. Preheat the oven to 350°F. Line two baking sheets with parchment paper.

3. Combine the apricot jam and walnuts in a small bowl.

4. Divide the dough into quarters and shape each portion into a rectangle. Lightly dust a work surface with confectioners' sugar. Working with one portion of dough at a time (keep the other portions in the refrigerator), roll out to form a long, narrow rectangle about 5 inches wide, 12 inches long, and ⅛ inch thick. Trim the edges of the dough to form an even rectangle. Save the trimmings. Spread the surface of the dough with one-quarter of the apricot mixture, leaving a 1- to 1½-inch border along the edge farthest from you. Brush the border with the beaten egg.

5. Starting with the side closest to you, roll up the dough to make a tight, even roll. Brush the roll with milk and sprinkle with granulated sugar. Cut the roll into 1-inch pieces and place them 1 inch apart on a prepared baking sheet. Repeat with the remaining dough, incorporating the saved trimmings.

6. Bake, one sheet at a time, for 22 to 25 minutes, until the cookies are golden.

7. Transfer the cookies to wire racks to cool.

Brandy Snaps

Brandy snaps, close cousins to gingersnaps, are cookies flavored with brandy, ginger, and molasses. They date at least as far back as the Middle Ages, when they were popular items at fairs in England. In particular, brandy snaps are associated with the Nottingham Fair, which was held annually on the first Thursday in October and was famous as the premier showcase for geese. People came from all over the English Midlands to select their geese, which were driven there in flocks by gooseherds armed only with crooks to keep the cantankerous geese in line.

Makes about 36 cookies

1 cup unbleached all-purpose flour	½ cup light molasses
½ cup sugar	½ cup (1 stick) butter
½ teaspoon ground ginger	2 tablespoons brandy
⅛ teaspoon salt	

1. Preheat the oven to 325°F.

2. Whisk the flour, sugar, ginger, and salt in a medium bowl.

3. Heat the molasses in a medium saucepan just to the boiling point. Stir in the butter. Add the flour mixture gradually and cook, stirring, until hot and blended. Remove from the heat. Stir in the brandy.

4. Place the pan over hot water to keep the mixture soft. Drop teaspoons of the dough 3 inches apart onto ungreased baking sheets. Allow only about 6 cookies to each sheet because they will spread as they bake.

5. Bake for 7 to 8 minutes, until the cookies are bubbly and golden.

6. Cool the cookies on the baking sheets for about 2 minutes, until the cookies hold together. Using a wide spatula, quickly loosen one cookie at a time and transfer to a wire rack or drape it over a rolling pin to cool in a curved shape. If the cookies harden before they are removed from the baking sheets, reheat in the oven for 1 minute.

7. When the cookies are cool, store immediately in an airtight container.

Sand Tarts

When a cookie is so rich and buttery that it crumbles like sand when you bite into it, chances are "sand" will be part of the title.

Makes 36 to 48 cookies

2 cups unbleached all-purpose flour
1 teaspoon baking powder
¼ teaspoon salt
1 cup plus 2 tablespoons sugar
½ cup (1 stick) butter, at room temperature

2 large eggs
1 teaspoon finely grated orange zest
1 teaspoon orange or vanilla extract
2 teaspoons water
½ teaspoon ground cinnamon
½ cup slivered almonds, to garnish

1. Sift the flour, baking powder, and salt into a medium bowl.

2. Beat together the 1 cup sugar and the butter in a large bowl until creamy. Separate one of the eggs. Beat one whole egg and one egg yolk and add to the butter mixture. Reserve the remaining egg white. Add the orange zest and orange extract to the mixture and beat until fluffy. Stir in the flour mixture, blending thoroughly.

3. Divide the dough in half and wrap each portion in plastic wrap. Refrigerate for 2 hours, until firm.

4. Preheat the oven to 350°F. Line two baking sheets with parchment paper.

5. Working with one portion of the dough at a time, roll out the dough to a thickness of ⅛ inch on a lightly floured work surface. Cut the dough into squares or diamonds. Carefully lift the cookies with a spatula and transfer to the prepared baking sheets, setting the cookies about 2 inches apart.

6. Make an egg wash by combining the remaining egg white with the water. Brush the tops of the cookies with the egg wash. Combine the 2 tablespoons sugar and the cinnamon and sprinkle on top of the cookies. Garnish with the slivered almonds.

7. Bake the cookies for 8 to 10 minutes, until their edges are golden.

8. Let the cookies cool on the baking sheets for a few minutes, and then use a spatula to carefully transfer them to wire racks to cool completely.

Pecan Tassies

Tarts, tartlets, tassies. Tassies are the tiniest of tarts, a finger tart that disappears in just two bites. Pecan Tassies are miniature pecan pies.

Makes 24 cookies

COOKIE SHELLS

½ cup (1 stick) butter, at room
   temperature
3 ounces cream cheese, at room
   temperature
1 cup unbleached all-purpose flour
⅛ teaspoon salt

FILLING

1 large egg
¾ cup firmly packed dark brown
   sugar
1 tablespoon butter, at room
   temperature
1 teaspoon vanilla extract
⅛ teaspoon salt
¾ cup chopped pecans
   Confectioners' sugar

1. To make the cookie shells, combine the butter and cream cheese in a large bowl and beat until well blended. Stir in the flour and salt, mixing until well combined. Gather the dough into a ball, wrap in plastic wrap, and chill for at least 1 hour.

2. Divide the dough into 24 pieces and roll each piece into a ball about 1 inch in diameter. Press a dough ball into each cup of a mini-muffin pan, lining the bottom and sides of the cups.

3. Preheat the oven to 325°F.

4. To make the filling, beat together the egg, brown sugar, butter, vanilla, and salt. Stir in the pecans. Spoon the filling into the cookie shells.

5. Bake for 20 to 25 minutes, until the cookie shells are golden and firm to the touch. The tops of the filling will be crazed.

6. Cool on wire racks for 20 to 25 minutes. To remove the pecan tassies from the pan, insert a thin-bladed knife around the edge of each cookie shell to loosen it, and then slip it out. When cool, sprinkle with confectioners' sugar.

Spritz Cookies

These pretty little cookies came to the United States with Scandinavian immigrants, who brought their cookie presses with them. The name comes from the German word *spritzen*, which means "to squirt or spray."

Makes 48 to 60 cookies

2¼ cups unbleached all-purpose flour	1 large egg or 2 large egg yolks
¼ cup cornstarch	1 teaspoon vanilla extract
½ teaspoon baking powder	½ teaspoon almond extract
¼ teaspoon salt	Colored sugar crystals, chocolate
1 cup (2 sticks) butter, at room	sprinkles, finely chopped nuts,
temperature	and halved candied cherries, to
¾ cup sugar	garnish

1. Preheat the oven to 375°F.

2. Sift the flour, cornstarch, baking powder, and salt into a medium bowl.

3. Beat together the butter and sugar in a large bowl until creamy. Beat in the egg. Mix in the vanilla and almond extracts, beating until fluffy. Stir in the flour mixture, mixing well.

4. Pack the dough into a cookie press fitted with a decorative plate. Press the dough onto ungreased baking sheets, 1 inch apart. Decorate with the assorted garnishes.

5. Bake for 10 minutes, until the edges of the cookies are lightly browned.

6. Transfer the cookies to wire racks to cool completely.

Baker's Tip

❊ If you don't have a cookie press, you can still make these cookies. Shape the dough into 1-inch balls. Flatten each ball with a glass that has been dipped in granulated sugar or make a crisscross design on the cookies by pressing down with a fork. Or roll the dough into ¼-inch ropes and form into pretzel shapes. Bake as instructed above.

Variations

Chocolate Spritz. Add 2 ounces of melted bittersweet, dark, or semisweet chocolate to the butter and sugar.

Spice Spritz. Add ½ teaspoon ground cinnamon, ¼ teaspoon ground cloves, and ¼ teaspoon freshly grated nutmeg to the flour mixture.

Cookie Slang

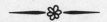

IN THE WILD WEST, a cookie was the cook or the cook's helper, not a delectable dessert. The name was one of the more benign slang terms that were used. Wouldn't you rather be called "cookie" than "bean master," "belly cheater," "biscuit roller," "dough puncher," "grease burner," "grub spoiler," "gut burglar," "hash slinger," "mess moll," "pot rustler," or "sizzler"? A waitress in a restaurant was known as a "cookie pusher."

Chocolate Coconut Macaroons

Sometimes called coconut drop kisses, these cookies are often featured on Jewish tables for the Passover holiday, during which no wheat, other than matzoh, is served. They make a delicious cookie any time of the year.

Makes about 40 cookies

- 1 (14-ounce) can sweetened condensed milk
- 1 teaspoon vanilla extract
- ⅓ cup unsweetened cocoa powder
- ¼ teaspoon salt
- 3 cups lightly packed, sweetened flaked coconut

1. Preheat the oven to 325°F. Line several baking sheets with parchment paper.

2. Combine the condensed milk, vanilla, cocoa, and salt in a large bowl, mixing until blended. Add the coconut and stir until well combined. Drop by large teaspoonfuls onto the baking sheets, placing them about 2 inches apart.

3. Bake, one sheet at a time, for about 10 minutes, until the cookies are firm. Watch carefully because the bottoms will burn quickly.

4. Let the cookies cool on the baking sheet for 10 to 15 seconds, and then use a spatula to carefully transfer them to wire racks to cool completely.

Chocolate Meringue Kisses

Old cookbooks might call these "forgotten cookies" because they were baked last, as the oven cooled after a session of baking breads or cakes. The baker would put the kisses in the "slack oven" and avoid looking into the oven as they slowly baked, lest more heat was lost. Under those circumstances, the cookies were sometimes forgotten.

Makes about 48 cookies

3 large egg whites, at room temperature	3 tablespoons unsweetened cocoa powder
⅛ teaspoon cream of tartar	1 cup chocolate chips
⅛ teaspoon salt	½ cup chopped hazelnuts or walnuts
1 cup sugar	½ teaspoon vanilla extract

1. Preheat the oven to 250°F. Line two baking sheets with parchment paper.

2. Beat the egg whites in a large, clean bowl with an electric mixer until foamy. Add the cream of tartar and salt and beat until soft peaks form. Gradually sprinkle in the sugar, 1 tablespoon at a time, beating well after each addition. Continue beating until the egg whites are stiff but not dry. The egg whites should hold their shape. Sift the cocoa over the mixture. With a rubber spatula, fold in the cocoa along with the chocolate chips, nuts, and vanilla.

3. Drop rounded teaspoons of the batter onto the prepared baking sheets, bringing up the spoon through each meringue to shape it like a Hershey's Kiss.

4. Bake for 25 to 30 minutes, until the cookies are crisp.

5. Let the cookies cool on the baking sheets for a few minutes, and then use a spatula to carefully transfer them to wire racks to cool completely. These cookies are best when freshly made, but they will keep for 3 to 4 days in an airtight container.

Baker's Tip

❋ To remove hazelnut skins, toast the nuts in a 300°F oven for 12 to 15 minutes, stirring occasionally. Then place the nuts in a towel and rub to remove the skins.

Whoopie Pies

Whoops of joy may have inspired the name of these cookie sandwiches, which are probably Pennsylvania Dutch in origin. Add chocolate frosting and you have a Moon Pie, which is the trademarked name for a cookie made by the Chattanooga Bakery in Chattanooga, Tennessee. Moon Pies have been made since 1917 and have proved to be so popular that the company now produces 300,000 Moon Pies a day. This recipe yields considerably fewer.

Makes 14 sandwich cookies

2 cups unbleached all-purpose flour	**FILLING**
½ cup unsweetened cocoa powder	
1 teaspoon baking soda	¾ cup vegetable shortening or butter, at room temperature
½ teaspoon salt	
1 cup granulated sugar	1½ cups confectioners' sugar, or more as needed
½ cup vegetable shortening	
1 large egg	6 tablespoons Marshmallow Fluff
1 teaspoon vanilla extract	1 egg white
½ cup buttermilk or plain yogurt	1 teaspoon vanilla extract
½ cup hot brewed coffee	Pinch of salt

1. Preheat the oven to 350°F. Grease several baking sheets.

2. Sift the flour, cocoa, baking soda, and salt into a medium bowl.

3. Beat the sugar and shortening in a large bowl until light and fluffy. Add the egg and vanilla and beat until thoroughly blended. Add one-third of the flour mixture alternately with one-third of the buttermilk and coffee and beat until smooth. Repeat, adding the flour mixture and liquids in thirds and then beating until smooth. The batter will be thicker than cake batter, thinner than cookie dough.

4. Using a small, trigger-style ice cream scoop, drop the batter onto the baking sheets about 2 inches apart.

5. Bake for about 8 minutes, until the tops of the cookies appear dry and cracked. Do not overbake.

6. Transfer the cookies onto a wire rack to cool.

7. To make the filling, combine the shortening, confectioners' sugar, Marshmallow Fluff, egg white, vanilla, and salt in a large bowl. Beat until light and smooth. If the filling seems loose (it will be if you have used butter), add a little more confectioners' sugar to stiffen.

8. Spread the filling on half of the cookie bottoms, and then sandwich each one with another cookie.

9. Serve immediately or cover well and store the whoopie pies in the refrigerator. Bring to room temperature before serving.

Baker's Tips

❋ The egg white in this recipe is not cooked. Please see "Egg Information" on page 388.

❋ The filling can be made with vegetable shortening (such as Crisco) or with butter, depending on the desired result. Using vegetable shortening results in a whoopie pie that tastes just like the kind you may remember from a bakery. It has a nice, smooth mouthfeel. Butter in the filling tastes richer, more homemade, and is slightly greasy. We prefer the taste and feel of Crisco but like the idea of butter.

❋ Using a small (1½-ounce), trigger-style ice cream scoop to portion out the dough guarantees that each cookie is roughly the same size and shape, making it easier to sandwich them. If you don't have a small ice cream scoop, make generously rounded tablespoonfuls.

Chocolate-Dipped Acorns

Although Native Americans did eat acorns, most of us haven't sampled their flavor. And these delicious meringues, though they do bear some resemblance to acorns in shape, are completely acorn-free. Instead, these are crunchy, chocolaty, almond meringues with a chocolate top and a winsome name.

Makes 60 to 72 cookies

6 ounces almonds, toasted
6 ounces dark or bittersweet
   chocolate
3 large egg whites, at room
   temperature
2 teaspoons white vinegar
⅛ teaspoon salt
1 cup sugar
1 teaspoon vanilla extract

TOPPING

6 ounces semisweet chocolate,
   chopped
1 tablespoon butter
¾ cup very finely chopped pistachio
   nuts or toasted almonds

1. Preheat the oven to 250°F. Position one rack in the lower third of the oven and the second rack in the upper third. Line two baking sheets with parchment paper or aluminum foil. Lightly grease the paper and then sprinkle with flour to coat. Shake off the excess flour.

2. Using a food processor or nut grinder, grate or grind the almonds. You want a coarse meal — do not grind to a powder. You should have 1½ cups. Repeat with dark chocolate. Again, avoid grinding to a powder. You should have 1⅓ cups.

3. Beat the egg whites in a large, clean bowl with an electric mixer until foamy. Add the vinegar and salt and beat until soft peaks form. Gradually sprinkle in the sugar, 1 tablespoon at a time, beating well after each addition. Beat until the egg whites form stiff peaks. Fold in the vanilla.

4. Drop rounded teaspoons of the batter onto the prepared baking sheets. Using two teaspoons, form into oval shapes about 1½ inches long and 1¼ inches wide, resembling pecans. If you prefer, spoon the mixture into a pastry bag with a plain #6 decorating tip and pipe out oval shapes.

5. Place the baking sheets in the upper and lower parts of the oven. Bake for 15 minutes. Reverse and rotate baking sheets, then bake for 15 minutes longer, until the cookies are firm and crisp.

6. Remove the meringues from the oven. Let cool a few minutes, and then remove the parchment or aluminum foil sheets, with the cookies on them, to cool on wire racks. When the cookies are completely cool, place them on waxed paper.

7. To prepare the topping, melt the chocolate and butter in the top of a double boiler set over simmering water. Stir until completely melted and smooth. Dip half of each meringue in the melted chocolate, and then sprinkle with finely chopped nuts. Place on waxed paper until firm.

As soon as school is out at night

All children, near and far,

Go rushing home, in one mad flight,

To find the Cooky jar!

(So keep it filled for their delight;

You know how children are.)

— **Anonymous**

Palmiers

These cookies have a long and distinguished lineage that harks back to a traditional Middle Eastern or Afghani pastry called *goash-e-feel*, meaning "elephant ears" — one of the many names for this cookie. In Afghanistan, elephant ears are usually served with tea. Often a bride's family will send them to the bride and groom the day after the wedding. Sometime in the early twentieth century, they were first made in either France or Vienna and dubbed *palmiers*, literally "palm leaves." Some people call them butterflies or bow knots or even Dutch girl cookies, because the shapes remind them of the traditional bonnet once worn by Dutch girls. Whatever you call them, sugar-encrusted puff pastries are crisp, flaky, and utterly delicious.

Makes about 42 cookies

....

> 2 cups unbleached all-purpose flour
> 1 cup (2 sticks) butter, chilled and
>   diced
> 6–7 tablespoons ice water
>   About ¾ cup sugar

....

1. Combine the flour and butter in a medium bowl. With a pastry blender or two knives, cut the butter into the flour until the mixture looks like small peas. Sprinkle the ice water over the mixture as you stir with a fork, until the dough is just moist enough to hold together. Shape the dough into a ball and knead a few times. Cut the ball in half and shape each portion into a 5-inch square with smooth edges. Wrap each half in plastic wrap and chill for at least 2 hours, up to 2 days.

2. Sprinkle ¼ cup of the sugar into a square in the center of the work surface, making the square a little larger than the chilled dough. Roll out one square of dough onto the sugar with a rolling pin, turning the dough to press in as much sugar as possible. Roll into an 8- by 11-inch rectangle, about ⅛ inch thick. Sprinkle with a little more sugar; roll it in. Using a ruler, lightly mark a line down the center of the 8-inch side, 4 inches from each edge. With your fingers, roll in both 8-inch sides of dough toward the middle. When the two rolls meet in the middle, squeeze together gently but firmly. Cover with plastic wrap and chill for 1 to 2 hours. Repeat with the second square of dough, once again sprinkling the work surface with ¼ cup of sugar. Refrigerate.

3. Remove one chilled piece of dough from the refrigerator. Sprinkle an additional tablespoon of sugar onto the work surface. With a sharp knife, cut the double rolls into ¼-inch slices. Press lightly into the sugar and then turn and sprinkle the other side with sugar. Place the cookies on ungreased baking sheets, 2 to 3 inches apart. The cookies will spread as they bake. Repeat with the second piece of dough. Chill in the refrigerator or freezer for at least 30 minutes, up to 2 hours, before baking.

4. Preheat the oven to 400°F.

5. Bake for 8 to 10 minutes, until the cookies are lightly browned. Remove the baking sheets from the oven and turn over the palmiers with a spatula. Continue baking for 3 to 5 minutes, until the second side is a light golden brown and slightly caramelized.

6. Remove from the oven. Cool the cookies, still on the baking sheets, on a wire rack for 5 minutes, then remove from the baking sheets before the cookies get cold. Store in an airtight container or tin box. Separate each layer with waxed paper.

Variation

Cinnamon Palmiers. Combine 2 teaspoons cinnamon and ½ cup granulated sugar in place of the sugar called for in the recipe. As the cookies bake, check frequently to avoid burning.

Ginger Spice Biscotti

Biscotti are twice-baked Italian cookies. The double baking makes them very dry and crunchy, the better to dip them in coffee or dessert wine for maximum eating pleasure.

Makes about 36 cookies

2 cups unbleached all-purpose flour
1½ teaspoons baking soda
½ teaspoon salt
1 teaspoon ground cinnamon
1 teaspoon ground ginger
¼ teaspoon ground cloves
¼ teaspoon freshly grated nutmeg
½ cup granulated sugar
½ cup firmly packed light brown sugar

⅓ cup canola or safflower oil
¼ cup light molasses
1 large egg plus 1 egg white
1 teaspoon vanilla extract
1 cup coarsely chopped, lightly toasted almonds
⅔ cup raisins
½ cup finely chopped crystallized ginger mixed with 2 tablespoons granulated sugar

1. Whisk the flour, baking soda, salt, cinnamon, ginger, cloves, and nutmeg in a medium bowl.

2. Beat together the granulated sugar, brown sugar, oil, and molasses in a large bowl. Add the egg and egg white and the vanilla; beat until well mixed. Stir in the flour mixture and mix thoroughly. Add the almonds and raisins and beat until well combined. The dough will be very thick; you may want to mix with your hands.

3. Preheat the oven to 350°F. Lightly grease two baking sheets or line with parchment paper.

4. On a lightly floured board, knead the dough eight to ten times. Cut the dough in half and roll each half into a log about 2 inches in diameter and 14 inches long. To make the dough easier to handle, cut the dough in half crosswise, so the logs will measure 7 inches long. Place a sheet of waxed paper on the board and put half of the crystallized ginger and sugar mixture down the center. Place a dough log on top of the mixture and roll and press the mixture into the log. Using the waxed paper, lift the log and place on the baking sheet with the ginger and sugar mixture on top. Repeat with the remaining dough. Arrange the logs, 3 inches apart, on the baking sheet (they will spread out and flatten while baking).

5. Bake for 20 to 25 minutes, until the logs are golden and slightly soft.

6. Cool the logs on the baking sheet on a wire rack for 10 minutes. Reduce the oven temperature to 300°F.

7. Place the biscotti on a cutting board. With a sharp knife, cut the biscotti crosswise on the diagonal into 1-inch-wide slices. Return the biscotti to the baking sheet.

8. Bake for 18 to 20 minutes, until the biscotti begin to get crisp and are light golden. Transfer to a rack. The biscotti will become firmer as they cool.

Biscotti Made Easy

BISCOTTI ARE EASY TO MAKE. The place where some people go wrong is in slicing the logs of dough after the first bake. Choose a heavy, straight-edged knife (not a serrated knife) and score the slices first. To make the cuts, put your full weight behind each slice. Place the tip of the knife on the cutting board about 1 inch from the first cut into the biscotti. Press down on the top of the handle with your other hand until you cut through to the cutting board and have made a slice. Use a rocking motion, not a sawing motion.

Chocolate Almond Biscotti

A good-quality chocolate is absolutely essential for good flavor in this recipe. Hazelnuts can replace the almonds if you wish.

Makes 36 cookies

2¼ cups unbleached all-purpose flour
1 teaspoon baking powder
½ teaspoon baking soda
¼ teaspoon salt
4½ ounces semisweet chocolate, coarsely chopped (about ¾ cup)
1 ounce unsweetened chocolate, coarsely chopped
½ cup (1 stick) butter, cut into large pieces

1 cup sugar
2 large eggs
2 teaspoons vanilla extract
1 cup toasted chopped almonds
6 ounces dark, bittersweet, or semisweet chocolate, chopped into ¼- to ⅜-inch chunks (about 1 cup)
3 ounces white chocolate, chopped, to decorate

1. Preheat the oven to 350°F. Line a baking sheet with parchment paper.

2. Whisk the flour, baking powder, baking soda, and salt in a medium bowl.

3. Combine the 4½ ounces semisweet chocolate, the unsweetened chocolate, and the butter in the top of a double boiler over barely simmering water. Stir frequently, until the chocolate and butter are melted and smooth. Remove the top of the double boiler from the hot water and set aside to cool for 5 minutes.

4. Whisk in the sugar. Beat in the eggs, one at a time, beating well after each addition. Add the vanilla. Gradually stir in the flour mixture, then the almonds and the 6 ounces dark chocolate chunks. The dough will be very stiff.

5. On a lightly floured surface, knead the dough a few times to bring it together. Divide the dough into three logs, 10 to 11 inches long and 3 inches in diameter.

6. Place the dough logs on the prepared baking sheet about 3 inches apart. They will spread as they bake. With wet fingers, press the top of the dough to flatten it somewhat, to a thickness of about 1 inch.

7. Bake for 25 minutes, until the logs are slightly firm and crackly on top. Remove from the oven and place the pan on a wire rack to cool for 15 minutes. Lower the oven temperature to 275°F.

8. Using a wide spatula, transfer one log to a cutting board. Slice the log into ¾- to 1-inch slices on the diagonal, using a heavy, straight-edged kitchen knife. Return the biscotti slices to the baking sheet cut-side down. Cut the remaining two logs into slices and transfer to the baking sheet.

9. Bake for 10 to 15 minutes, until the biscotti are firm. If the biscotti need to bake longer, turn off the oven and leave the door ajar until the biscotti are cold.

10. To decorate the biscotti, melt the white chocolate in the top of a double boiler set over simmering water. Stir until completely melted and smooth. Remove the top of the double boiler from the heat and let cool slightly. Put the chocolate in a pastry bag or small plastic bag. (Cut off a tiny corner if using a plastic bag.) Squeeze out the melted chocolate to make a squiggly design on top of each cookie.

Baker's Tip

❋ Chocolate biscotti are more fragile when they're hot than are other kinds of biscotti.

Brownies and Bars

Brownies get their name from their deep, rich color — but who made the first one is not known. Some claim that the brownie was invented as a portable dessert at the Palmer House Hotel in Chicago during the 1892 Columbian Exposition. The name "brownie" first appeared in the 1896 *Boston Cooking-School Cook Book,* but that bar cookie was flavored and colored by molasses, not chocolate. The earliest published recipe for chocolate brownies appeared in the *Boston Daily Globe* on April 2, 1905.

Brownies and bars are welcome everywhere, from potlucks to picnics. They are easy to make.

Ingredients

○ **Chocolate should be melted over low heat to avoid scorching.** The easiest way to do this is in a double boiler set over a pan of barely simmering water. If you don't have a double boiler, fashion one by placing a metal bowl over a saucepan of simmering water.

○ **You can also melt chocolate in the microwave if you are very careful.** Using 50 percent power, heat the chocolate in short bursts of 10 to 20 seconds, and check frequently. Stir the chocolate between bursts of heat. You can figure that 4 ounces of chopped chocolate will take about 3 minutes total at 50 percent power.

○ **Chocolate that has been stored in a cold, damp place may develop a "bloom," which is just tiny crystals of sugar.** The chocolate is still usable.

○ **For the best flavor, bake with butter instead of margarine.**

Techniques

○ **Always start by preheating the oven.** Place an oven rack in the center of the oven.

○ **For ease of serving butter the baking dish.** Then line your baking dish with aluminum foil or parchment paper with overhanging edges. Then butter the foil, if using. When the brownies or bar cookies are done, lift up the liner from the baking dish by holding on to the edges, and set the brownie or bar on a cutting board. When completely cool, it should be easy to cut the bars into even-size pieces.

○ **Do not overbeat brownie batter.** Fudge brownie recipes are best mixed by hand in a large bowl with a mixing spoon.

○ **Brownie batter is thick.** Use a spatula to spread out the batter and move it into the corners of the pan.

○ **To create brownies without crumbled edges, bake them a day in advance.**

○ **Do not overbake brownies! Remove fudge brownies from the oven when the top appears dry and shiny and the brownie begins to pull away from the sides of the pan.** Generally, bar cookies are done when a wooden pick inserted into the center comes out clean or with moist (not wet) crumbs adhering to it.

○ **Dress up brownies by adding a frosting** (see pages 131 to 145).

○ **For the best-looking bar cookies, cool completely, then put in the freezer for a few minutes to harden.** Cut with a long, sharp knife and trim away any dry, overly brown edges.

○ **Brownies and bars can be stored in the pan in which they were baked, covered, for several days.** If they contain cream cheese, however, they must be refrigerated.

○ **Brownies and bars freeze best when pieces are individually wrapped.** Double-wrap in plastic wrap and aluminum foil, then place in an airtight bag. Thaw still wrapped, at room temperature.

Chocolate Fudge Brownies

One often reads about the importance of the Sears, Roebuck catalog to rural America in the nineteenth century — but who would have guessed that it popularized brownies by printing a recipe for them in 1897?

Makes 16 bars

- 2 ounces semisweet chocolate or ⅛ cup semisweet chocolate chips
- 2 ounces unsweetened chocolate
- ½ cup (1 stick) butter
- 1 cup sugar
- ¼ teaspoon salt
- 1 teaspoon vanilla extract
- 2 large eggs
- ½ cup unbleached all-purpose flour
- ½ cup chopped walnuts

1. Preheat the oven to 350°F. Lightly grease and flour an 8-inch square baking pan.

2. Melt the chocolates and butter in the top of a double boiler set over simmering water. Stir until completely smooth and glossy. Remove the top of the double boiler from the heat and stir in the sugar and salt.

3. Transfer the chocolate mixture to a medium bowl and add the vanilla and eggs, one at a time, beating well after each addition. Stir in the flour and nuts, mixing until blended. Spoon the batter into the prepared pan.

4. Bake for about 25 minutes, until the top feels dry and looks shiny. The inside will be soft but will firm up when cooled.

5. Cool the brownies completely in the pan on a wire rack, then cut into 2-inch squares.

Cocoa Brownies

When the urge to bake strikes but there is only cocoa in the house, you can still make delicious, chewy brownies. This old-fashioned brownie isn't "death by chocolate" but it is happiness in a square pan.

Makes 16 bars

- 4 tablespoons butter
- 1 cup firmly packed light brown sugar
- 1 large egg
- 1½ teaspoons vanilla extract
- ½ cup sifted all-purpose flour
- 3 tablespoons unsweetened cocoa powder
- ⅛ teaspoon salt
- ¾ cup chopped walnuts
- Confectioners' sugar, to dust

1. Preheat the oven to 325°F. Grease an 8-inch square baking pan.

2. Melt the butter in a heavy saucepan over low heat. Remove the pan from the heat and stir in the sugar. Let cool.

3. Mix in the egg and vanilla, beating until light and smooth.

4. Whisk the flour, cocoa, and salt in a small bowl until well mixed. Fold into the chocolate mixture, stirring until combined. Spoon the batter into the prepared pan. Use a spatula to spread the batter into the corners of the pan.

5. Bake for 20 minutes, until the top of the brownie feels dry and the edges pull away from the sides of the pan. Do not overbake.

6. Cool the brownie completely in the pan on a wire rack, then cut into 2-inch squares. Sprinkle lightly with confectioners' sugar. Serve immediately or store in an airtight container for 2 to 3 days.

Marbled Cheesecake Brownies

These brownies are rich, indulgent, and sinful — or about as sinful as most of us would ever contemplate. Cut them into small pieces.

Makes 32 bars

8 ounces semisweet, dark, or bittersweet chocolate	2 cups sugar
	6 large eggs
¾ cup (1½ sticks) butter, at room temperature	1¼ cups unbleached all-purpose flour
	2 teaspoons vanilla extract
1 (8-ounce) package cream cheese, at room temperature	1½ teaspoons baking powder
	½ teaspoon salt

1. Preheat the oven to 350°F. Grease a 9- by 13-inch baking pan and line it with a large sheet of parchment paper or aluminum foil, leaving handles of paper extending over the rim of the pan.

2. Melt the chocolate with ½ cup of the butter in the top of a double boiler set over simmering water. Stir until completely smooth. Remove from the heat.

3. To make the cheesecake batter, beat the remaining ¼ cup butter with the cream cheese in a large bowl until smooth. Gradually add ½ cup of the sugar and beat until fluffy. Beat in two of the eggs, ¼ cup of the flour, and 1 teaspoon vanilla.

4. To make the brownie batter, beat the remaining 4 eggs and 1½ cups sugar in a large bowl until frothy. Slowly incorporate the chocolate mixture. Beat in the remaining teaspoon vanilla.

5. Stir together the remaining 1 cup flour and the baking powder and salt. Add to the chocolate brownie batter, beating until smooth.

6. Spread half the brownie batter in the prepared pan. Smooth the cheesecake mixture over the batter. Drop spoonfuls of the remaining brownie batter on top of the cheese layer. Swirl a knife through the batter to marble in the chocolate.

7. Bake for about 35 minutes, until the top is firm and a tester inserted into the center comes out almost clean. Do not overbake.

8. Cool the brownie completely in the pan on a wire rack. Lift the entire brownie out of the pan using the paper handles. Cut into small squares.

Peanut Butter Brownies

Peanut butter and chocolate is a marriage made in heaven, calling forth a sublime harmony and bringing out the best in each partner.

Makes 16 bars

- 2 ounces dark or bittersweet chocolate, coarsely chopped
- 4 tablespoons butter
- ½ cup firmly packed dark brown sugar
- ½ cup granulated sugar
- ½ cup chunky peanut butter
- 2 large eggs
- 1½ teaspoons vanilla extract
- 6 tablespoons unbleached all-purpose flour
- ¼ teaspoon baking powder
- ⅛ teaspoon salt
- ¼ cup finely chopped peanuts, plus 2 tablespoons for topping
- ¾ cup chocolate chips

1. Preheat the oven to 350°F. Grease a 9-inch square baking pan.

2. Melt the chocolate and butter in the top of a double boiler set over simmering water. Stir until completely smooth and glossy. Remove the top of the double boiler from the heat and add the brown sugar and the granulated sugar, mixing until thoroughly combined.

3. Transfer the chocolate mixture to a medium bowl and mix in the peanut butter, beating until smooth. Mix in the eggs, one at a time, beating well after each addition. Stir in the vanilla.

4. Whisk the flour, baking powder, and salt in a small bowl until thoroughly combined. Fold the flour mixture into the chocolate mixture, stirring until combined. Stir in the ¼ cup peanuts and the chocolate chips. Spoon the batter into the prepared pan. Sprinkle the top with the 2 tablespoons peanuts.

5. Bake for 25 to 28 minutes, until the edges begin to firm up and the center of the brownie appears dry.

6. Cool the brownie completely in the pan on a wire rack. To serve, run a knife around the sides and cut into squares. Store for up to 2 days or freeze.

Cherry Almond Brownies

With the availability of quality dark chocolates, the good old American brownie has undergone a transformation. It is impossible to resist updating this classic. Here the brownie is made with rich dark chocolate and Kirsch-soaked dried cherries.

Makes 16 to 20 bars

⅔ cup dried cherries
3 tablespoons Kirsch
6 ounces dark or bittersweet chocolate, broken into pieces
½ cup (1 stick) butter, cut up

3 large eggs
¾ cup sugar
¾ cup unbleached all-purpose flour
¼ teaspoon salt
½ cup flaked almonds

1. Preheat the oven to 325°F. Grease an 8-inch square baking dish.

2. Combine the cherries and Kirsch in a small, microwave-safe bowl. Heat in the microwave for 1 minute on high. Set aside; the cherries will plump up and absorb most or all of the Kirsch.

3. Melt the chocolate and butter in the top of a double boiler set over simmering water. Stir until completely smooth and glossy. Remove the top of the double boiler from the heat and let cool slightly.

4. Beat the eggs with a spoon in a medium bowl until well combined. Add the sugar and beat until smooth. Scrape in the chocolate mixture and beat until smooth. Stir in the flour and salt. Stir in the cherries, any remaining Kirsch, and the almonds. Transfer the batter to the prepared pan.

5. Bake for about 35 minutes, until the top is shiny and somewhat firm. Do not overbake.

6. Cool the brownie completely in the pan on a wire rack before cutting into squares.

Peppermint Patty Brownies

Which came first: the candy or the cartoon character? York Peppermint Patties pre-date Charlie Brown's often misguided friend by decades. The candy was invented by Henry C. Kessler in 1940. Its chocolate coating, sweet mint center, and firm texture made instant fans. The character Peppermint Patty was introduced in 1966, and she, too, was an instant hit. Brownies (no relation to Charlie Brown) are a perfect match for Peppermint Patties, the candy.

Makes 16 bars

- 2 ounces unsweetened chocolate
- ½ cup (1 stick) butter
- 1 cup granulated sugar
- 1 teaspoon vanilla extract
- 2 large eggs
- ¾ cup unbleached all-purpose flour
- ¼ teaspoon baking powder
- ¼ teaspoon salt
- 16 peppermint patties

FROSTING

- 1½ cups sifted confectioners' sugar
- 3 tablespoons butter, at room temperature
- 1–1½ tablespoons milk
- ½–1 teaspoon peppermint extract
  Few drops green food coloring (optional)
  Green crystallized sugar sprinkles (optional)

1. Preheat the oven to 350°F. Grease an 8-inch square baking pan.

2. Melt the chocolate and butter in the top of a double boiler set over simmering water. Stir until completely smooth and glossy. Remove the top of the double boiler from the heat and stir in the sugar.

3. Transfer the chocolate mixture to a medium bowl and add the vanilla and eggs, one at a time, beating well after each addition. Stir until blended.

4. Whisk the flour, baking powder, and salt in a small bowl until well mixed. Fold the flour mixture into the chocolate mixture, stirring until combined.

5. Spread 1 cup of the brownie batter over the bottom of the prepared baking pan. Arrange peppermint patties in rows on top of the batter, setting them about ¼ inch away from the edges of the pan and ⅛ to ½ inch apart. Spread the rest of the batter gently over the patties, completely covering them. Use a spatula to spread the batter into the corners of the pan.

6. Bake for about 25 minutes, until the top feels dry and the edges pull away from the sides of the pan. If they have not pulled away, bake the brownie for 2 to 3 minutes longer. Do not overbake.

7. Cool the brownie completely in the pan on a wire rack.

8. To make the frosting, beat together the confectioners' sugar and butter until smooth. Gradually add the milk, mixing in a teaspoon at a time. Add a few drops of peppermint extract at a time, tasting for desired peppermint flavor. Add food coloring (if using) to make a pale green frosting. When the frosting is a spreading consistency, spread over the brownie. Top with the crystallized sugar sprinkles (if using).

9. Allow the frosting to set, 40 to 45 minutes. Cut into squares. Serve immediately or store in an airtight container for 2 to 3 days.

Dark or Bittersweet Chocolate

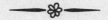

ONE CONSEQUENCE of America's recent discovery of quality chocolate has been some name changes. What used to be called "bittersweet" chocolate is now often called "dark" chocolate. To avoid confusion, we use "dark or bittersweet chocolate" in the recipes. These are chocolates that must contain at least 35 percent chocolate liquor (sometimes written as 35 percent cacao), but often contain more.

Chocolate Raspberry Brownies

Chocolate is always available, but the season for fresh raspberries is fleeting. No problem here: These brownies get their fruit flavor from raspberry jam and raspberry liqueur. The result? Very chocolaty. Very fruity. Very delicious.

Makes 32 bars

4 ounces semisweet, dark, or bittersweet chocolate
2 ounces unsweetened chocolate
1 cup (2 sticks) butter, cut up
4 large eggs
1¼ cups sugar
⅔ cup raspberry jam
2 tablespoons Chambord or other raspberry liqueur (or substitute Kirsch)
¼ teaspoon salt
1 cup unbleached all-purpose flour

1. Preheat the oven to 350°F. Grease a 9- by 13-inch baking pan. Line the pan with a large sheet of parchment paper or aluminum foil, leaving handles of paper extending over the rim of the pan. Grease the foil liner.

2. Melt the semisweet chocolate, unsweetened chocolate, and butter in the top of a double boiler set over simmering water. Stir until completely smooth and glossy. Remove the top of the double boiler from the heat and let cool.

3. Beat the eggs in a large bowl until light and fluffy. Slowly beat in the sugar until the mixture is light and fluffy. Beat in the jam, liqueur, and salt. Scrape in the chocolate mixture and beat until smooth. Fold in the flour. Spoon the batter into the prepared pan.

4. Bake for about 25 minutes, until the top feels dry and looks shiny. The inside will be soft but will firm up when cooled.

5. Cool the brownie completely in the pan on a wire rack. Lift the entire brownie out of the pan using the paper handles. Cut into squares.

Mississippi Mud Brownies

The chocolate chip meringue topping creates a frosting that looks a bit like mud. And if it is mud, it must be Mississippi mud. Some Mississippi mud bars are made with a marshmallow or marshmallow crème topping. However, this meringue topping is simple to make and doesn't require a special trip to the store for the marshmallows.

Makes 16 brownies

2 *ounces dark or bittersweet chocolate*
2 *ounces unsweetened chocolate*
½ *cup (1 stick) butter*
1 *cup granulated sugar*
¼ *teaspoon salt*
1 *teaspoon vanilla extract*
2 *large eggs*
½ *cup unbleached all-purpose flour*
½ *cup chopped walnuts or pecans*

TOPPING

1 *egg white, at room temperature*
Pinch of salt
2 *tablespoons granulated sugar*
¼ *cup firmly packed light brown sugar*
½ *teaspoon vanilla extract*
¾ *cup chocolate chips*

1. Preheat the oven to 350°F. Lightly grease and flour an 8-inch square baking pan.

2. Melt the dark chocolate, unsweetened chocolate, and butter in the top of a double boiler set over simmering water. Stir until completely smooth and glossy. Remove the top of the double boiler from the heat and stir in the sugar and salt.

3. Transfer the chocolate mixture to a medium bowl and add the vanilla and eggs, one at a time, beating well after each addition. Stir in the flour and nuts, mixing until blended. Spoon the batter into the prepared pan.

4. For the topping, beat the egg white until foamy. Add the salt and beat until soft peaks form. Gradually sprinkle in the granulated sugar and beat until stiff but not dry. Fold in the brown sugar and vanilla, mixing until combined. Stir in the chocolate chips. Spread the topping evenly over the top of the brownie batter.

5. Bake for 30 minutes.

6. Cool the brownie completely in the pan on a wire rack. Cut into squares.

Low-Fat Chocolate Brownie Squares

In every life, a little rain must fall, and in every life, a little dieting must be considered. So here it is: The best low-fat brownies you're ever likely to encounter.

Makes 16 brownies

3	ounces unsweetened chocolate, coarsely chopped	3	tablespoons prune purée (puréed prune baby food)
1½	tablespoons butter	¾	cup unbleached all-purpose flour
1⅓	cups sugar	3	tablespoons unsweetened cocoa
2	large eggs	¼	teaspoon baking soda
2	teaspoons vanilla extract	¼	teaspoon salt

1. Preheat the oven to 350°F. Grease a 9-inch square baking pan.

2. Melt the chocolate and butter in the top of a double boiler set over simmering water. Stir until completely smooth and glossy. Remove the top of the double boiler from the heat and stir in the sugar.

3. Transfer the chocolate mixture to a medium bowl and add the eggs, one at a time, beating until light and smooth. Mix in the vanilla and the prune purée.

4. Whisk the flour, cocoa, baking soda, and salt in a small bowl until well mixed. Fold the flour mixture into the chocolate mixture, stirring until combined. Spoon the batter into the prepared pan.

5. Bake for 22 to 24 minutes, until the top feels dry and the edges pull away from the sides of the pan. Do not overbake.

6. Cool the brownie completely in the pan on a wire rack. Cut into squares. Serve, or store in an airtight container in the refrigerator for 2 to 3 days.

Brownie Pizza

Brownie pizzas are always a hit, whether they are an excuse for decorating with colorful candies or for making a faux pizza, with grated white chocolate standing in for mozzarella. Let your imagination be your guide! Thin rounds of red licorice can simulate bits of pepperoni or tomato and thin strips of leaf-shaped green jelly candies can stand in for strips of green peppers or basil. In fine pastry shops, you can sometimes find little marzipan candies shaped like vegetables, which are also fun to use. But no one will object to a shower of M&Ms or a topping of sliced fruit drizzled with chocolate syrup.

Makes 12 slices

4½ ounces unsweetened chocolate	1½ cups unbleached all-purpose flour
¾ cup (1½ sticks) butter, cut up	2 ounces white chocolate
2 cups sugar	½ cup assorted candies (such as jelly
3 large eggs, lightly beaten	beans, sliced gumdrops, sliced
1 tablespoon vanilla extract	licorice)

1. Preheat the oven to 350°F. Grease a 12-inch round pizza pan.

2. Melt the unsweetened chocolate and butter in the top of a double boiler set over simmering water. Stir until completely smooth and glossy. Remove the top of the double boiler from the heat and let cool for 1 minute.

3. Stir the sugar, eggs, and vanilla into the melted chocolate mixture and transfer to a medium bowl. Stir in the flour until smooth. Pour into the prepared pan and spread evenly with a spatula.

4. Bake for about 18 minutes, until the top springs back when touched lightly.

5. While the brownie bakes, grate the white chocolate using the largest holes on a box grater. Sprinkle the grated chocolate over the hot brownie and top with the candies. Let cool in the pan. To serve, cut into 12 wedges using a large knife or pizza wheel.

Chocolate Chip–Nut Bars

When you want a chocolate chip cookie without the fuss of scooping out dozens of cookies and baking multiple batches, turn to this bar cookie. The batter can be made quickly with a food processor. Truthfully, the only tricky parts are smoothing the cookie dough in the pan (it takes a little wrestling) and not overbaking. Well, maybe restricting yourself to just one . . .

Makes 32 bars

2 cups unbleached all-purpose flour	3 large eggs
1 teaspoon baking powder	1 teaspoon vanilla extract
1 teaspoon salt	1½ cups chocolate chips
¼ teaspoon baking soda	1½ cups walnuts or pecans
¾ cup (1½ sticks) butter, softened	
2 cups firmly packed light or dark brown sugar	

1. Preheat the oven to 325°F. Generously grease a 9- by 13-inch baking pan.

2. Stir together the flour, baking powder, salt, and baking soda in a medium bowl.

3. Combine the butter and brown sugar in a food processor and process until light and fluffy. Add the eggs and vanilla and process until light. Add the flour mixture and process until just combined. Add the chocolate chips and nuts and pulse until just mixed in.

4. Spoon the dough into the prepared pan. Use a spatula to move the dough into the corners and to level the surface.

5. Bake for 40 to 45 minutes, until a tester inserted near the center comes out clean. Do not overbake.

6. Cool the brownie completely in the pan on a wire rack. Cut into squares.

Lemon Bars

This recipe makes a rich, buttery cookie. It is a good idea to place the cut bars on paper towels to absorb some of the excess butter. For variation, consider sprinkling the bars with coconut flakes instead of the confectioners' sugar.

Makes 32 bars

COOKIE CRUST

- 2 cups unbleached all-purpose flour
- ½ cup plus 2–3 tablespoons confectioners' sugar
  Pinch of salt
- 1 teaspoon finely grated lemon zest
- 1 cup (2 sticks) butter, at room temperature

LEMON FILLING

- 4 large eggs
- 2 cups granulated sugar
- 1 tablespoon finely grated lemon zest
- 6 tablespoons fresh lemon juice
- 2 tablespoons unbleached all-purpose flour
- 1 teaspoon baking powder

1. Preheat the oven to 350°F. Lightly grease a 9- by 13-inch baking pan.

2. To make the cookie crust, combine the flour, the ½ cup confectioners' sugar, and salt in a food processor. Add the lemon zest and butter, processing until thoroughly blended. Spread the mixture in the prepared pan and press gently to form an even layer. Bake for 20 minutes.

3. While the crust is baking, prepare the filling. Beat the eggs until light. Gradually add the granulated sugar, beating until thick and lemon-colored. Add the lemon zest, lemon juice, flour, and baking powder, blending until well combined.

4. Pour the lemon mixture over the still-warm cookie crust.

5. Bake for 20 to 25 minutes, until the top is golden brown. The filling should be soft; do not overbake.

6. To garnish, sift the remaining 2 to 3 tablespoons confectioners' sugar over the cookies while they are still warm. Cool in the pan on a wire rack for at least 30 minutes before cutting into squares or bars.

Tropical Lime Squares

Prefer limes over lemons? Have a hankering for something new? These lime-flavored bar cookies are a wonderful variation on lemon squares.

Makes about 32 bars

COOKIE CRUST

2 cups unbleached all-purpose flour
½ cup confectioners' sugar
Pinch of salt

1 cup (2 sticks) butter, at room temperature

LIME FILLING

4 large eggs
2 cups granulated sugar
1 tablespoon finely grated lime zest
6 tablespoons fresh lime juice
2 tablespoons unbleached all-purpose flour

1 teaspoon baking powder
Few drops green food coloring (optional)
½ cup lightly packed, sweetened flaked coconut, to garnish

1. Preheat the oven to 350°F. Lightly grease a 9- by 13-inch baking pan.

2. To make the cookie crust, combine the flour, confectioners' sugar, and salt in a food processor. Add the butter and process until thoroughly blended. Spread the mixture in the prepared pan and press gently to form an even layer. Bake for 20 minutes.

3. While the crust is baking, prepare the filling. Beat the eggs until light. Gradually add the sugar, beating until thick and lemon-colored. Add the lime zest, lime juice, flour, and baking powder, blending until well combined. Stir in the food coloring (if using).

4. Pour the lime mixture over the still-warm cookie crust.

5. Bake for 20 to 25 minutes, until the top is golden. The filling should be soft.

6. Sprinkle the coconut over the cookie while it is still warm. Cool in the pan on a wire rack for at least 30 minutes before cutting into squares or bars.

Raspberry Bars

Raspberries are our favorite, but any berry can be used to make these bar cookies, including blueberries, blackberries, or hulled and chopped strawberries.

Makes 32 bars

BOTTOM LAYER

2 cups unbleached all-purpose flour
¾ cup confectioners' sugar

½ cup (1 stick) butter, melted
½ teaspoon vanilla extract

FILLING

2 cups fresh or frozen (thawed) raspberries

½ cup granulated sugar
2 tablespoons quick-cooking tapioca

TOP LAYER

2 cups rolled oats (or 1 cup rolled oats and 1 cup quick oats)
1 cup firmly packed light brown sugar

½ cup (1 stick) butter, melted
1 teaspoon ground cinnamon

1. Preheat the oven to 325°F. Lightly grease a 9- by 13-inch baking pan.

2. To make the bottom layer, combine the flour, confectioners' sugar, butter, and vanilla. Mix with a fork until the butter is evenly distributed and the mixture is crumbly. Firmly pat the mixture into the bottom of the baking dish. Bake for 15 minutes, then set aside to cool.

3. While the bottom layer bakes, make the filling. Combine the raspberries, granulated sugar, and tapioca. Set aside for at least 30 minutes to allow the tapioca to blend with the raspberry juice.

4. To make the top layer, mix the oats, brown sugar, butter, and cinnamon and stir until the mixture is crumbly.

5. When the bottom layer is cool, spread the filling evenly over it. Sprinkle the oat mixture over the raspberries. Bake for 25 to 30 minutes, until the top is golden.

6. Cool completely in the pan on a wire rack. Cut into squares or rectangles.

Blondies

Difficult though it is to imagine, there are people who don't care for chocolate. Even more painful to contemplate is that some people are allergic to chocolate. For these souls, the blondie was invented: a chocolate-free brownie.

Makes 16 bars

4 tablespoons butter	1 teaspoon vanilla extract
1 cup firmly packed light brown sugar	½ cup unbleached all-purpose flour
⅛ teaspoon salt	¼ teaspoon baking soda
1 large egg	1 cup coarsely chopped walnuts, lightly toasted

1. Preheat the oven to 350°F. Lightly grease and flour an 8-inch square baking pan.

2. Melt the butter over low heat in a medium saucepan. Remove from the heat and stir in the brown sugar and salt. Beat in the egg and vanilla. Stir in the flour and baking soda, mixing until blended. Mix in the nuts. Spoon the batter into the prepared pan.

3. Bake for 18 to 20 minutes, until the blondie begins to pull away from the sides of the pan and is still slightly soft in the middle. Do not overbake.

4. Cool the blondie completely in the pan on a wire rack. Cut into squares or rectangles.

Baker's Tip

※ To toast the walnuts, place in a shallow baking pan and toast in the preheated 300°F oven for 7 to 10 minutes, until fragrant.

Dream Bars

hy are these tooth-achingly sweet bar cookies called dream bars? Perhaps because they are the perfect answer to the recurrent waking nightmare every parent experiences. It happens just as you tuck the little darlings into bed and one of them says, "Oh, I forgot to tell you, but I have to bring in something for the school bake sale tomorrow." These cookies are also known as seven-layer bars and lazy layer bars, for obvious reasons: All you have to do is layer up the ingredients, no mixing, no fussing.

Makes 32 bars

½ cup (1 stick) butter, melted
1¼ cups graham cracker crumbs
1 cup chocolate chips
1 cup butterscotch morsels
1 cup lightly packed, sweetened
       flaked coconut

1 (14-ounce) can sweetened
       condensed milk
1 cup chopped pecans

1. Preheat the oven to 350°F. Spread the butter in a 9- by 13-inch baking pan.

2. Sprinkle the graham cracker crumbs evenly over the butter. Pat to make a firm, level surface with the crumbs. Sprinkle the chocolate chips over the crumbs. Sprinkle the butterscotch morsels over the chocolate. Then sprinkle the coconut over the butterscotch. Drizzle the condensed milk evenly over the entire pan. Sprinkle the pecans over all.

3. Bake for about 20 minutes, until the bar is golden.

4. Cool completely in the pan on a wire rack, and then cut into bars. These bars improve in flavor after a day.

Baker's Tips

※ If you are using a glass baking dish, you can melt the butter in the baking dish in a microwave set on high for about 1 minute.

※ Graham cracker crumbs are easily made in a food processor. It takes about nine sheets of graham crackers to make 1¼ cups of crumbs.

Blueberry Cheesecake Squares

When you need a high-yield dessert for a bake sale or party, this is a terrific recipe — delicious, very easy to prepare, and conveniently made with fresh or frozen blueberries. It is made in a jelly-roll pan, which is also known as a rimmed baking sheet, and is found in the cupboard of most bakers.

Makes 36 squares

CRUST AND CRUMBLE TOPPING

2¾ cups all-purpose flour
½ cup firmly packed light brown sugar
½ cup granulated sugar
1 teaspoon ground cinnamon
½ teaspoon salt
¼ teaspoon freshly grated nutmeg
1 cup (2 sticks) butter, melted

FILLING

2 (8-ounce) packages cream cheese, at room temperature
1½ cups granulated sugar
3 large eggs
1 teaspoon vanilla extract
3 cups fresh or thawed frozen blueberries

1. Preheat the oven to 350°F. Grease a 10- by 15-inch jelly-roll pan.

2. To make the crust and topping, stir together the flour, brown sugar, granulated sugar, cinnamon, salt, and nutmeg. Stir in the butter until the mixture is crumbly. Put two-thirds of the mixture into the prepared pan and press gently to form an even layer. Reserve the remaining mixture for the topping.

3. To make the filling, beat together the cream cheese, sugar, eggs, and vanilla with an electric mixer on medium speed until smooth.

4. Spread the blueberries over the crust in the pan, then pour the cream cheese mixture over the berries. Sprinkle with the reserved crumble mixture.

5. Bake for 35 to 40 minutes, until the topping is golden brown and the cream cheese mixture is set.

6. Cut into squares immediately, but allow them to cool completely in the pan before serving. Store in an airtight container in the refrigerator for up to 3 days or freeze for up to 1 month.

Chinese Chews

There is nothing Chinese about this bar cookie recipe, which has its origins in the 1920s. Whoever named it must have thought that dates are so exotic that the recipe must be Chinese. Recipes for Chinese chews were popular through the 1960s and appeared in hundreds of community cookbooks.

Makes 36 squares

1¾ cups unbleached all-purpose flour
¾ cup (1½ sticks) butter, chilled and diced
¼ cup granulated sugar
2 cups firmly packed light or dark brown sugar

1½ cups chopped dates
1 cup lightly packed, sweetened flaked coconut
3 large eggs
½ cup confectioners' sugar

1. Preheat the oven to 350°F. Grease a 10- by 15-inch jelly-roll pan.

2. Combine 1¼ cups of the flour, the butter, and the granulated sugar in a food processor and process until crumbly. (Alternatively, you can mix together the flour and sugar and rub in the butter with your fingertips until the mixture is crumbly.) Transfer the mixture to the prepared jelly-roll pan and pat to make an even layer.

3. Bake for about 12 minutes, until light brown. Reduce the oven temperature to 325°F.

4. Meanwhile, combine the remaining ½ cup flour and the brown sugar, dates, coconut, and eggs and mix well. Spread over the baked mixture. Try to make the layer as even as possible by spreading with a palette knife or offset spatula.

5. Bake for about 25 minutes, until brown.

6. Cut into bars while still warm. Sift the confectioners' sugar over the bars. Let cool before removing from the pan.

Fig Newtons

When Massachusetts schoolchildren petitioned the state legislature to make the chocolate chip cookie the state cookie, it created a huge controversy because many people, including Governor William Weld, preferred fig Newtons, which were also invented in the state, and named after the town of Newton. Finally, in 1997, Massachusetts bill S-1716 named the chocolate chip cookie the official state cookie. The sore losers declared the fig Newton the unofficial state "fruit cookie." These cookies are a little more difficult to make than the other bar cookies in this chapter, but well worth the effort.

Makes 40 to 42 bar cookies

COOKIE DOUGH

1¾ cups unbleached all-purpose flour
½ cup whole-wheat flour
¼ teaspoon baking soda
¼ teaspoon ground cinnamon
¼ teaspoon salt
½ cup (1 stick) butter, at room temperature

½ cup firmly packed light brown sugar
¼ cup granulated sugar
1 teaspoon freshly grated orange zest
2 large eggs, at room temperature
1 teaspoon vanilla extract

FIG FILLING

1 pound dried figs, stems removed, finely chopped
2–2½ cups water
⅓ cup granulated sugar, plus more as needed

2 teaspoons grated orange zest
Confectioners' sugar

1. To make the cookie dough, whisk the all-purpose flour, whole-wheat flour, baking soda, cinnamon, and salt in a medium bowl.

2. Beat the butter in a large bowl until creamy. Gradually add the brown sugar, granulated sugar, and orange zest, beating until thoroughly combined. Add the eggs, one at a time, beating well after each addition. Mix in the vanilla. Gradually mix in the flour mixture, stirring until well combined. Dust the dough with a little flour,

shape into a ball, and wrap in plastic wrap, and refrigerate for at least 2 hours, until the dough is easy to handle.

3. To make the filling, put the figs in a small saucepan and cover with water. Bring to a boil, reduce the heat, and simmer, covered, for 25 to 30 minutes, until the figs are soft. Add the sugar and orange zest and simmer, uncovered, for 10 to 15 minutes, stirring occasionally, until most of the liquid has been absorbed and the mixture has the consistency of jam. Taste and add more sugar if needed. Set aside to cool.

4. Cover a baking sheet with parchment paper.

5. On a lightly floured surface, knead the dough five or six times to make a smooth ball. Divide the ball into two equal portions. Flatten each into a rectangle about ½ inch thick. Return one portion, wrapped in plastic wrap, to the refrigerator. Place the first rectangle between two long sheets of waxed paper lightly dusted with flour. Roll out the dough into a straight-edged rectangle measuring 7 inches by 15 inches. Pull off the top sheet of waxed paper. Cut the dough lengthwise into two strips; each strip should measure 3½ by 15 inches. Divide the filling into four equal parts. Spoon one-quarter of the filling in a mound down the center of one of the strips of dough. Using a long spatula or pastry scraper, gently lift the sides of each strip of dough over the filling, overlapping the dough slightly on top to enclose it. Press the dough together lightly to seal. To make the bars easier to handle, cut them in half, crosswise, and transfer them to the baking sheet, seam-side down. Repeat the rolling and filling process using another one-fourth of the filling on each of the three remaining strips.

6. Preheat the oven to 375°F. Refrigerate the filled bars for about 15 minutes before baking.

7. Bake for 20 to 22 minutes, until the bars are lightly browned.

8. Cool on a wire rack for 10 minutes. With a sharp, serrated knife, trim off the ends of each strip, and then slice each strip into 1½-inch bars. Dust lightly with confectioners' sugar.

Matrimonial Bars

Why the name "matrimonial bar?" Research into historical cookbooks didn't yield a clue. But the answer may be obvious: If you have plenty of dates, you will probably wind up finding someone to marry. These orange-scented date bars may be proposal-worthy.

Makes 32 bars

FILLING

- 1 pound pitted dates, chopped
- ½ cup water
- ½ cup firmly packed light brown sugar
- 1 tablespoon finely grated orange zest
- ⅔ cup freshly squeezed orange juice
- 1 teaspoon ground cinnamon

CRUST

- 1½ cups all-purpose flour
- 1 cup firmly packed light brown sugar
- 1 teaspoon baking powder
- ½ teaspoon baking soda
- ½ teaspoon salt
- 1 cup (2 sticks) butter, chilled and diced
- 2 cups rolled oats (not quick-cooking)

1. To prepare the filling, combine the dates, water, brown sugar, orange zest, orange juice, and cinnamon in a small saucepan. Cook over medium heat until thick and smooth, about 20 minutes, stirring frequently and breaking up the dates with the back of a spoon. Set aside to cool.

2. Preheat the oven to 350°F. Grease a 9- by 13-inch baking pan.

3. To make the crust, combine the flour, brown sugar, baking powder, baking soda, and salt in a food processor. Add the butter and process until the mixture has the texture of coarse crumbs. Add the oats and pulse to mix in.

4. Press half of the oat mixture into the prepared baking pan, patting until smooth. Drop dollops of the cooled date filling over the mixture and spread evenly with a palette knife or offset spatula. Sprinkle the remaining crust over the filling and pat to make an even layer.

5. Bake for 40 to 45 minutes, until the topping is golden brown and the juices are bubbling.

6. Cut into bars immediately, but allow them to cool completely in the pan on a wire rack before serving.

The Secrets of Success

BAR COOKIES AND BROWNIES should come out of the pan with precise, square corners and neat straight edges. What's the secret to success? Let them cool completely in the pan, preferably overnight. If you are baking for your family, then by all means make up a batch of brownies and serve them warm, right out of the oven. Nothing tastes better. But if you are making brownies, blondies, or bar cookies for a dessert buffet or bake sale, it is best to make them the day before. Then when you cut them, the edges will be straight and a neat appearance will be accomplished.

Another way to guarantee straight edges is to bake the bar cookies in a pan lined with aluminum foil or parchment paper. Cut the foil long enough to overhang the edges of the pan. Grease the foil if the recipe calls for a greased pan. Once the cookies are baked and cooled, use the overhanging foil to lift the entire batch of cookies out of the pan. Then cut the cookies with a long knife — you can even use a straight-edge ruler to guarantee equal-size pieces. The foil will also save on cleanup and prevent knife marks in the pan.

Fancy Cakes

We like to celebrate special occasions with cake, probably because no other confection allows us so many opportunities for decorating and writing out our thoughts. But cakes are more than special-occasion message boards; they are an expression of love, generosity, and homemade goodness.

In the old days, bakers used teacups and spoons of varying sizes for measuring. After Fanny Farmer standardized our measuring cups and spoons, recipes could be written down and shared with some degree of accuracy from cook to cook, mother to daughter, and cookbook writer to reader. But even with standardized recipes, a few helpful hints from an experienced baker can speed up the learning curve.

Preparing Cake Pans

✪ **Shiny baking pans reflect heat and produce cakes with a tender crust.**

✪ **When baking fancy cakes, the last thing you want is for the cake to stick to the pan.** Nonstick cake pans are great; to prepare them, all you need to do is grease with shortening. When we bake with nonstick bakeware, we usually grease the pans, then dust with flour, just to play it safe.

✪ **If you have them, use nonstick pans except for angel food and sponge cakes.** With those cakes, you want the batter to cling to the sides of the pan and rise as high as possible.

✪ **Regular aluminum pans, without a nonstick coating, should be greased, then lined with parchment paper.** Parchment paper has a thin coating of silicon on both sides that prevents foods from sticking. It is more expensive than waxed paper, but well worth it.

✪ **We used to use waxed paper to line our cake pans because parchment paper wasn't available.** The problem with using waxed paper was that sometimes the cake would stick, so it was necessary to grease the pan, line it with waxed paper, then grease again and dust with flour. If you are going to line your pans with waxed paper, you will need to perform these extra steps.

✪ **To grease a pan, scoop a little solid shortening or butter onto a piece of paper towel, a bit of waxed paper, or the wrapping from a stick of butter.** Spread the shortening or butter over the bottom and up the sides of the pan. Line the greased pan with parchment paper or dust with flour, depending on the recipe.

✪ **To dust a greased pan with flour, sprinkle 1 to 2 tablespoons of flour inside the pan and shake the pan to spread the flour more evenly.** Invert the pan and shake or tap out the excess flour.

Ingredients

✪ **Your cakes will rise to their fullest potential if all the ingredients are at room temperature.**

✪ **Always use fresh eggs.** Eggs separate best when cold, but egg whites whip up best at room temperature.

✪ **Milk, yogurt, and sour cream combine best at room temperature.**

✪ **Ground spices lose their pungency and aroma quickly, so buy them in small quantities, label the date of purchase, and discard them after 6 months.** For instance, freshly grated nutmeg is incomparable in flavor to ground nutmeg, which is why we recommend purchasing whole nutmegs and grating what you need.

✪ **If a recipe calls for cake flour and you have only all-purpose flour, don't despair.** Substitute 1 cup of all-purpose flour minus 2 tablespoons plus 2 tablespoons of cornstarch for every cup of cake flour.

✪ **Pieces of fruit, nuts, and chocolate chips are less likely to sink in a batter if they are tossed with flour.**

Techniques

✪ **Always preheat the oven and set out your baking pans when you start to make**

a cake. Make sure the oven rack is in the center of the oven, unless a recipe specifies otherwise.

☙ **Most recipes call for beating together the butter and sugar until light and fluffy.** Don't shortchange this step! Thorough beating creates a light-textured cake; insufficient beating results in a heavy, dense cake.

☙ **To allow enough room for the cake to rise, do not fill baking pans more than two-thirds to three-quarters full.**

☙ **Transfer the filled pans into the preheated oven as soon as possible.** The leaveners start reacting as soon as they are moistened, and beaten egg whites start deflating after 5 minutes.

☙ **Quickly put the pans in the oven as soon as you open its door, placing them as near the center (both vertical and horizontal center) as possible.** Allow at least 2 inches of space on all sides and between the pans, so the heat can circulate. If you need to use two oven racks, stagger the pans between the lower-third and upper-third shelves. Rotate the pans halfway through baking.

☙ **Don't open the oven door during the first 15 minutes of baking or your cake may not rise properly.**

☙ **Oven temperatures can vary.** Start testing a cake for doneness 5 to 15 minutes before the recipe says it should be done.

☙ **To test a cake for doneness, insert a bamboo skewer into the center of the cake.** It should come out without any batter clinging to it. You'll know a cake is done when the center isn't wobbly or wet. Most cakes are done if they quickly spring back like a sponge when touched with your fingertip. The sides of the cake also shrink away from the sides of the pan when done.

☙ **Cool cakes in the pans for 10 to 15 minutes before running a knife around the edges to loosen them.** Turn out the cakes onto wire racks to cool.

☙ **To prevent a wire rack from leaving an imprint on the cake surface, cover the rack with a double thickness of paper towel.** Place the covered rack over the top of the cake, then invert the cake and rack. Remove the pan.

☙ **Cool the cake out of the pan for at least 1 hour before decorating.** Then brush loose crumbs off the cake.

☙ **Apply a thin layer of frosting to the cake, then refrigerate until it is set before applying the final, heavier layer of frosting.** This will seal in the crumbs, ensuring a clean final appearance.

Devil's Food Cake

The first printed recipe for devil's food cake appeared around 1905 — but how did this cake earn its name? Was it because the cake was so rich it tasted like sin to our grand-mothers? Some writers hold that theory and propose that some wit named devil's food cake to contrast with angel food cake, an earlier creation. Another theory suggests that when baking soda interacts with cocoa, it gives a reddish tint to the cake, hence the association with the devil. Some recipes in the 1950s called for adding an entire bottle of red food col-oring to the batter to enhance the red tint.

Serves 10 to 12

2½ cups sifted unbleached all-purpose flour	5 large eggs
⅔ cup unsweetened cocoa powder	1⅓ cups buttermilk or plain yogurt
1 tablespoon baking soda	1 teaspoon vanilla extract
¼ teaspoon salt	Fudge Frosting (page 131), Rich Fudge Frosting (page 135), or Seven-Minute Frosting (page 138)
½ cup (1 stick) butter, at room temperature	
1⅔ cups sugar	

1. Preheat the oven to 350°F. Grease and flour two 9-inch round nonstick cake pans. If you are using uncoated aluminum bakeware, grease the cake pans and line with parchment paper.

2. Sift the flour, cocoa, baking soda, and salt into a medium bowl.

3. Beat the butter in a large bowl until creamy. Gradually add the sugar and beat until fluffy. Add the eggs, one at a time, beating well after each addition.

4. Add the flour mixture to the egg mixture alternately with the buttermilk and beat until smooth. Mix in the vanilla. Pour the batter into the prepared pans.

5. Bake for 30 to 35 minutes, until a tester inserted into the center of one of the cake layers comes out clean.

6. Cool on wire racks for about 10 minutes. Remove the cakes from the pans and cool completely.

7. Fill between the layers and frost with your choice of frosting.

Chocolate Layer Cake

The Latin name for chocolate is *theobroma* — "food of the gods." Can a birthday party be complete without a chocolate layer cake? This is a dark, moist cake with a tender texture.

Serves 8

- 2 cups sifted cake flour
- 1 teaspoon baking soda
- ½ teaspoon salt
- 6 tablespoons butter, at room temperature
- 1½ cups sugar
- 2 large eggs
- 3 ounces unsweetened chocolate, melted
- 1 teaspoon vanilla extract
- ¾ cup milk
- ½ cup sour cream
- Chocolate Frosting (page 133)
- 8 walnut halves, to garnish (optional)

1. Preheat the oven to 350°F. Grease and flour two 8-inch round nonstick cake pans. If you are using uncoated aluminum bakeware, grease the cake pans and line with parchment paper.

2. Sift the flour, baking soda, and salt into a medium bowl.

3. Beat the butter in a large bowl until creamy. Gradually add the sugar, beating until fluffy. Add the eggs, one at a time, beating well after each addition. Blend in the melted chocolate and the vanilla. Add the flour mixture alternately with the milk and sour cream, mixing just until the batter is smooth and blended. Spoon the batter into the prepared pans.

4. Bake for 30 to 35 minutes, until a tester inserted into the center of one of the cake layers comes out clean.

5. Cool on wire racks for about 10 minutes. Remove the cakes from the pans and cool completely.

6. Frost with the Chocolate Frosting. Garnish with the walnut halves (if using).

German Chocolate Cake

One would think that this cake originated in Germany or with German settlers in Pennsylvania or the Midwest, but it isn't so. It seems that when Walter Baker, grandson of the founder of Baker's chocolate, teamed up with a gentleman named German, they created a sweet baking chocolate such as the one used here. This cake owes its name to the "German" chocolate that is used in the recipe. The original recipe was printed on a box of German sweet chocolate. Although you can use just about any frosting for this cake, a coconut pecan frosting is traditional.

Serves 12 to 14

- 6 ounces dark or bittersweet chocolate, cut into small pieces
- ½ cup water
- 2⅓ cups sifted cake flour
- 1 teaspoon baking soda
- ½ teaspoon salt
- 1 cup (2 sticks) butter, at room temperature
- 1¾ cups sugar
- 4 large eggs, separated
- 1 teaspoon vanilla extract
- 1 cup buttermilk or plain yogurt
- ¼ teaspoon cream of tartar
- Coconut Pecan Frosting (page 142)

1. Preheat the oven to 350°F. Grease and flour three 9-inch round nonstick cake pans. If you are using uncoated aluminum bakeware, grease the cake pans and line with parchment paper.

2. Combine the chocolate and water and melt in the top of a double boiler set over simmering water. Stir until completely smooth and glossy. Remove the top of the double boiler from the heat and set aside to cool.

3. Sift the flour, baking soda, and salt into a medium bowl.

4. Beat the butter in a large bowl until creamy. Gradually add 1½ cups of the sugar, beating until fluffy. Add the egg yolks, one at a time, beating well after each addition. Blend in the melted chocolate and the vanilla. Add the flour mixture alternately with the buttermilk, mixing just until the batter is smooth and blended.

5. In another bowl, beat the egg whites until foamy. Add the cream of tartar and beat until soft peaks form. Add the remaining ¼ cup sugar gradually and beat until stiff but not dry. The egg whites should hold their shape and remain moist. Stir one-quarter of the egg white mixture into the batter, then gently fold in the remainder. Spoon the batter into the prepared pans.

6. Bake for 30 to 35 minutes, until a tester inserted into the center of one of the cake layers comes out clean.

7. Cool on wire racks for 10 minutes. Remove the cakes from the pans and cool completely.

8. Frost with the Coconut Pecan Frosting.

When You Don't Have the Right-Size Pan

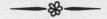

OF COURSE, IT'S BEST TO USE THE PAN SIZE SPECIFIED IN A RECIPE, but that isn't always possible. You may substitute another pan as long as the cake batter fills it at least 1 inch deep; otherwise, the cake won't rise properly. For most cakes, fill the pans half to two-thirds full. Bundt, tube, and loaf pans may be filled a little higher. If you have too much batter, use the excess to fill muffin tins or custard cups.

The baking time may need to be adjusted if you're using a different-size pan. Check for doneness by inserting a cake tester into the center of the cake. If it comes out clean, the cake is done. You can double-check by seeing that the cake pulls away from the sides of the pan and springs back when lightly pressed in the center.

Chocolate Marble Cake

Marble cakes — made with molasses rather than chocolate — were probably the invention of Mennonites from Pennsylvania. The Pennsylvania Dutch were known for their vast repertoire and skill when it came to cooking, and they particularly excelled at dessert making.

Serves 12 to 16

2 cups granulated sugar	1½ teaspoons vanilla extract
½ cup unsweetened cocoa powder	4 large eggs
¼ cup strong brewed coffee	1⅔ cups buttermilk or plain yogurt, at room temperature
3 cups sifted cake flour	Zest of 1 orange, finely grated
2 teaspoons baking powder	Sifted confectioners' sugar, to garnish (optional)
1 teaspoon baking soda	
½ teaspoon salt	
¾ cup (1½ sticks) butter, at room temperature	

1. Preheat the oven to 350°F. Thoroughly grease and flour a 9-inch tube or Bundt pan.

2. In a medium bowl, mix ¼ cup of the granulated sugar and the cocoa. Add the coffee gradually and stir until blended. Set aside.

3. Sift the flour, baking powder, baking soda, and salt into a medium bowl.

4. Beat the butter in a large bowl until creamy. Gradually add the remaining 1¾ cups sugar and the vanilla, beating until fluffy. Add the eggs, one at a time, beating well after each addition. Add the flour mixture alternately with the buttermilk, mixing just until the batter is smooth and blended.

5. Remove about one-third of the batter and add it to the cocoa mixture, blending well.

6. To the remaining batter in the bowl, stir in the orange zest.

7. Using a tablespoon, put alternate spoonfuls of the white and chocolate batters into the prepared baking pan. Swirl a spatula through the batter to give a marbled effect.

8. Bake for 55 to 60 minutes, until a tester inserted into the center of the cake comes out clean.

9. Cool on a wire rack for about 10 minutes. Run a spatula carefully around the sides and center tube of the pan before turning out the cake onto the rack. The cake should cool right-side up.

10. Sprinkle with confectioners' sugar (if using) just before serving.

Handling Eggs for Cakes

EGGS SEPARATE BEST WHEN CHILLED. When separating eggs, use three bowls. Separate an egg over a clean bowl, dropping the egg white into the bowl. Drop the yolk into the second bowl and then transfer the whites into the third bowl. Repeat, always combining the whites in a bowl other than the one you are separating the eggs over. That way if a little yolk gets into the white as you separate the egg, only one egg white is ruined, not the whole batch of whites.

For best results, eggs should be at room temperature when added to a cake batter. Bring chilled eggs to room temperature quickly by leaving them in a pan of very warm water for 10 to 15 minutes.

Chocolate Sheet Cake

For big birthday bashes, graduation parties, and classroom events, a sheet cake is a giant message board on which to write your thoughts. But it is surprisingly difficult to find recipes big enough to accommodate a baker's half sheet pan. This cake will make a crowd happy to see you.

Serves 32

2½ cups sifted unbleached all-purpose flour
1   cup unsweetened cocoa powder (preferably Dutch-processed cocoa)
2   teaspoons baking soda
½   teaspoon salt
1   cup (2 sticks) butter, at room temperature
2   cups granulated sugar
1½ teaspoons vanilla extract
2   large eggs
2½ cups buttermilk, at room temperature

Mocha Frosting

1   cup (2 sticks) butter, at room temperature
6   cups sifted confectioners' sugar
6   tablespoons unsweetened cocoa powder
6–7 tablespoons strong brewed coffee
2   teaspoons Kahlua or other coffee liqueur

1. Preheat the oven to 350°F. Grease and flour a 12- by 17-inch half sheet pan.

2. Sift the flour, cocoa, baking soda, and salt into a medium bowl.

3. Beat the butter in a large bowl with an electric mixer until creamy. Gradually add the sugar and vanilla, beating until fluffy. Add the eggs, one at a time, beating well after each addition. Add the flour mixture alternately with the buttermilk. Scrape the sides of the bowl frequently. When the mixture is combined, beat on medium speed for 1 minute. Pour the batter into the prepared pan. Use a spatula to spread out the batter and move it into the corners of the pan.

4. Bake for 30 to 35 minutes, rotating the pan after 20 minutes for even baking. Bake until a tester inserted into the center of the cake comes out clean and the cake starts to pull away from the sides of the pan.

5. Cool the cake on a wire rack.

6. To make the frosting, beat the butter in a large bowl with an electric mixer at medium speed until creamy. Gradually add the confectioners' sugar and cocoa, blending thoroughly. Add half of the coffee, scraping the sides of the bowl as needed. Beat on high, adding the remaining coffee and the Kahlua 1 tablespoon at a time, to make a creamy frosting of spreading consistency. Spread the frosting on the cooled cake.

TAKE FORTY EGGS and divide the whites from the yolks, and beat them to a froth.

Then work four pounds of butter to a cream, and put the whites of the eggs to it, a tablespoonful at a time, until it is well worked.

Then put four pounds of sugar, finely powdered, to it in the same manner.

Then put in the yolks of eggs and five pounds of flour and five pounds of fruit.

Two hours will bake it.

Add to it one-half an ounce of mace, one nutmeg, one-half pint of wine and some French brandy.

— "How to Make a Great Cake," from *Mrs. Colquitt's Savannah Cook Book.* This recipe was copied from an older manuscript from Mount Vernon, 1781, by Martha Custis who later married and became Martha Washington.

Frosted Chocolate-Zucchini Layer Cake

This is a rich, dark chocolate cake. The zucchini is barely noticeable, except to give the cake an unusually moist texture.

Serves 10 to 12

4 ounces unsweetened chocolate
½ cup canola oil
2 cups sifted unbleached all-purpose flour
⅓ cup unsweetened cocoa
2 teaspoons baking powder
2 teaspoons baking soda
1 teaspoon salt
½ teaspoon ground cinnamon
½ cup (1 stick) butter, at room temperature

2 cups sugar
3 large eggs
2 teaspoons vanilla extract
⅓ cup buttermilk, yogurt, or sour cream
3 cups grated zucchini or summer squash
Chocolate Frosting (page 133), Fudge Frosting (page 131), or Rich Fudge Frosting (page 135)

1. Preheat the oven to 350°F. Grease and flour two 9-inch round nonstick cake pans. If you are using uncoated aluminum bakeware, grease the cake pans and line with parchment paper.

2. Combine the chocolate and oil in the top of a double boiler set over simmering water. Stir until completely smooth and glossy. Remove the top of the double boiler from the heat and set aside.

3. Sift together the flour, cocoa, baking powder, baking soda, salt, and cinnamon.

4. Cream the butter and sugar in a large bowl until light. Add the eggs, one at a time, beating well after each addition. Beat in the melted chocolate mixture and the vanilla. Add the flour mixture and the buttermilk and beat just until combined. Fold in the zucchini. Divide the batter evenly between the prepared pans.

5. Bake for 40 minutes, until a tester inserted into the center of one of the cake layers comes out clean.

6. Cool on wire racks for about 10 minutes. Remove the cakes from the pans and cool completely.

7. Fill between the layers and frost with the frosting of your choice.

Cakes through the Ages

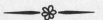

CAKES PREDATE WRITTEN HISTORY. Archaeological evidence suggests that Neolithic people baked cakes made of crushed grains on hot stones. The Egyptians developed ovens, which made cake-making more predictable, though their cakes were still primitive compared with the confections we serve today. The Egyptians and the Greeks used honey-sweetened cakes as offerings to their gods. These cakes were also served at weddings and other special occasions.

Skip ahead to the Romans, whose cakes were flat and heavy and made with barley, raisins, pine nuts, pomegranate seeds, and sweet wine. Cato published a recipe for cheesecake sweetened with honey in his treatise *On Agriculture* in A.D. 75. The Romans introduced the idea of yeast-raised cakes, and for a while there wasn't much difference between cakes and breads.

The word *cake* comes from an Old Norse word, *kaka*, which in Middle English became cake. The saying "You can't have your cake and eat it, too" first appeared in print in 1562 in John Heywood's *Proverbs and Epigrams*.

During the Middle Ages, Italian cooks became famous for their baking skills and were often employed by wealthy households in England and France. These cooks are credited with inventing the sponge cake, which was called "biscuit" at the time. The earliest recipe for sponge cake appeared in print in 1615.

In the 1700s, bakers used eggs to leaven their cakes. The eggs were often beaten for hours. The batters were sometimes poured into elaborate molds, but more often, cakes were baked in loaf pans. Tea cakes are a direct descendant of those early cakes.

It wasn't until the development of reliable baking soda and baking powder, and the availability of modern ovens after 1870, that cakes as we know them today emerged.

Dark Chocolate Cupcakes

Those are rich chocolate cupcakes for grown-ups who like to indulge — not too sweet, very chocolaty. The frosting, piped in a spiral on top of the cupcakes, gives them a sophisticated look. If you don't have a pastry bag, fill a plastic sandwich bag with the frosting, snip off the tip, and pipe out the frosting with gentle pressure on the bag. It really works!

Makes 12 cupcakes

1¼ cups all-purpose flour
¼ cup unsweetened cocoa powder
1½ teaspoons baking powder
1 teaspoon baking soda
¼ teaspoon salt
½ cup (1 stick) butter, at room temperature
1 cup firmly packed light brown sugar

1 large egg
⅓ cup sour cream
⅓ cup strong brewed coffee
1 teaspoon vanilla extract
2 ounces dark or bittersweet chocolate, melted

FROSTING

6 ounces dark or bittersweet chocolate, chopped
3 tablespoons butter

¾ cup heavy cream
3 tablespoons granulated sugar

1. Preheat the oven to 350°F. Line a 12-cup muffin pan with paper liners.

2. Sift the flour, cocoa, baking powder, baking soda, and salt into a medium bowl.

3. Cream the butter and brown sugar in a large bowl until light and fluffy. Beat in the egg until light. Add the sour cream, coffee, vanilla, and melted chocolate and beat until well combined. Add the flour mixture and beat until just combined. Divide the batter evenly among the paper liners, filling them about three-quarters full.

4. Bake for about 15 minutes, until a tester inserted into the middle of one of the cupcakes comes out clean.

5. Cool in the pan on a wire rack for 10 minutes. Using a small spatula or knife, remove the cupcakes from the pan. Continue to cool on a wire rack to room temperature.

6. To make the frosting, melt the chocolate and butter in the top of a double boiler set over barely simmering water. Whisk in the cream and granulated sugar until smooth. Let sit until it reaches a spreading consistency, about 1 hour. Spoon the frosting into a piping bag fitted with a plain tip. Pipe a spiral of frosting on top of each cupcake.

Chocolate Chat

EVER SINCE A CERTAIN DR. JAMES BAKER invested in the first chocolate mill in the New World, Americans have conducted a love affair with chocolate. They buy Baker brand chocolate to this day for their cakes, brownies, and cookies.

Recently, though, Americans have begun to take note of other high-quality brands, imported and domestic. Only the good brands contain cocoa butter; look for it in the ingredients list. Other brands use less-expensive vegetable oils, which extend the shelf life of the chocolate by maintaining its fresh appearance.

Chocolate quality is actually determined during the manufacturing process. After they are picked, cocoa beans are fermented; then they are processed to separate the cocoa butter from the rest of the bean. What is left is called chocolate liquor. During the manufacture of high-quality chocolate, the cocoa butter is remixed with the chocolate liquor. Sugar may be added to make semisweet, bittersweet, dark, or sweet chocolate; milk solids may be added for milk chocolate. Lecithin may also be added to improve the viscosity and heighten the chocolate flavor.

In a pinch, you can substitute unsweetened cocoa powder for unsweetened chocolate, using 3 tablespoons of cocoa plus 1 tablespoon of vegetable oil for every ounce of chocolate.

Vanilla Cupcakes

Cupcakes remain the staple of kids' birthday parties and school bake sales — and more. Since the late '90s, a cupcake craze has swept the nation, with tiers of cupcakes replacing the traditional wedding cake at hundreds of weddings, and with dozens of cupcake bakeries opening from coast to coast. Most people agree that the current craze dates back to a single episode of *Sex in the City*, in 1997, when Carrie (Sarah Jessica Parker) and Miranda (Cynthia Nixon) ate Magnolia Bakery's miniature treats. Since then, cupcakes were featured on the cover of *Martha Stewart Living* and have appeared on TV shows as diverse as *Saturday Night Live* and *Oprah*. Why are cupcakes so popular? Many think it is the high frosting-to-cake ratio that makes them so appealing.

Makes 24 cupcakes

½ cup (1 stick) butter, at room temperature	2 teaspoons baking powder
1½ cups sugar	½ teaspoon salt
4 large egg whites	1 cup milk
1½ teaspoons vanilla extract	Rich Fudge Frosting (page 135),
2 cups unbleached all-purpose flour	Vanilla Frosting (page 137), or another frosting of your choice

1. Preheat the oven to 350°F. Line two 12-cup muffin pans with paper liners.

2. Beat the butter and sugar in a large bowl with an electric mixer until light and fluffy. Beat in the egg whites, one at a time, until well combined and light. Beat in the vanilla. Scrape the bowl.

3. Combine the flour, baking powder, and salt in a sifter and sift over the butter mixture. Mix at low speed for 2 minutes. Scrape the bowl. Add the milk gradually and beat at high speed until fluffy and smooth, about 2 minutes. Fill the paper liners one-half to two-thirds full of batter. Do not overfill.

4. Bake for about 20 minutes, until a tester inserted into the middle of one of the cupcakes comes out clean.

5. Cool in the pan on a wire rack for 10 minutes. Using a small spatula or knife, remove the cupcakes from the pan. Finish cooling on wire racks.

6. Frost as desired.

Gold Cake

This is the yellow cake that simply doesn't come out of a box. We give the cake a hint of orange flavor, which you can highlight with a tangy orange frosting, but this cake is also delicious with chocolate frosting.

Serves 8

....

1¾ cups sifted cake flour	1 teaspoon orange juice concentrate,
2 teaspoons baking powder	at room temperature, or
¼ teaspoon salt	½ teaspoon orange extract
½ cup (1 stick) butter, at room	8 large egg yolks (about ½ cup)
temperature	½ cup milk
1 cup sugar	Chocolate Frosting (page 133) or
1 teaspoon finely grated orange zest	Orange Frosting (page 141)

....

1. Preheat the oven to 350°F. Grease and flour two 8-inch round nonstick cake pans. If you are using uncoated aluminum bakeware, grease the cake pans and line with parchment paper.

2. Sift the flour, baking powder, and salt into a medium bowl.

3. Beat the butter in a large bowl until creamy. Gradually add the sugar, orange zest, and orange juice concentrate, beating until fluffy.

4. Beat the egg yolks in a small bowl until thick and lemon-colored. Add to the butter mixture. (If you are using an electric mixer, add the egg yolks to the butter mixture one at a time, beating thoroughly after each addition.)

5. Add about one-quarter of the flour mixture to the creamed mixture, beating until blended, and then add one-third of the milk. Repeat the procedure, alternating the flour and milk, ending with the flour. Mix just until smooth and blended. Divide the batter between the prepared pans.

6. Bake for 25 to 30 minutes, until a tester inserted into the center of one of the cakes comes out clean.

7. Cool on wire racks for 10 minutes. Remove the cakes from the pans and cool completely.

8. Frost with the Chocolate Frosting or the Orange Frosting.

Golden Sheet Cake with Chocolate Fudge Frosting

When you need a big cake to serve a crowd, this one is perfect. It requires a standard baker's half sheet pan, which measures 12 by 17 inches and is about 1 inch deep.

Serves 32

4½ cups sifted unbleached all-purpose flour

1½ tablespoons baking powder

1½ teaspoons salt

1¼ cups (2½ sticks) butter, at room temperature

2¼ cups granulated sugar

1 tablespoon vanilla extract

4 whole eggs, plus 8 egg yolks

1¼ cups milk

CHOCOLATE FUDGE FROSTING

½ cup (1 stick) butter, cut up

8 ounces dark or bittersweet chocolate

4 cups sifted confectioners' sugar, one (1-pound) box

4–6 tablespoons milk or cream

2 teaspoons vanilla extract

1. Preheat the oven to 350°F. Grease and flour a 12- by 17-inch half sheet pan.

2. Sift the flour, baking powder, and salt into a large bowl.

3. Beat the butter in a large bowl until creamy. Gradually add the sugar and vanilla, beating until fluffy.

4. Beat the eggs and egg yolks in a small bowl until thick and lemon-colored. Add to the butter mixture. (If you are using an electric mixer, add the eggs and egg yolks to the butter mixture one at a time, beating thoroughly after each addition.)

5. Add about one-quarter of the flour mixture to the creamed mixture, beating until blended, then add about one-third of the milk. Repeat the procedure, alternating the flour and milk, ending with the flour. Mix just until smooth and blended. Scrape the batter into the prepared pan and smooth the top.

6. Bake for 35 to 45 minutes, until a tester inserted into the center of the cake comes out clean.

7. Cool the cake on a wire rack.

8. To make the frosting, melt the butter and chocolate in the top of a double boiler set over simmering water. Stir until completely smooth and glossy. Remove the top of the double boiler from the heat and transfer to a medium bowl; let cool slightly. Gradually add half of the confectioners' sugar, beating thoroughly. Beat in 2 tablespoons of the milk, the vanilla, then the remaining confectioners' sugar. Add enough of the remaining milk to make a smooth frosting of spreading consistency. Spread the frosting on the cooled cake.

The Non-Fermentation Movement

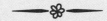

THE TEMPERANCE MOVEMENT of the 1800s had its impact on cake baking, strange though that may sound. One arm of the movement — the religiously inspired Non-Fermentation Movement — wanted to ban the use of yeast in breads and cakes because yeast produces alcohol in the rising process, albeit in minute amounts. The use of baking powder, which produces a gas that raises the batter, was promoted instead. Some manufacturers of baking powder and other "safe, non-fermenting yeasts" also claimed that their products prevented rickets, cholera, and tooth decay while promoting muscle and bone growth. The Non-Fermentation Movement got a boost when agents for Horsford's Self-Raising Bread Preparation distributed for free *The Good Cook's Hand Book* in the 1860s and 1870s, which provided plenty of recipes using baking powder.

Coconut Cake

Baking with coconut got a big boost when Franklin Baker accepted a cargo of coconuts from Cuba in lieu of cash for a shipment of flour to Havana. When he found it difficult to market the whole nuts, he bought machinery and developed a method for making the flaked coconut we are accustomed to purchasing in plastic bags. As a convenience food, coconut was readily adopted by American bakers, who turned it into delicious cream pies and layer cakes.

We are among those who believe that every good cake deserves a little chocolate, so this snowy white cake is filled with a chocolate buttercream between the layers. Billowy clouds of lemony or vanilla buttercream and toasted coconut make a luscious topping for this three-layer cake.

Serves 8 to 10

- 3 cups cake flour
- 4 teaspoons baking powder
- 1 teaspoon salt
- ½ teaspoon cream of tartar
- 1 cup lightly packed, sweetened flaked coconut
- ½ cup (1 stick) butter, at room temperature
- ½ cup white solid vegetable shortening
- 1¾ cups granulated sugar
- 6 egg whites
- 1⅓ cups coconut or regular milk
- 1½ teaspoons coconut extract
- 1½ teaspoons lemon extract

BUTTERCREAM FROSTING

- 1 cup lightly packed, sweetened flaked coconut
- ½ cup (1 stick) plus 2 tablespoons butter, at room temperature
- 5 cups sifted confectioners' sugar
  Pinch of salt
- 4–5 tablespoons half-and-half or light cream
- 1 teaspoon lemon or vanilla extract
- 1½ ounces unsweetened chocolate, melted

1. Preheat the oven to 350°F. Grease and flour three 8-inch round nonstick cake pans. If you are using uncoated aluminum bakeware, grease the cake pans and line with parchment paper.

2. Sift the flour, baking powder, salt, and cream of tartar into a medium bowl. Sift two more times. Stir in the coconut.

3. Cream the butter and shortening in a large bowl with an electric mixer. Gradually add the sugar and beat for 5 minutes.

4. Beat the egg whites in a large bowl with a fork or whisk for 1 minute. Add the coconut milk and whisk until well blended.

5. Add one-third of the flour mixture and one-third of the egg whites to the butter and shortening mixture. Beat until well blended. Add the rest of flour mixture and egg whites in thirds until all is combined. Add the coconut and lemon extracts and beat for about 1 minute, until well combined. The batter will be thick. Spoon the batter into the prepared cake pans and smooth the tops.

6. Bake for 25 to 35 minutes, rotating the pans in the oven after 20 minutes for even baking. A tester inserted into the center of one of the cakes should come out clean.

7. Cool on wire racks for 10 minutes. Remove the cakes from the pans and cool completely.

8. To make the frosting, preheat the oven to 300°F. Spread the coconut on a baking sheet and toast for 5 to 10 minutes. Watch carefully and shake the pan from time to time. Once the coconut begins browning, it will scorch quite easily. Remove from the hot pan and set it aside to cool.

9. Whip the butter with an electric mixer until light and fluffy. Add half the sugar and the salt and beat until combined. Add the remaining sugar and 3 tablespoons of the half-and-half. Beat until very smooth, adding more half-and-half as needed for a good spreading consistency.

10. Remove about three-quarters of the buttercream to a bowl. Mix in the lemon flavoring and set aside. To the remaining buttercream, beat in the chocolate until smooth.

11. Spread the chocolate buttercream between the cake layers. Cover the top and sides with the white buttercream, swirling the frosting to make swirls and peaks. Sprinkle the toasted coconut on top.

Banana Cake

The Koran says that the forbidden fruit in the Garden of Eden was a banana, not an apple. Bananas were cultivated in India at least as far back as 2000 BC. Alexander the Great found the wise men of India eating bananas when he crossed the Indus in 327 BC, hence the banana's botanical name, *Musa sapientum*, "of the wise muse."

Serves 10 to 12

- 2 cups sifted unbleached all-purpose flour
- 1 teaspoon baking powder
- 1 teaspoon baking soda
- ½ teaspoon salt
- ⅛ teaspoon freshly grated nutmeg
- ½ cup (1 stick) butter or vegetable shortening, at room temperature
- 1½ cups sugar
- 2 large eggs
- 1 teaspoon vanilla extract
- 1¼ cups mashed ripe bananas
- ⅔ cup buttermilk or plain yogurt
- ½ cup toasted chopped walnuts (optional)
- Chocolate Frosting (page 133), Vanilla Frosting (page 137), or Sea Foam Frosting (page 143)

1. Preheat the oven to 350°F. Grease and flour two 9-inch round nonstick cake pans. If you are using uncoated aluminum bakeware, grease the cake pans and line with parchment paper.

2. Sift the flour, baking powder, baking soda, salt, and nutmeg into a medium bowl.

3. Beat the butter in a large bowl until creamy. Gradually add the sugar, beating until fluffy. Add the eggs, one at a time, beating well after each addition. Add the vanilla. Add the flour mixture alternately with the bananas and buttermilk, mixing just until batter is smooth and blended. Fold in the chopped nuts (if using). Spoon the batter into the prepared pans.

4. Bake for 25 to 30 minutes, until a tester inserted into the center of one of the cakes comes out clean.

5. Cool on wire racks for about 10 minutes. Remove the cakes from the pans and cool completely.

6. Fill between the layers and top with your choice of frosting.

Troubleshooting Cake Problems

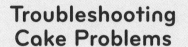

The cake is dense and heavy:

- The eggs were too small. Always use large eggs when baking.
- Insufficient air was whisked into the egg and sugar mixture.
- The butter, sugar, and eggs were not beaten together long enough.
- The flour was not folded in gently or was beaten at too high a speed.
- Too much flour was used.
- The oven temperature was too low.

The cake rose unevenly in the oven:

- The flour was not blended evenly in the batter.
- The temperature inside the oven was uneven, or the oven temperature was too high.

The top of the cake sank:

- The oven temperature was too hot.
- The cake was not baked long enough.
- The oven door was opened too soon.

The top of the cake peaked or cracked:

- The oven temperature was too hot, causing the outside of the cake to bake and form a crust too quickly.
- The cake wasn't baked on the center rack of the oven.

Lady Baltimore Cake

A largely forgotten 1906 romance novel by Owen Wister entitled *Lady Baltimore* is responsible for spreading the fame of this cake. Mr. Wister enjoyed the cake at the Lady Baltimore Tea Room in Charleston, South Carolina, and lovingly described the cake in his book. With its filling of sherry-soaked dried fruits and nuts, the cake is even more memorable than Mr. Wister's prose.

Serves 8

2½ cups sifted cake flour
2½ teaspoons baking powder
½ teaspoon salt
½ cup (1 stick) butter, at room temperature
1¼ cups plus 1 tablespoon sugar
1 teaspoon vanilla extract
1 cup milk, at room temperature
4 large egg whites, at room temperature
¼ teaspoon cream of tartar

FILLING AND FROSTING

½ cup chopped raisins
⅓ cup finely chopped dried cherries
⅓ cup finely chopped moist figs
¼ cup sherry
½ cup chopped pecans
Seven-Minute Frosting (page 138)

1. Preheat the oven to 350°F. Grease and flour two 8-inch round nonstick cake pans. If you are using uncoated aluminum bakeware, grease the cake pans and line with parchment paper.

2. Sift together the flour, baking powder, and salt. Sift two more times.

3. Beat the butter in a large bowl until creamy. Gradually add the 1¼ cups sugar and the vanilla. Beat until fluffy. Add the flour mixture alternately with the milk, mixing just until the batter is smooth and blended.

4. In another bowl, beat the egg whites until foamy. Add the cream of tartar and beat until soft peaks form. Add the 1 tablespoon sugar gradually and beat until the egg whites are stiff but not dry. The egg whites should hold their shape and remain moist. Stir one-quarter of the egg whites into the batter, and then gently fold in the remainder. Spoon the batter into the prepared pans.

5. Bake for 25 to 30 minutes, until a tester inserted into the center of one of the cakes comes out clean.

6. Cool on wire racks for 10 minutes. Remove the cakes from the pans and cool completely.

7. While the cakes cool, make the filling. Combine the raisins, cherries, figs, and sherry in a medium bowl. Set aside.

8. Prepare Seven-Minute Frosting according to the recipe directions.

9. Drain off the excess liquid from the dried fruits. Stir in the pecans. Fold one-third of the frosting into the filling mixture and blend until combined evenly.

10. Spread the filling between the two cake layers. Spread the remaining frosting over the top and sides of the cake.

Preparing Pans for Baking

MOST OF THE CAKE RECIPES in this book call for greasing a pan, then lining the pan with parchment paper. Reusable silicone liners will also work well.

Although you can use butter for greasing pans, we prefer solid vegetable shortening. It is more neutral in flavor, burns at a much higher temperature, and leaves less residue in the pan.

Spice Cake

A cup of coffee and a frosty fall afternoon do justice to this moist, light spice cake. The coffee-flavored whipped cream is just the right complement to the lively combination of spices.

Serves 8 to 12

2¼ cups unbleached all-purpose flour
1½ teaspoons baking powder
1½ teaspoons ground cinnamon
1 teaspoon baking soda
½ teaspoon ground ginger
½ teaspoon freshly grated nutmeg
½ teaspoon salt
¼ teaspoon ground allspice
¼ teaspoon ground cloves

½ cup (1 stick) butter or vegetable shortening, at room temperature
1 cup granulated sugar
½ cup firmly packed dark brown sugar
2 large eggs
1 teaspoon vanilla extract
1 cup buttermilk, plain yogurt, or sour milk

COFFEE WHIPPED CREAM

1 cup whipping cream
1 tablespoon instant coffee powder

¼ cup sifted confectioners' sugar
½ teaspoon vanilla extract

1. Preheat the oven to 350°F. Grease and flour two 8-inch round nonstick cake pans. If you are using uncoated aluminum bakeware, grease the cake pans and line with parchment paper.

2. Sift together the flour, baking powder, cinnamon, baking soda, ginger, nutmeg, salt, allspice, and cloves.

3. Beat the butter in a large bowl until creamy. Gradually add the granulated sugar and brown sugar, beating until fluffy. Add the eggs, one at a time, beating well after each addition. Add the vanilla. Add the flour mixture alternately with the buttermilk, mixing just until the batter is smooth and blended. Divide the batter between the prepared pans.

4. Bake for 30 minutes, until a tester inserted into the center of one of the cakes comes out clean.

5. Cool on wire racks for about 10 minutes. Remove the cakes from the pans and cool completely.

6. To make the whipped cream, combine the cream and coffee powder in a large bowl. Refrigerate for 15 minutes, and then beat until soft peaks form. Add the confectioners' sugar and vanilla and beat until stiff.

7. Spread the cream between the layers and over the top and sides of the cake. Keep the frosted cake refrigerated.

Cake Chemistry 101

—❀—

CAKE BATTERS that use baking soda for leavening require an acid ingredient. When heat is applied, the acid activates the baking soda, causing it to release bubbles of carbon dioxide, which raise the cake. The acid can be supplied by buttermilk, yogurt, or sour milk, interchangeably. Buttermilk and yogurt are both dairy products made by culturing sweet milk with friendly bacteria. Sour milk can be made at home by adding 1 teaspoon of lemon juice or vinegar to 1 cup of milk at room temperature, then setting it aside for 15 minutes.

Boston Cream Pie

How did a dessert that is so clearly a cake come to be named a pie? No one seems to know. Boston cream pie was on the menu when the famed Parker House in Boston opened its doors in 1856, but at the time it was called a Parker House chocolate pie. Although they did not invent this delectable dessert, they did add the chocolate glaze topping. Cakes with a cream filling between the layers do exist in earlier cookbooks. Boston cream pie was adopted as the official state dessert of Massachusetts in 1996.

Serves 8

CAKE LAYERS

1½ cups sifted cake flour
1½ teaspoons baking powder
¼   teaspoon salt
3   large eggs

1⅓ cups granulated sugar
1½ teaspoons vanilla extract
2   tablespoons butter
¾   cup hot (not boiling) milk

PASTRY CREAM FILLING

¼   cup granulated sugar
2½ tablespoons unbleached all-
    purpose flour
¼   teaspoon salt
1   cup hot (not boiling) milk or
    half-and-half

3   large egg yolks, lightly beaten
1   teaspoon vanilla extract
1   tablespoon butter, cut into small
    pieces

CHOCOLATE GLAZE

⅔   cup semisweet chocolate chips
3   tablespoons milk
1   tablespoon butter

1   cup sifted confectioners' sugar
1   teaspoon vanilla extract

1. To make the cake, preheat the oven to 350°F. Grease and flour two 8-inch round nonstick cake pans. If you are using uncoated aluminum bakeware, grease the cake pans and line with parchment paper.

2. Sift together the flour, baking powder, and salt. Sift two more times. Return the flour mixture to the sieve and set aside over a bowl.

3. Beat the eggs in a large bowl with an electric mixer for 3 to 4 minutes, until thick and lemon-colored. Gradually add the sugar and beat for 5 minutes longer (if by hand, beat for 8 minutes). Add the vanilla, mixing until blended.

4. Melt the butter in the hot milk, then pour it into the egg mixture all at once. The batter will be thin.

5. Sift half the flour mixture into the batter and quickly fold it in. Repeat with the second half of the flour. The folding in of the milk and flour mixture should take only about 1 minute. Divide the batter between the prepared pans.

6. Bake for 20 to 25 minutes, until a tester inserted into the center of one of the layers comes out clean.

7. Cool on wire racks for about 10 minutes. Remove the layers from the pans and cool completely.

8. To prepare the pastry cream filling, combine the sugar, flour, and salt in a heavy saucepan. Add the hot milk gradually, stirring constantly with a wire whisk to remove any lumps. Cook over medium-high heat, stirring constantly, until the mixture is bubbly. Cook and stir for 2 minutes, until it begins to thicken. Remove from the heat.

9. Stir the hot milk mixture into the egg yolks a few teaspoonfuls at a time, beating constantly until well blended. Return the egg yolk mixture to the saucepan. Stir and cook for 2 minutes longer, until thick and smooth. Remove from the heat.

10. Add the vanilla. Gradually stir in the butter. Cover the surface of the pastry cream with plastic wrap. When the pastry cream is cool, refrigerate.

11. To make the chocolate glaze, combine the chocolate chips, milk, and butter in a small saucepan. Cook over very low heat until the mixture is smooth. Remove from the heat and gradually add the confectioners' sugar, beating until smooth. Stir in the vanilla. Cool until thick enough to spread.

12. When the cake is completely cooled, the pastry cream is cold, and the glaze is thick enough to spread, spread the pastry cream filling between the cake layers and the glaze over the top cake layer.

13. Allow the glaze to set for about 2 hours before serving.

Carrot Cake

Those who scoffed at seed-eaters and granola-crunchers were forced to rethink their prejudices when it came to carrot cake. And why did carrot cake become the standard for health-food aficionados? It could have been because the moist cake stands up even to the assault of whole wheat, or perhaps because it is packed with fiber and vitamins and low in animal fats. Perhaps people adopted it because the recipe is so often foolproof and lends itself to multiplication for huge wedding cakes. Or, perhaps, carrot cake became universally popular because it tastes so good.

Serves 14 to 16

2 cups sifted unbleached all-purpose flour	1 tablespoon finely grated orange zest
2 teaspoons baking powder	1 teaspoon vanilla extract
1½ teaspoons baking soda	3 cups lightly packed, finely shredded carrots
1½ teaspoons ground cinnamon	
1 teaspoon salt	8 ounces crushed pineapple, drained
¼ teaspoon ground allspice	
¾ teaspoon freshly grated nutmeg	1 cup toasted chopped walnuts
1 cup vegetable oil	Cream Cheese Frosting (page 140)
1 cup granulated sugar	Toasted coconut, to garnish (optional)
¾ cup firmly packed light brown sugar	
4 large eggs	

1. Preheat the oven to 350°F. Thoroughly grease and flour a 9- by 13-inch baking pan.

2. Sift the flour, baking powder, baking soda, cinnamon, salt, allspice, and nutmeg into a medium bowl.

3. Beat the oil, granulated sugar, and brown sugar in a large bowl until thoroughly combined. Add the eggs, one at a time, beating well after each addition. Add the orange zest and vanilla; continue beating until fluffy. Gradually add the flour mixture, mixing just until the batter is smooth and blended. Fold in the carrots, pineapple, and walnuts. Spoon the batter into the prepared pan.

4. Bake for 35 minutes, until a tester inserted into the center of the cake comes out clean.

5. Cool the cake on a wire rack.

6. Frost with Cream Cheese Frosting when completely cool. Sprinkle with the toasted coconut (if using).

Fresh Coconut

THE FLAVOR OF FRESH COCONUT is far superior to that of the dried, packaged flakes. To prepare a fresh coconut: Pierce two of the eyes with a strong, sharp instrument, such as a metal skewer or ice pick. Shake out the juice. Smell it for rancidity. If it tastes and smells fresh, serve it in a drink; otherwise, discard the juice. The flesh will be fine regardless of the state of the juice.

Bake the empty nut in a 400°F oven for 15 minutes. Lay the hot nut on a table or counter and give it a sharp blow with a hammer right at the center of the shell. It will break cleanly in two. Pare away the brown skin with a sharp knife and grate the white flesh in a food processor.

Angel Food Cake

A great, billowy cloud of a cake, yes. But surely not invented by angels? More than one story is attached to the origins of this celestial dessert. The most credible tale is that it was invented by a frugal Pennsylvania Dutch cook who sought to use up egg whites left from the making of egg noodles. Another story credits an Indian cook who somehow sent the recipe to the United States. The recipe wound up in the hands of a baker who baked the cakes behind shuttered windows to prevent competitors from stealing the recipe. At this time, the cake was also known as "mystery cake."

Still another story sets down St. Louis as the location of the divine inspiration that led a certain Mr. Sides to make the cake with a secret recipe, which he sold for $25. The catch was that the cake could be made only with a secret white powder, which Mr. Sides also sold. The secret white powder was shortly revealed to be cream of tartar, which whitened the cake and made it tender, and soon the dish was seen on restaurant menus throughout St. Louis — a secret no longer.

Serves 10 to 12

....

1¼ cups sifted cake flour	¼ teaspoon salt
1½ cups sifted granulated sugar	1 teaspoon vanilla extract
1¾ cups (12–14) egg whites, at room temperature	½ teaspoon almond extract
1¼ teaspoons cream of tartar	Sifted confectioners' sugar, to garnish

....

1. Preheat the oven to 300°F. Set out a 10-inch tube or angel cake pan. Do not grease.

2. Sift the flour with ½ cup of the granulated sugar. Sift three more times.

3. Beat the egg whites in a large bowl with an electric mixer until foamy. Add the cream of tartar and salt and beat until soft peaks form. Continue beating the egg whites until stiff but not dry. The egg whites should hold their shape and remain moist.

4. Beat in the remaining 1 cup granulated sugar, 1 tablespoon at a time, beating well after each addition, until stiff peaks form. Beat in the vanilla and almond extracts.

5. Sift the flour mixture over the egg whites, about one-quarter of it at a time. Using a rubber spatula or flat wire whisk, fold in the flour gently as you rotate the bowl. Continue folding in the flour by quarters until it is all incorporated.

6. Carefully spoon the batter into the ungreased pan. Pass a knife through the batter, going around the pan twice to break up any air bubbles. Smooth the top.

7. Bake for 50 to 60 minutes, until the cake is golden brown and the top springs back when gently pressed.

8. Invert the cake in the pan and let it cool upside down for 1 to 2 hours. If the pan doesn't have feet, place the center tube of the pan over the narrow neck of a bottle or an inverted funnel to enable the air to circulate freely under the cake.

9. When the cake is completely cool, run a thin spatula around the sides and center tube of the pan. Tap the bottom and sides of the pan to release the cake. Invert the cake and turn it out onto a platter. Sprinkle with the confectioners' sugar.

Variation

Layered Angel Cake. For a more elaborate presentation, horizontally slice the angel cake into three layers. Spread each layer with crushed sweetened strawberries or drained crushed pineapple. Cover with whipped cream. Reassemble the layers, and then coat the sides of the cake with whipped cream.

Angel Food Flops?

IF YOUR ANGEL FOOD CAKE hasn't risen enough, your mixing method was probably the problem. Either you:

- **overbeat** the egg whites until they were stiff and dry, rather than moist and glossy, or
- **underbeat** the egg whites so they didn't hold enough air, or
- **overmixed** the batter when the flour was folded in and deflated the batter.

Sponge Cake

Few people regard sponge cake as an end in itself, but rather as the base for a luscious layering of cake, fruit, and cream. You can use sponge cake in trifles with custard and fruit, smother it under fresh summer berries, or marry it to ice cream. This cake is light, airy, and golden yellow.

Serves 10 to 12

> 1½ cups sifted cake flour
> 1½ teaspoons baking powder
> ½ teaspoon salt
> ½ cup egg yolks (about 8)
> 1½ cups granulated sugar
> 6 tablespoons boiling water
> 1 tablespoon fresh lemon juice or
>   1½ teaspoons vanilla extract
>
> 1 cup egg whites (about 8), at room
>   temperature
> ½ teaspoon cream of tartar
>   Sifted confectioners' sugar, to
>   garnish

1. Preheat the oven to 325°F. Set out a 10-inch tube or angel food cake pan. Do not grease.

2. Sift together the flour, baking powder, and salt. Sift two more times. Return the mixture to the sieve and set aside over a bowl.

3. Beat the egg yolks in a large bowl with an electric mixer until thick and lemon-colored, about 5 minutes. Gradually add 1¼ cups of the granulated sugar and beat for 5 minutes longer. Continue beating, and add the boiling water in a steady stream. Beat until the mixture is light and fluffy. Add the lemon juice.

4. Sift one-third of the flour mixture at a time over the egg yolk mixture. Using a rubber spatula, gently fold in the flour as you rotate the bowl. The folding in of the flour should take 2 to 3 minutes. Work carefully to avoid deflating the batter.

5. In another bowl, beat the egg whites until foamy. Add the cream of tartar and beat until soft peaks form. Beat in the remaining ¼ cup granulated sugar, 1 tablespoon at a time, beating well until the egg whites are stiff but not dry. The egg whites should hold their shape and remain moist.

6. Stir one-quarter of the egg whites into the batter and then gently fold in the remainder, just until incorporated. Spoon the batter into the pan.

7. Bake for 50 to 55 minutes, until a tester inserted into the center of the cake comes out clean.

8. Immediately invert the pan and let the cake cool upside down in the pan for about 2 hours. If the pan doesn't have feet, place the center tube of the pan over the narrow neck of a bottle or an inverted funnel to enable the air to circulate freely under the cake.

9. When the cake is completely cool, carefully cut away any crust that is stuck to the tube or rim of the pan. Run a thin spatula around the sides of the pan and center tube. Tap the bottom and sides of the pan to help release the cake. Invert the cake and turn it out onto a platter. Sprinkle with the confectioners' sugar.

Cake Flour for Tender Cakes

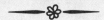

CAKE FLOUR PRODUCES CAKES that are lighter and more tender than cakes made with all-purpose flour. Cake flour is high in starch and low in protein (gluten), which enables it to blend more easily into a batter. If you don't have cake flour on hand, you can make a substitute with all-purpose flour and cornstarch. For each cup of cake flour, measure out 1 cup all-purpose flour. Remove 2 tablespoons four and replace with 2 tablespoons cornstarch.

Jelly Roll

Since the mid-1800s, jelly rolls have been a popular dessert. They are made from a thin sponge cake that is spread with jelly (or cream) and then rolled. When sliced, each piece presents an attractive pinwheel pattern. Jelly rolls are sometimes called Swiss rolls.

Serves 12

¾	cup sifted cake flour	1 teaspoon vanilla extract
1	teaspoon baking powder	¼ teaspoon cream of tartar
¼	teaspoon salt	About ⅔ cup sifted confectioners' sugar
4	large eggs, separated	
¾	cup granulated sugar	10–12 ounces raspberry or other jam

1. Preheat the oven to 375°F. Grease a 10- by 15-inch jelly-roll pan and line with parchment paper.

2. Sift together the flour, baking powder, and salt. Sift two more times.

3. Beat the egg yolks in a large bowl until thick and lemon-colored. Gradually add ½ cup of the granulated sugar and beat until fluffy. Blend in the vanilla. Beat for 5 minutes. Stir in half the flour mixture, mixing until blended. Add the remaining flour mixture, mixing until well combined. The batter will be stiff.

4. In another bowl, beat the egg whites until foamy. Add the cream of tartar and beat until soft peaks form. Add the remaining ¼ cup granulated sugar gradually, and beat until the egg whites are stiff but not dry. The egg whites should hold their shape and remain moist. Stir one-quarter of the egg whites into the batter and then gently fold in the remainder. Spoon the batter into the prepared pan, spreading it to the corners of the pan.

5. Bake for 12 to 15 minutes, until the cake is golden and the top of the cake springs back when lightly pressed with a finger.

6. Generously sprinkle a kitchen towel with the confectioners' sugar. Invert the cake onto the towel. Carefully peel off the parchment paper. Cut off any crisp edges. While the cake is still hot, roll it up in the towel from the long side, jelly-roll fashion.

7. Cool the cake in the towel, seam-side down, on a wire rack for about 30 minutes.

8. Unroll the cake, remove the towel, and spread the cake with the jam. Roll up, place on a serving platter, and sprinkle with additional confectioners' sugar.

Baker's Tip

※ To use this sponge cake for Baked Alaska (page 380), prepare the cake in a 9-inch round cake pan or springform pan lined with parchment paper or aluminum foil. Lightly grease and flour the liner but not the sides of the pan. Bake at 350°F for 25 to 28 minutes, until a tester inserted into the center of the cake comes out clean and the sides of the cake begin to pull away from the pan. Cool in the pan on a wire rack for about 30 minutes. Then invert the cake onto a foil-lined board or platter and carefully peel off the parchment paper.

The baking is the most critical part of cake making. Test the oven with a piece of white paper. If it turns a light yellow in five minutes, it is ready for sponge cake; if a dark yellow in five minutes it is ready for cup cakes.

— *The All-Ways Preferable Cook Book*, compiled by Miss Ada A. Hillier, prepared for The Malleable Steel Range Mfg. Co., South Bend, Indiana (date unknown)

Orange Chiffon Cake

Most recipes are variations on other recipes. It is a rare event, indeed, when a chef invents a dish that is truly new. It is even more rare for an amateur to produce an absolutely original recipe. But such was the case in 1927, when Harry Baker, a Los Angeles insurance agent, is said to have invented the original chiffon cake, which, according to General Mills, was the first really new cake in 100 years.

Baker was hounded for his recipe, but he kept it a secret and made the cake only for screen stars and Hollywood power brokers, many of whom enjoyed it at the Brown Derby Restaurant. Eventually Baker sold the recipe to General Mills so "Betty Crocker could give the secret to the women of America." The secret was revealed in the May 1948 *Better Homes and Gardens* magazine. And the secret? The recipe replaces the usual butter or shortening with vegetable oil, which makes an unusually light-textured cake.

Serves 12 to 14

2¾ cups sifted cake flour	1 teaspoon orange liqueur (Triple Sec, Cointreau, or Grand Marnier) or vanilla extract
1½ cups granulated sugar	
1 tablespoon baking powder	
½ teaspoon salt	9 large egg whites, at room temperature
7 large egg yolks, at room temperature	¾ teaspoon cream of tartar
½ cup vegetable oil	Pinch of salt
2 tablespoons freshly grated orange zest	Confectioners' sugar, whipped cream, or Orange Marmalade Frosting (see page 136)
¾ cup freshly squeezed orange juice	

1. Preheat the oven to 325°F. Set out an ungreased 10-inch tube pan, preferably with feet and a removable bottom.

2. Sift the flour, 1¼ cups of the granulated sugar, the baking powder, and the salt into a large bowl. Make a well in the center of the flour mixture.

3. With an electric mixer fitted with a whisk attachment, beat together the egg yolks, vegetable oil, zest, juice, and liqueur. Beat for about 2 minutes, until thoroughly mixed. Pour the yolk mixture into the center of the flour mixture and whisk it into the flour, until the batter is smooth and well blended. Do not overmix.

4. Thoroughly clean the electric mixer bowl and beaters with white vinegar. Beat the egg whites in the clean bowl until foamy. Add the cream of tartar and salt and beat until soft peaks form. Add the remaining ¼ cup granulated sugar gradually, beating the egg whites until they hold stiff, shiny peaks. Stir one-third of the whites into the batter and then gradually fold in the remainder in thirds. Spoon the batter into the pan. The batter should fill the pan to within 1 inch of the top.

5. Bake for 60 to 70 minutes, until a tester inserted into the center of cake comes out clean and the top of the cake springs back when lightly pressed.

6. Immediately invert the pan and let the cake cool upside down in the pan for about 1½ hours. If the pan doesn't have feet, place the center tube of the pan over the narrow neck of a bottle or an inverted funnel to enable the air to circulate freely under the cake.

7. To remove the cake from the pan, run a long, thin-bladed knife or spatula around the sides and center tube of the pan. Invert onto a wire rack.

8. Cool completely. Serve with whipped cream, a sprinkling of confectioners' sugar, or frosted with Orange Marmalade Frosting.

Judging When a Cake Is Done

AN UNDERBAKED CAKE will be dense, overly moist, and sunken in the center. An overbaked cake will be dry. Removing a cake at the perfect moment of doneness is not difficult:

• The cake should shrink slightly from the edges of the pan.

• The cake top should spring back when lightly pressed with a fingertip.

• A cake tester or wooden pick inserted near the center of the cake should come out clean, with no batter or moist crumbs clinging to it.

Applesauce Cake

One of the pleasures of fall is going to a nearby orchard and picking apples. We make a stop at the bin of "drops" for bargain-priced sauce apples, which we cook down, strain, and flavor with cinnamon, no sugar needed. Some of that sauce makes its way into this moist cake.

Serves 12 to 14

½ cup dried currants
½ cup raisins
1⅔ cups plus 1 tablespoon sifted unbleached all-purpose flour
1 teaspoon baking powder
1 teaspoon ground cinnamon
½ teaspoon baking soda
½ teaspoon ground cloves
½ teaspoon freshly grated nutmeg
¼ teaspoon salt
½ cup (1 stick) butter, at room temperature

¾ cup granulated sugar
½ cup firmly packed dark brown sugar
2 large eggs
1 teaspoon vanilla extract
1 cup applesauce (purchased or homemade, page 292), warmed
2 tablespoons milk
Brown Sugar Frosting (page 144)
Chopped peanuts or toasted almonds, to garnish

1. Preheat the oven to 350°F. Thoroughly grease and flour a 9-inch tube or Bundt pan.

2. Toss the currants and raisins in a small bowl with the 1 tablespoon flour.

3. Sift together the 1⅔ cups flour and the baking powder, cinnamon, baking soda, cloves, nutmeg, and salt.

4. Beat the butter in a large bowl until creamy. Gradually add the granulated sugar and brown sugar, beating until fluffy. Add the eggs, one at a time, beating well after each addition. Add the vanilla. Add the flour mixture alternately with the applesauce and milk, mixing just until the batter is smooth and blended. Fold in the currants and raisins. Spoon the batter into the prepared pan.

5. Bake for 45 to 50 minutes, until a tester inserted into the center of the cake comes out clean.

6. Cool on a wire rack for about 10 minutes. Run a spatula carefully around the sides and center tube of the pan before turning out the cake onto the rack. The cake should cool right-side up.

7. Frost the top of the cake with Brown Sugar Frosting when completely cool. Sprinkle with the chopped nuts.

LET ALL THINGS BE DONE DECENTLY and in order and the first thing to put in order when you are going to bake is yourself. Secure the hair in a net or other covering, to prevent any from falling, and brush the shoulders and back to be sure none are lodged there and might blow off; make the hands and fingernails clean, roll the sleeves up above the elbows, and put on a large clean apron. Clean the kitchen table of utensils and everything not needed, and provide everything that will be needed until the cake is baked, not forgetting even the broom-splints previously picked off a new broom and laid away carefully in a little box. (A knitting needle may be kept for testing cake instead of splints.)

If it is warm weather, place the eggs in cold water, and let stand for a few minutes, as they will then make a finer froth; and be sure they are fresh, as they will not make a stiff froth from any amount of beating if old. The cake-tins should be prepared before the cake, when baking powder is used, as it effervesces but once, and there should be no delay in baking, as the mixture should be made firm by the heat, while the effervescing process is going on.

— Mrs. Florence K. Stanton, *The Practical Housekeeper*, 1898

Pumpkin Spice Cake

Pumpkin cakes are sweet, moist, and a welcome change from pumpkin pie. If you like, you can substitute any winter squash purée for the pumpkin.

Serves 8

- 2 cups sifted cake flour
- 2 teaspoons baking powder
- 2 teaspoons ground ginger
- 1 teaspoon baking soda
- 1 teaspoon ground cinnamon
- ½ teaspoon salt
- ¼ teaspoon ground cloves
- ¼ teaspoon freshly grated nutmeg
- 1 cup cooked or canned pumpkin
- ½ cup buttermilk, at room temperature
- 1 teaspoon vanilla extract
- ½ cup (1 stick) butter, at room temperature
- 1 cup lightly packed brown sugar
- ½ cup granulated sugar
- 2 large eggs
- 3 tablespoons ginger marmalade

GINGER CREAM CHEESE FROSTING

- 4 tablespoons butter, at room temperature
- 1 (8-ounce) package cream cheese, at room temperature
- 2 tablespoons ginger marmalade
- 1 cup sifted confectioners' sugar
- ¼ cup finely chopped crystallized ginger, for garnish

1. Preheat the oven to 350°F. Lightly grease and flour two 8-inch round nonstick cake pans. If you are using uncoated aluminum bakeware, grease the cake pans and line with parchment paper.

2. Sift together the flour, baking powder, ginger, baking soda, cinnamon, salt, cloves, and nutmeg. Sift two more times. Return the flour mixture to the sifter and set aside over a bowl.

3. Thoroughly combine the pumpkin, buttermilk, and vanilla in a medium bowl.

4. Beat the butter in a large bowl, with an electric mixer or by hand, until creamy. Gradually add the brown sugar and granulated sugar, beating until thoroughly combined. Add the eggs, one at a time, beating well after each addition. Add the

flour mixture alternately with the pumpkin mixture, mixing just until the batter is smooth and blended. Divide the batter between the prepared pans.

5. Bake for 30 to 35 minutes, until a tester inserted into the center of one of the cakes come out clean and the cake pulls away from the side of the pan.

6. Cool on wire racks for 5 minutes. While the cake is still warm, brush 1½ tablespoons of ginger marmalade on each layer of cake. (If the marmalade is too thick to spread easily, put the marmalade in a custard cup and warm it in a small pan of boiling water until softened.) Cool the cake layers for 5 minutes longer, then remove from pans and cool completely.

7. To prepare the frosting, beat the butter and cream cheese until creamy and well blended. Mix in the 2 tablespoons ginger marmalade. Gradually add the confectioners' sugar, beating until smooth.

8. Spread the frosting between the layers and over the top of cake. Sprinkle with crystallized ginger. Keep the frosted cake refrigerated.

A Buttery Nursery Rhyme

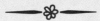

Come, butter, come,

Come, butter, come;

Peter stands at the gate

Waiting for a butter cake,

Come, butter, come.

According to the *Oxford Dictionary of Nursery Rhymes* (1951), this old English nursery rhyme made it across the Atlantic and was heard chanted by a butter maker as she churned, as recently as 1936 in southern Indiana. Marjorie Kinnan Rawlings reported a similar version of the rhyme in Florida in her book *Cross Creek Cookery* (1942).

Lindy's New York Cheesecake

Cheesecakes were known to the ancient Greeks and popular over the centuries through-out Europe. The quintessential American cheesecake, a sweet, creamy, sinfully rich cake, was developed at Lindy's in New York, a restaurant known more for its clientele of celebrities than for its food. According to legend, waiters at Lindy's could be bribed to reveal the "secret" recipe. No doubt the bribery has been widespread because this version is quite well known.

Serves 10 to 16

COOKIE DOUGH CRUST

1 cup unbleached all-purpose flour
3 tablespoons sugar
1 teaspoon finely grated lemon zest
⅛ teaspoon salt
½ cup (1 stick) butter, cut into ¼-inch cubes
1 large egg yolk
½ teaspoon vanilla extract

CHEESE FILLING

5 (8-ounce) packages cream cheese (2½ pounds), at room temperature
1¾ cups sugar
3 tablespoons unbleached all-purpose flour
2 teaspoons finely grated lemon zest
1 teaspoon fresh lemon juice
1 teaspoon vanilla extract
5 large eggs
2 large egg yolks
¼ cup whipping cream

1. To make the crust, combine the flour, sugar, lemon zest, and salt in a large bowl or food processor. With a pastry blender, with your fingertips, or with the food processor, cut or rub the butter into the flour mixture until it has the consistency of coarse crumbs. Add the egg yolk and the vanilla. Mix until combined. Gather the dough into a ball, wrap in plastic wrap, and refrigerate for 45 minutes.

2. Preheat the oven to 400°F. Pat out the dough over the bottom and 2 inches up the sides of a 9-inch springform pan.

3. Bake the crust for 10 minutes. Remove the pan from the oven and set aside to cool. Reduce the oven temperature to 325°F.

4. To make the cheese filling, beat the batter by hand. If you use an electric mixer, avoid beating on very high speed because this incorporates too much air into the cheesecake and causes it to rise (and fall) like a soufflé. Beat the cream cheese in a large bowl until it is creamy and smooth. Combine the sugar and flour and beat into the cream cheese. Add the lemon zest, lemon juice, and vanilla. Beat in the eggs and egg yolks, one at a time. Mix well after each addition. Beat in the cream, mixing until smooth. Pour the cheese mixture into the crust-lined pan and smooth the surface.

5. Bake the cake for 60 to 75 minutes, until the center appears set but not firm.

6. Set the cake in a draft-free place until completely cooled; the cake will become firm as it cools.

7. Gently run a sharp knife around the edge of the pan. Refrigerate until thoroughly chilled. Remove the sides of the pan and serve.

Baker's Tip

✳ The original Lindy's recipe used a cookie-dough crust, but if you prefer, follow the recipe on page 265 to prepare a graham cracker crust instead.

Black Walnut Cake

If you grew up in the Midwest, particularly Kansas, you might have especially fond memories of this rich, crunchy moist cake studded with black walnuts. If you don't live near a source of black walnuts, substitute toasted English walnuts.

Serves 14 to 16

2¾ cups sifted cake flour
2½ teaspoons baking powder
¾ teaspoon salt
⅔ cup (about 1¼ sticks) butter, at room temperature
1 cup granulated sugar
⅔ cup firmly packed dark brown sugar

3 large eggs
1 teaspoon vanilla extract
1 cup milk
1½ cups finely chopped black walnuts or toasted English walnuts
Burnt Sugar Icing (page 139)
½ cup walnut halves, to garnish

1. Preheat the oven to 350°F. Lightly grease and flour a 9- by 13-inch baking pan.

2. Sift together the flour, baking powder, and salt.

3. Beat the butter in a large bowl until creamy. Gradually add the granulated sugar and brown sugar, beating until fluffy. Add the eggs, one at a time, beating well after each addition. Add the vanilla. Add the flour mixture alternately with the milk, mixing just until the batter is smooth and blended. Fold in the nuts. Spoon the batter into the prepared pan.

4. Bake for 30 to 35 minutes, until a tester inserted into the center of the cake comes out clean.

5. Cool the cake on a wire rack.

6. Frost with the Burnt Sugar Icing when completely cool. Garnish with the walnut halves.

Fudge Frosting

Frosting for two 8- or 9-inch layers, one 9- by 13-inch cake, or 20 to 24 cupcakes

....

4 ounces semisweet chocolate	½ cup milk, or more as needed
4 tablespoons butter	1 teaspoon vanilla extract
4 cups sifted confectioners' sugar (one 1-pound box)	⅛ teaspoon salt

....

1. Melt the chocolate and butter in the top of a double boiler set over simmering water. Stir until completely smooth and glossy. Remove the top of the double boiler from the heat and let cool slightly.

2. Combine the confectioners' sugar, milk, vanilla, and salt. Beat until well combined. Add the chocolate mixture and beat until smooth. If the frosting is too thick, thin with a little more milk, added a teaspoon at a time. If the frosting is too thin, allow it to stand for a few minutes, stirring occasionally. Once it is the right consistency, work quickly because the frosting becomes hard upon standing.

Recommended for:

Devil's Food Cake, page 88 ❄ Chocolate Layer Cake, page 89 ❄ Frosted Chocolate-Zucchini Layer Cake, page 96 ❄ Vanilla Cupcakes, page 100 ❄ Gold Cake, page 101

Frosted to Perfection

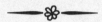

EVEN A PERFECTLY BAKED CAKE may suffer a tarnished reputation if its frosting isn't up to par. Making the frosting is only half the battle; many would say that correctly applying the frosting is more difficult.

The techniques below explain how to frost a layer cake, which is a challenging cake to frost; modify these techniques for other types of cakes. After all, it's only fair that your cake look as good as it tastes!

1. Start with a completely cooled cake. Brush off any crumbs and, if necessary, cut away any crisp edges. (Professionals often frost frozen cakes, which is why many bakery cakes taste stale. Don't go that route.)

2. Most frostings work best if made just before they are spread. Creamy, uncooked frostings can be held in the refrigerator for a few hours if they are kept tightly covered. Warm to room temperature and stir well before using.

3. To keep the cake plate clean, place strips of waxed paper around the edges of the plate and remove them when you are done.

4. Place the first layer, top-side down, on the cake plate. Using a frosting spatula, spread the frosting almost to the edge,

5. Place the second layer, top-side up, on the bottom layer.

6. Spread about three-quarters of the remaining frosting on the sides. Hold the frosting spatula so that the tip rests on the cake plate. The straight edge of the blade should be held against the frosting so that the flat side of the blade forms a 30-degree angle with the side of the cake. Spread the frosting evenly on the sides. Don't worry about the ridge of frosting that piles up on the top of the cake; you will use that to cover the top.

7. Spread the remaining frosting on top of the cake, working from the edge to the center with the spatula held horizontally and level.

8. If you want a smooth top, dip the spatula in water before smoothing the top. Use cold water for creamy or butter-based frostings; use hot water for cooked frostings. To make swirled circles and wavy lines in the frosting, use the back of a spoon. Pull up for peaks.

9. Before putting a design or writing on a cake, mark your lines with a toothpick and smooth over mistakes with the back of a spoon.

Chocolate Frosting

Frosting for two 8- or 9-inch layers, one 9- by 13-inch cake, or 20 to 24 cupcakes

3 ounces unsweetened chocolate
3 tablespoons butter
3 cups sifted confectioners' sugar
   Pinch of salt
7 tablespoons milk, at room temperature
1 teaspoon vanilla extract

1. Melt the chocolate and butter in the top of a double boiler set over simmering water. Stir until completely smooth and glossy. Remove the top of the double boiler from the heat and let cool slightly.

2. Blend in the confectioners' sugar and salt, alternating with the milk and vanilla. Mix until the frosting is smooth and has a good consistency for spreading.

Recommended for:

Devil's Food Cake, page 88 ✳ Chocolate Layer Cake, page 89 ✳ Vanilla Cupcakes, page 100 ✳ Gold Cake, page 101 ✳ Banana Cake, page 106 ✳ Carrot Cake, page 114 ✳

Glossy Chocolate Glaze

Glaze for the top and sides of an 8- or 9-inch layer cake

....

1 cup semisweet chocolate chips or 6 ounces semisweet chocolate, chopped	4 tablespoons butter 1 tablespoon light corn syrup

....

1. Combine the chocolate, butter, and corn syrup in a heavy saucepan. Cook over low heat, stirring until the mixture is melted and smooth.

2. Cool for about 10 minutes, stirring occasionally, then spread or pour over the cake.

Recommended for:

Chocolate Layer Cake, page 89 ❋ Gold Cake, page 101 ❋ Angel Food Cake, page 116 ❋ Sponge Cake, page 118

Many families have owed their prosperity full as much to the propriety of female management, as to the knowledge and activity of the father.

— *Mrs. J. S. Bradley's Housekeeper's Guide,* 1853

Rich Fudge Frosting

Frosting for the tops of two 8- or 9-inch layers, one 9- by 13-inch cake, or 20 to 24 cupcakes

....

½ cup whipping cream	3 ounces unsweetened chocolate,
¾ cup sugar	cut into small pieces
½ teaspoon instant coffee powder	4 tablespoons butter, softened

....

1. Combine the cream and sugar in a small saucepan. Bring to a boil, stirring until the sugar dissolves. Decrease the heat so the mixture boils slowly. Cook, stirring often, for 6 to 7 minutes, until mixture thickens and becomes syrupy. Watch carefully so the mixture doesn't burn. The syrup will look almost like fine bubbly marshmallow.

2. Remove the pan from the heat and stir in the coffee powder until dissolved. Add the chocolate and butter and stir until smooth. The frosting will gradually thicken to a spreading consistency. If it is too soft to spread, dip bottom of the saucepan in a shallow pan of cold water for a few seconds while stirring. Immediately spread the frosting over the top of the cake, before it cools like fudge.

Recommended for:

Devil's Food Cake, page 88 ✳ Chocolate Layer Cake, page 89 ✳ Frosted Chocolate-Zucchini Layer Cake, page 96 ✳ Vanilla Cupcakes, page 100 ✳ Gold Cake, page 101

Orange Marmalade Frosting

Frosting for two 8-inch or 9-inch layers, one 9- by 13-inch cake, or 20 to 24 cupcakes

- 5 tablespoons orange marmalade
- 6 tablespoons butter, at room temperature
- 4 cups sifted confectioners' sugar (one 1-pound box)
- 2 teaspoons finely grated orange zest
- 2–4 tablespoons fresh orange juice

1. In a microwave or small saucepan, heat the marmalade until runny. Cool to room temperature.

2. Beat the butter in a medium bowl until light and fluffy. Beat in half the confectioners' sugar, mixing it in as much as possible. The mixture will be lumpy. Beat in the marmalade, the remaining confectioners' sugar, and orange zest. Stir in 2 tablespoons of the orange juice, mixing until almost combined. Beat in additional orange juice, a half tablespoon at a time, until the frosting has a creamy, spreadable consistency.

Recommended for:

Gold Cake, page 101 ❋ Orange Chiffon Cake, page 122 ❋ Pumpkin Spice Cake, page 126 ❋ Vanilla Cupcakes, page 100

Vanilla Frosting

Frosting for two 8- or 9-inch layers, one 9- by 13-inch cake, or 20 to 24 cupcakes

....

4 tablespoons butter, at room temperature	3 cups sifted confectioners' sugar
2 teaspoons finely grated lemon zest	2–3 tablespoons cream or milk
	1 teaspoon vanilla extract

....

1. Beat the butter with the lemon zest until creamy. Gradually add 1½ cups of the confectioners' sugar, blending thoroughly.

2. Beat in 2 tablespoons of the cream, the vanilla, and the remaining 1½ cups confectioners' sugar. Add enough cream to make a smooth frosting of spreading consistency.

Recommended for:

Devil's Food Cake, page 88 ❋ Chocolate Layer Cake, page 89 ❋ Banana Cake, page 106 ❋ Vanilla Cupcakes, page 100

Improvising a Pastry Bag

IF YOU DON'T HAVE A PASTRY BAG to use to for piping a message across a cake, improvise with a plastic ziplock bag. Fill the bag with frosting. Snip off the tip of one corner and squeeze out the frosting from the bag as you would with a pastry bag.

Seven-Minute Frosting

Frosting for two 8- or 9-inch layers, one 9- by 13-inch cake, or 20 to 24 cupcakes

2 large egg whites	¼ teaspoon cream of tartar
1½ cups sugar	Pinch of salt
⅓ cup water	1 teaspoon vanilla extract

1. Combine the egg whites, sugar, water, cream of tartar, and salt in the top of a double boiler. Place over simmering water (upper pan should not touch water) and beat with an electric hand mixer or rotary beater for 7 minutes, until stiff peaks form.

2. Remove the pan from the boiling water, add the vanilla, and beat for another minute on high speed, until frosting has a spreadable consistency.

Recommended for:

Devil's Food Cake, page 88 ※ Chocolate Layer Cake, page 89 ※ Lady Baltimore Cake, page 108 ※ Spice Cake, page 110 ※ Black Walnut Cake, page 130 ※ Vanilla Cupcakes, page 100

Burnt Sugar Icing

Frosting for two 8- or 9-inch layers, one 9- by 13-inch cake, or 20 to 24 cupcakes

¼ cup granulated sugar
⅓ cup boiling water
3 tablespoons butter, at room
      temperature

2¼ cups sifted confectioners' sugar
1 teaspoon vanilla extract

1. Cook the granulated sugar in a small heavy saucepan or skillet over medium heat, without stirring, until the sugar melts and the syrup becomes a deep golden brown, about 5 minutes.

2. Remove from the heat. Slowly and carefully pour in the boiling water. (The water will steam and boil up as it hits the caramelized sugar.) Return the pan to low heat and stir the mixture until the sugar is completely dissolved. Allow to cool.

3. Beat the butter in a medium bowl until creamy. Gradually add half of the confectioners' sugar, blending well. The mixture will be lumpy. Beat in 3 tablespoons of the cooled burnt sugar syrup and the vanilla. Blend in the remaining confectioners' sugar and additional syrup to make a smooth frosting of spreading consistency.

Recommended for:

Spice Cake, page 110 ※ Black Walnut Cake, page 130 ※ Pound Cake, page 161

Cream Cheese Frosting

Frosting for two 8- or 9-inch layers, one 9- by 13-inch cake, or 20 to 24 cupcakes

....

1 (8-ounce) package cream cheese, at room temperature

½ cup (1 stick) butter, at room temperature

2 teaspoons finely grated orange zest

2 cups sifted confectioners' sugar

....

Beat the cream cheese and butter in a large bowl until creamy and well blended. Beat in the orange zest. Gradually add the confectioners' sugar, beating until smooth.

Recommended for:

Chocolate Layer Cake, page 89 ❄ German Chocolate Cake, page 90 ❄ Spice Cake, page 110 ❄ Carrot Cake, page 114 ❄ Pumpkin Spice Cake, page 126

Stack Cakes

ONE TYPE OF CAKE you don't see very often anymore is a stack cake, a kind of pioneer potluck cake. Guests invited to a wedding would each bring a cake layer — any flavor — to make the wedding cake. The layers were held together by applesauce. A bride's popularity was gauged by the number of stacks and their heights.

Orange Frosting

Frosting for two 8- or 9-inch layers, one 9- by 13-inch cake, or 20 to 24 cupcakes

....

4 tablespoons butter, at room
   temperature
1 tablespoon finely grated orange
   zest

3 cups sifted confectioners' sugar
  About ¼ cup freshly squeezed
   orange juice

....

1. Beat the butter and the orange zest in a large bowl until creamy. Gradually add 1½ cups of the confectioners' sugar, blending thoroughly.

2. Beat in 2 tablespoons of the orange juice; then add the remaining 1½ cups confectioners' sugar. Add enough orange juice to make a creamy frosting of spreading consistency.

Recommended for:

Gold Cake, page 101 ✳ Sponge Cake, page 118 ✳ Orange Chiffon Cake, page 122

Coconut Pecan Frosting

Frosting for two 8- or 9-inch layers, one 9- by 13-inch cake, or 20 to 24 cupcakes

....

3 large egg yolks	1 teaspoon vanilla extract
1 cup evaporated milk	1¼ cups lightly packed, sweetened
¾ cup firmly packed light brown	flaked coconut
sugar	1 cup chopped pecans
½ cup (1 stick) butter	

....

1. Beat the egg yolks lightly with a wire whisk in a heavy saucepan. Add the evaporated milk, brown sugar, and butter. Cook over low heat, stirring, until the mixture thickens, 8 to 10 minutes. Do not boil.

2. Remove the saucepan from the heat. Stir in the vanilla. Cool, stirring frequently.

3. Add the coconut and pecans and beat until the frosting is of spreading consistency.

Recommended for:

German Chocolate Cake, page 90 ❋ Spice Cake, page 110 ❋ Pumpkin Spice Cake, page 126

Sea Foam Frosting

Frosting for two 8- or 9-inch layers, one 9- by 13-inch cake, or 20 to 24 cupcakes

....

2 large egg whites
1½ cups firmly packed light brown
    sugar
⅓ cup water

¼ teaspoon cream of tartar
    Pinch of salt
1 teaspoon vanilla extract

....

1. Combine the egg whites, brown sugar, water, cream of tartar, and salt in the top of a double boiler. Place over simmering water (the water should not touch the bottom of the pan) and beat with an electric hand mixer or rotary beater for 7 minutes, until the mixture forms stiff peaks.

2. Remove the pan from the boiling water, add the vanilla, and beat for another minute on high speed, until the frosting is thick enough to spread.

Recommended for:

Banana Cake, page 106 ✳ Spice Cake, page 110 ✳ Black Walnut Cake, page 130

Brown Sugar Frosting

Frosting for a 9-inch square or tube cake

....

1½ cups firmly packed dark brown
    sugar
5 tablespoons cream or half-and-
    half

1 tablespoon butter
   Pinch of salt
½ teaspoon vanilla extract

....

1. Combine the brown sugar, cream, butter, and salt in a small saucepan. Cook over medium heat, stirring constantly, until the mixture comes to a boil. Boil for 1 minute, reduce the heat, and simmer for about 3 minutes, stirring until slightly thickened. Stir in the vanilla.

2. Place the saucepan in a bowl of cool water and stir constantly for 1 to 2 minutes, until cool. Remove the pan from the water and continue stirring until the frosting thickens and starts to stiffen. Work quickly to spread the frosting because it hardens quickly. If the frosting gets too stiff, add a few drops of cream.

Recommended for:

Applesauce Cake, page 124 ❋ Poppy Seed Cake, page 163

Chocolate Ganache

Y ou can use ganache to frost or fill a cake or cookies. To make a smooth frosting, allow the ganache to cool slightly, then pour over the cake. If you want to use the ganache for spreading on a cookie or between cake layers, chill in the refrigerator, stirring occasionally, until the ganache is slightly thickened. For a fluffy frosting or filling, let the ganache cool until thickened, then beat with a whisk until fluffy.

Makes 1¾ cups, enough to fill one 8- or 9-inch layer cake or 14 sandwich cookies

- 1 *cup whipping cream*
- 8 *ounces good-quality dark or*
  bittersweet chocolate, chopped
- 1 *tablespoon rum or brandy*
  (optional)

1. Bring the cream to a simmer in a medium saucepan over medium heat. Watch carefully to avoid having the cream boil up the sides and over the top of the pan.

2. Put the chocolate in a medium bowl. Immediately pour the cream over the chocolate. Let stand for a few minutes, and then whisk the mixture until the chocolate is melted. Add the rum (if using).

Recommended for:

Oatmeal Sandwich Cookies, page 12 ❋ Vanilla Sandwich Cookies, page 13 ❋ Devil's Food Cake, page 88 ❋ Chocolate Layer Cake, page 89 ❋ Frosted Chocolate-Zucchini Layer Cake, page 96 ❋ Gold Cake, page 101 ❋ Banana Cake, page 106

Everyday Cakes, Muffins & Scones

When there is no holiday, special occasion, or birthday to celebrate, try an everyday cake. Think gingerbread, coffee cakes, and loaf cakes. The cakes may be filled with fruit, nuts, or chocolate.

Muffins and quick breads are very similar, just baked in a different shape. Scones, on the other hand, are similar to biscuits, and are at their best when served warm and fresh, and with either lemon curd or jam and clotted cream (Devonshire cream). All of them are easily served at brunch, where the distinction between dessert and the rest of the meal is never particularly rigid. Novice bakers find these sweet treats simple to make.

Ingredients

○ **Freshly grated nutmeg is incomparable in flavor to ground nutmeg;** we recommend purchasing whole nutmegs and grating what you need.

○ **Pieces of fruit, nuts, and chocolate chips are less likely to sink in a batter if they are tossed with flour.**

Equipment

○ **Always preheat the oven and set out your baking pans when you start to bake.** Make sure the oven rack is in the center of the oven, unless a recipe specifies otherwise.

○ **Shiny baking pans reflect heat and produce baked goods with a tender crust.**

Techniques

○ **Loaf cakes will release from their pans easily if you grease the bottom of the pans and then line with parchment paper, waxed paper, or aluminum foil.** Muffin pans can be greased or lined with paper liners.

○ **Do not overmix when stirring the wet ingredients into the dry ingredients.** It is fine to have lumps. An overmixed batter creates tough and rubbery muffins and loaf cakes.

○ **Use a standard (3-ounce), trigger-style ice cream scoop to portion the batter into muffin tins.** It keeps your hands from getting messy and ensures uniform-size muffins.

○ **Use a light touch when making scones and do not handle the dough more than necessary.** Overhandling causes tough scones.

○ **Scones can be cut into any shape you desire.** Use a drinking glass to make circles, or cut the dough into squares or wedges with a knife. Dip the edges of the cutter in flour to prevent the dough from sticking. Leave the cuts as sharp as possible to allow the scones to rise in layers. Place scones closely together on the baking sheet to encourage them to rise up rather than spread out.

○ **To allow enough room for cakes to rise, do not fill baking pans more than two-thirds to three-quarters full.** Muffin cups should be filled about two-thirds full.

○ **Fill any empty muffin cups with an inch or two of water.** Muffins tend to burn faster in a pan with empty cups.

○ **Put the pan in the oven as soon as possible after making the batter for the best results.**

○ **If the cake appears to be browning darkly but a tester inserted near the center of the cake shows it is not done, put a tent of foil over the cake and lower the oven temperature by 25 degrees, so the top of the cake doesn't burn before the middle has time to catch up.**

○ **To test a cake or muffin for doneness, insert a bamboo skewer or toothpick into the center of the cake.** It should come out without any batter clinging to it.

○ **Cool cakes, muffins, and scones in the pans for 10 to 15 minutes before running a knife around the edges to loosen them and turning them out onto a wire rack.** Turn right-side up to finish cooling. Muffins and scones can be eaten warm. Most of the loaf cakes taste better the next day.

Chocolate Dump Cake

A dump cake is one in which all the ingredients are "dumped" into a bowl and mixed together, without the refinement of creaming the butter and sugar, beating in the eggs, and so on. And it works just fine. This is a delicious cake to make when you are too busy to fuss. If you don't want to bother with the frosting, just dust with confectioners' sugar — no one will complain!

Serves 12 to 16

2 cups unbleached all-purpose flour
2 cups sugar
1½ teaspoons baking soda
¼ teaspoon salt
1 cup warm brewed coffee
¾ cup (1½ sticks) butter
3 ounces unsweetened chocolate, cut into small pieces

¾ cup sour cream, at room temperature
2 large eggs, at room temperature, lightly beaten
1 teaspoon vanilla extract
Chocolate Fudge Frosting (page 102)

1. Preheat the oven to 350°F. Grease and flour a 9- by 13-inch baking pan.

2. Combine the flour, sugar, baking soda, and salt in a large bowl.

3. Combine the coffee, butter, and chocolate in a saucepan over low heat. Stir occasionally until the butter and chocolate have melted. Remove from the heat.

4. Make a well in the center of the flour mixture. Pour in the coffee mixture and whisk until combined and smooth. Whisk in the sour cream, eggs, and vanilla, mixing thoroughly. Spoon the batter into the prepared pan, spreading the mixture into the corners.

5. Bake for 35 minutes, until a tester inserted into the center of the cake comes out clean.

6. Cool on a wire rack for about 30 minutes. Frost the still-warm cake in the pan with the frosting.

Chocolate Snack Cake

A snack cake is one that is easily made and can be tucked into a lunch box or eaten out of hand. This cake is so moist that it doesn't need a frosting — a light dusting of confectioners' sugar can finish this cake. However, if you want to frost it, go right ahead; it will no longer be a snack cake but it will make a terrific dessert.

Serves 8 or 9

- 2 ounces semisweet chocolate, chopped
- ⅔ cup hot brewed coffee
- 1¾ cups all-purpose flour
- 1½ cups granulated sugar
- ¾ cup unsweetened cocoa powder
- 2 teaspoons baking soda
- ¾ teaspoons salt
- 2 large eggs
- ⅔ cup vegetable oil
- ¾ cup buttermilk
- 1 teaspoon vanilla extract
- Confectioners' sugar, to dust

1. Preheat the oven to 350°F. Grease and flour an 8-inch square baking pan.

2. Combine the chocolate and coffee in a bowl and stir until the chocolate is melted and the mixture is smooth.

3. Combine the flour, sugar, cocoa powder, baking soda, and salt in a large bowl. Make a well in the center.

4. In a separate bowl, whisk the eggs, oil, buttermilk, vanilla, and melted chocolate mixture until combined well. Add to the center of the flour mixture and mix until smooth. Pour the batter into the prepared baking pan.

5. Bake for about 45 minutes, until a tester inserted into the center of the cake comes out clean.

6. Cool on a wire rack. Dust the cake with confectioners' sugar before serving.

Troubleshooting

BAKING ISN'T ROCKET SCIENCE. Most recipes will turn out delicious, whether or not you are an experienced baker. But if success eludes you, maybe the answer lies here.

Cake or muffin sticks to the pan:

- The pan was not well greased. (Buying high-quality, nonstick metal baking pans will prevent the problem in the future.)
- The cake or muffins were left in the pan too long.

Big holes and "tunnels" in the cake or muffin and/or the texture is tough:

- The batter was overmixed.

Big crack down the middle of the loaf:

- The top of the loaf "set" in the heat of the oven before the loaf finished rising. Drizzle the loaf with icing or dust with confectioners' sugar to conceal the crack.

Cake is uncooked in the center:

- Oven temperature was too high. (Check the accuracy of the oven temperature with a thermometer.)
- Wrong-size pan was used.

Chocolate Zucchini Cake

Zucchini, originally a New World squash, was popular in Italy for decades before it reached mainstream American kitchens. In the 1960s, zucchini was adopted by American gardeners, who were thrilled with this easy-to-grow vegetable. But "easy-to-grow" soon gave way to "overabundant," and recipes for using up squash were immediately adopted. The zucchini disappears in this orange-scented cake, but the sneaky vegetable lends its moisture to its texture, and keeps it fresh-tasting for several days longer than most cakes. This cake recipe was developed with Renee Shepherd for *Renee's Garden Recipes*.

Serves 12 to 16

2 cups sifted unbleached all-purpose flour
⅓ cup unsweetened cocoa powder
1 teaspoon baking powder
1 teaspoon baking soda
½ teaspoon ground cinnamon
½ teaspoon salt
1¾ cups granulated sugar
½ cup vegetable oil
2 teaspoons finely grated orange zest

1 large egg
3 large egg whites, slightly beaten
2 cups finely shredded raw zucchini (do not peel)
⅓ cup buttermilk or plain yogurt, at room temperature
1 teaspoon vanilla extract
½ cup chocolate chips
Sifted confectioners' sugar, to garnish

1. Preheat the oven to 350°F. Grease and flour a 10-inch springform pan.

2. Sift together the flour, cocoa, baking powder, baking soda, cinnamon, and salt. Sift two more times.

3. Combine the sugar, oil, and orange zest in a large bowl, mixing well. Add the egg and the egg whites, one at a time, beating well after each addition. Stir in the zucchini.

4. Combine the buttermilk and vanilla.

5. Add the flour mixture to the egg mixture alternately with the buttermilk, beating until the batter is smooth. Stir in the chocolate chips, mixing just until combined. Pour the batter into the prepared pan.

6. Bake for 30 to 40 minutes, until a tester inserted into the center of the cake comes out clean.

7. Cool on a wire rack for about 10 minutes. Run a thin knife around the edge of the springform pan, between the pan and the cake. Set aside for about 30 minutes, until cool, and then remove the sides of the pan.

8. When the cake is completely cool, sprinkle with confectioners' sugar.

Vegetables are a must on a diet.

I suggest carrot cake, zucchini bread,

and pumpkin pie.

— **Jim Davis, creator of the *Garfield* comic strip**

Chocolate Chip Coffee Cake

When the occasion is appropriate for coffee cake but you want chocolate, you can have both. Mini chocolate morsels work better in this recipe, but full-size chocolate chips can be substituted.

Serves 10 to 12

CHOCOLATE STREUSEL

- ½ cup mini chocolate morsels
- ½ cup chopped pecans or walnuts
- ¼ cup unsweetened cocoa powder

COFFEE CAKE

- 2 cups unbleached all-purpose flour
- 1 tablespoon baking powder
- ½ teaspoon salt
- 6 tablespoons butter, at room temperature
- 1 cup granulated sugar

- 2 large eggs
- ½ teaspoon vanilla extract
- ¼ teaspoon almond extract
- ⅔ cup sour cream
  Confectioners' sugar, to dust (optional)

1. Preheat the oven to 350°F. Grease and flour a 10-inch tube pan.

2. To make the streusel, combine the chocolate morsels, nuts, and cocoa. Set aside.

3. To make the cake, sift the flour, baking powder, and salt into a medium bowl.

4. Beat the butter and granulated sugar in a large bowl until pale and fluffy. Add the eggs, one at a time, beating well after each addition. Beat in the vanilla and almond extracts.

5. Alternately fold the flour mixture and sour cream into the butter mixture, one-third at a time. Mix until smooth.

6. Spoon about half the batter into the prepared pan and spread to evenly cover the bottom of the pan. Sprinkle with half the streusel. Spread the remaining cake mixture over the streusel. Evenly sprinkle the remaining streusel over the top. With a knife, cut through the mixture a few times to marble in the streusel.

7. Bake for about 45 minutes, until a tester inserted into the center of the cake comes out clean.

8. Cool on a wire rack for 10 minutes. Then run a knife around the edge of the cake and invert onto the rack. Use a second rack to turn the cake right-side up and let cool completely.

9. If using, dust with confectioners' sugar just before serving.

Coffee Cakes over Time

THE ORIGINAL COFFEE CAKES were more like bread than cake; they were made with yeast, flour, eggs, sugar, nuts, dried fruit, and sweet spices. Over time, coffee cake recipes changed. Today's American coffee cake recipes often contain sugared fruit, cheese, yogurt, and other creamy fillings. Many of the American-style recipes came from German, Scandinavian, and Dutch settlers.

Chocolate Pudding Cake

The mixing method for pudding cakes is different from the mixing method for most other cakes. As this cake bakes, it separates into a gooey chocolate pudding on the bottom and a chocolate sponge cake on top.

Serves 6 to 8

1 cup unbleached all-purpose flour	4 tablespoons butter, melted and cooled
⅔ cup unsweetened cocoa powder	2 teaspoons vanilla extract
½ teaspoon baking powder	¾ cup firmly packed dark or light brown sugar
½ teaspoon salt	
½ teaspoon ground cinnamon	3 ounces dark or bittersweet chocolate, grated
2 large eggs	
1 cup granulated sugar	1½ cups hot brewed coffee
¾ cup whole milk	

1. Preheat oven to 350°F. Lightly grease an 8-inch square baking pan.

2. Stir the flour, ⅓ cup of the cocoa, the baking powder, the salt, and the cinnamon into a medium bowl.

3. Whisk the eggs, granulated sugar, milk, butter, and vanilla in a medium bowl. Add to the flour mixture and stir until just combined. Spread the batter evenly in the prepared baking pan.

4. Whisk the remaining ⅓ cup cocoa, the brown sugar, and the chocolate in a medium bowl. Sprinkle over the batter. Pour the hot coffee evenly over the batter; do not mix.

5. Bake for 30 to 35 minutes, until a tester inserted into the center of the cake comes out without crumbs sticking to it.

6. Cool the cake on a wire rack for 10 minutes. Serve warm.

Lemon Pudding Cake

As the title suggests, this lovely, lemony dessert is a cross between a pudding and a cake. To gild this lily, serve with cream, fresh berries, or a raspberry sauce made by puréeing a 10-ounce package of sweetened frozen berries.

Serves 6

1 cup sugar	5 tablespoons fresh lemon juice
¼ cup unbleached all-purpose flour	3 large egg yolks
⅛ teaspoon salt	1½ cups milk
2 tablespoons butter, melted	3 egg whites, at room temperature
1 tablespoon finely grated lemon zest	⅛ teaspoon cream of tartar

1. Preheat the oven to 350°F. Lightly grease a 1½-quart baking dish, an 8-inch square baking pan, or six custard cups. Set into a slightly larger pan that is at least 2 inches deep.

2. Combine ¾ cup of the sugar, the flour, and the salt in a medium bowl. Add the butter, zest, and juice, and mix until thoroughly blended.

3. In another bowl, beat the egg yolks with a whisk until thick and lemon-colored. Add the milk and mix well. Combine with the lemon mixture, stirring until blended.

4. In another bowl, beat the egg whites until foamy. Add the cream of tartar and beat until soft peaks form. Add the remaining ¼ cup sugar gradually and beat until the egg whites are stiff but not dry. The egg whites should hold their shape and remain moist. Fold the whites into the lemon mixture. Spoon into the baking dish or custard cups. Pour 1 inch of water into the larger pan, surrounding the dish or cups with the water.

5. Bake in the baking dish for 45 minutes or in the custard cups for 35 minutes, until the pudding is set and the top is golden brown.

6. Remove the baking dish or custard cups from the water and cool on a wire rack. Serve warm or chilled.

Lazy Daisy Oatmeal Cake

Lazy daisy cakes were popularized when a recipe appeared on a Quaker Oats carton in the 1960s. The "lazy" refers to the ease of making both the cake and the frosting. This is a casual cake, a snack cake, something to feed the family when there is no special occasion to justify a special effort.

Serves 6 to 9

1¼ cups boiling water	1 teaspoon vanilla extract
1 cup rolled oats (not quick-cooking)	2 large eggs, at room temperature
½ cup (1 stick) butter, at room temperature	1½ cups unbleached all-purpose flour
1 cup firmly packed light brown sugar	1 teaspoon baking soda
	¾ teaspoon ground cinnamon
	½ teaspoon salt
	¼ teaspoon freshly grated nutmeg

LAZY DAISY FROSTING

4 tablespoons butter, melted	¾ cup lightly packed, sweetened flaked coconut
½ cup firmly packed light brown sugar	½ cup chopped pecans
3 tablespoons cream or half-and-half	

1. Pour boiling water over the oats in a large bowl and stir to combine. Cover and let stand for 20 minutes.

2. Preheat the oven to 350°F. Grease and flour a 9-inch square baking pan.

3. Beat the butter in a large bowl until creamy. Gradually add the brown sugar, beating until fluffy. Stir in the vanilla. Add the eggs, one at a time, beating well after each addition. Add the oat mixture and blend well.

4. In another bowl, mix together the flour, baking soda, cinnamon, salt, and nutmeg. Add to the butter mixture and blend well. Spoon the batter into the prepared baking pan.

5. Bake the cake for 50 to 55 minutes, until the cake starts to pull away from the sides of the pan.

6. While the cake is baking, prepare the frosting. Combine the melted butter, brown sugar, cream, coconut, and pecans in a medium bowl. Mix well.

7. When the cake is done, transfer it to a rack, but do not remove the cake from the pan. Let stand for 5 minutes, while you preheat the broiler. Spread the frosting on top of the warm cake by dropping teaspoons of the frosting on the cake and spreading with the back of the spoon.

8. Place the cake 3 inches from the heat source and broil until the frosting becomes light brown and bubbly. Watch carefully because the topping browns very quickly. Serve warm or cold.

Praline Sour Cream Coffee Cake

We don't have time for morning coffee klatches anymore. The term comes from the German *Kaffeeklatsch*, which translates as "coffee gossip." Coffee klatches were informal gatherings over coffee, particularly popular during the 1950s and 1960s with stay-at-home moms. Still, the need for coffee cakes remains constant — for brunches, office treats, and bake sales. This recipe is a classic.

Serves 10 to 12

2 cups unbleached all-purpose flour
1½ teaspoons baking powder
½ teaspoon baking soda
¼ teaspoon salt
1 cup (2 sticks) butter, at room temperature
2 cups sugar
2 teaspoons vanilla extract
2 large eggs
2 cups sour cream

PRALINE

1 cup chopped pecans
2 tablespoons sugar
2 teaspoons ground cinnamon

1. Preheat the oven to 350°F. Grease and flour a 9-inch tube or Bundt pan.

2. Sift the flour, baking powder, baking soda, and salt into a medium bowl.

3. Beat the butter in a large bowl until creamy. Gradually add the sugar and the vanilla, beating until fluffy. Add the eggs, one at a time, beating well after each addition. Add the sour cream, mixing until smooth. Fold in the flour mixture and beat just until blended. Be sure to avoid overmixing.

4. To make the praline, combine the pecans, sugar, and cinnamon in a small bowl.

5. Spoon half the batter into the prepared pan. Sprinkle the praline evenly over the batter. Top with the remaining batter. With a knife, cut through the batter to distribute the praline.

6. Bake for 55 to 60 minutes, until a tester inserted into the center comes out clean.

7. Cool on a wire rack for 20 minutes. Run a spatula carefully around the sides and center tube of the pan before turning out the cake onto the rack. Serve warm.

Pound Cake

In the days before our heavy reliance on cookbooks, many cakes were reduced to easily remembered formulas. A one-two-three-four cake required 1 cup butter, 2 cups sugar, 3 cups flour, and 4 eggs. Likewise, the pound cake had an easily remembered formula: 1 pound (2 cups) butter, 1 pound (2 cups) sugar, 1 pound (4 cups) flour, and 1 pound (about 9) eggs. Those proportions make two 9-inch loaves or a single 10-inch tube cake. We don't follow those exact proportions anymore because our ingredients have changed. Butter has more fat and less water than it used to; flour, too, is less moist; and sugar is cleaner and therefore sweeter. This variation on the "half-pound" cake delivers good old-fashioned taste and a dense, velvety texture.

Serves 10 to 12

2 cups unbleached all-purpose flour	1½ teaspoons vanilla extract or 1 tablespoon finely grated lemon zest with 1 tablespoon lemon juice
¼ teaspoon salt	
1 cup (2 sticks) butter, at room temperature	
1¾ cups granulated sugar	Sifted confectioners' sugar, to garnish (optional)
5 large eggs	

1. Preheat the oven to 325°F. Lightly grease a 9- by 5-inch loaf pan and line with parchment paper.

2. Sift the flour and salt into a medium bowl.

3. Beat the butter in a large bowl with an electric mixer until very light and creamy. Add the granulated sugar gradually and continue beating for 5 minutes, until the mixture is very fluffy. Beat in the eggs, one at a time, beating well after each addition. Add the vanilla. Fold in the flour mixture, mixing just until the batter is smooth and blended. Spoon the batter into the prepared pan.

4. Bake for 1 hour 15 minutes, until a tester inserted into the center of the cake comes out clean.

5. Cool on a wire rack for about 10 minutes. Remove the cake from the pan and cool completely. If using, sprinkle with the confectioners' sugar just before serving.

Gingerbread

Ginger isn't native to the New World, but it made an early appearance with the English colonists, who frequently made gingerbread. A recipe appeared in Amelia Simmons's *American Cookery* in 1796. A dessert that has stood the test of time, gingerbread is to some the quintessential comfort food — wildly appetizing as it bakes, filling the house with the warm scent of ginger. Richly satisfying to eat, it's wonderfully pleasing as an excuse for whipped cream. It's also delicious served with applesauce or rhubarb sauce and vanilla ice cream.

Serves 8 to 9

1½ cups sifted unbleached all-purpose flour	¾ cup firmly packed dark brown sugar
2 teaspoons ground ginger	1 large egg, lightly beaten
1 teaspoon baking soda	½ cup dark molasses (not blackstrap)
¾ teaspoon ground cinnamon	½ cup boiling hot brewed coffee
¼ teaspoon ground cloves	Confectioners' sugar, to garnish (optional)
¼ teaspoon salt	
½ cup (1 stick) butter, at room temperature	

1. Preheat the oven to 350°F. Grease and flour an 8-inch square baking pan.

2. Sift the flour, ginger, baking soda, cinnamon, cloves, and salt into a medium bowl.

3. Beat the butter in a large bowl until creamy. Gradually add the brown sugar, beating until fluffy. Add the egg and beat until smooth. Beat in the molasses. Add the flour mixture alternately with the coffee, mixing until just combined. The batter will be thin. Pour the batter into the prepared pan.

4. Bake for about 35 minutes, until a tester inserted into the center of the cake comes out clean.

5. Cool on a wire rack. Dust the cake with the confectioners' sugar, if using.

Poppy Seed Cake

Cookbooks are always advising the reader that fresh is better, and in the case of poppy seeds, this advice is especially true. Consider growing a patch of Oriental poppies and tasting the difference. The sight of the flowers swaying on their delicate stems is a bonus.

Serves 12 to 18

1 cup poppy seeds	2 tablespoons cream sherry
1 cup milk	2 teaspoons vanilla extract
3 cups sifted cake flour	6 large egg whites, at room temperature
2½ teaspoons baking powder	¼ teaspoon cream of tartar
½ teaspoon salt	Sifted confectioners' sugar, to garnish
1 cup (2 sticks) butter, at room temperature	
2 cups granulated sugar	

1. Combine the poppy seeds and milk and let stand for several hours or overnight. If pressed for time, stir the seeds into warm milk and set aside for 1 hour.

2. Preheat the oven to 350°F. Thoroughly grease and flour a 10-inch tube or Bundt pan or two 9- by 5-inch loaf pans.

3. Sift the flour, baking powder, and salt into a medium bowl.

4. Beat the butter in a large bowl until creamy and then gradually add 1¾ cups of the granulated sugar, beating until fluffy. Mix in the sherry and vanilla. Add the flour mixture alternately with the poppy seed mixture, stirring just until the batter is smooth and blended.

5. In another bowl, beat the egg whites until foamy. Add the cream of tartar and beat until soft peaks form. Add the remaining ¼ cup granulated sugar gradually. Beat until stiff but not dry. The egg whites should hold their shape and remain moist. Stir one-quarter of the egg whites into the batter, then gently fold in the remainder. Spoon the batter into the prepared pan(s).

6. Bake a tube or Bundt cake for 50 to 60 minutes or bake loaf pans for 40 to 50 minutes, until a tester inserted into the center of the cake comes out clean.

7. Cool on a wire rack for about 10 minutes. Remove the cake from the pan and cool completely. Sprinkle with the confectioners' sugar.

Honey Cake

Honey cakes were standard fare at teas given by abolitionists in the early 1800s. They were popular because honey replaced the more common molasses, a sweetener produced by slave labor. Today, honey cake is a traditional dessert on Rosh Hashanah, the Jewish New Year, when honey is eaten in hopes of having a sweet year. The rich honey cake goes well with raw apples dipped in honey, another Jewish New Year tradition.

Serves 12

- 1 cup dark honey, such as buckwheat
- ½ cup strong brewed coffee
- 2½ cups sifted unbleached all-purpose flour
- 2 teaspoons baking powder
- 1 teaspoon ground cinnamon
- ½ teaspoon ground allspice
- ½ teaspoon baking soda
- ½ teaspoon ground ginger
- ¼ teaspoon salt
- ⅛ teaspoon ground cloves

- 3 large eggs
- ¾ cup firmly packed dark brown sugar
- ⅓ cup vegetable oil
- 2 teaspoons finely grated orange zest
- ½ cup chopped walnuts
- 2 tablespoons finely chopped candied orange peel (optional)
- Sifted confectioners' sugar, to garnish

1. Preheat the oven to 300°F. Grease a 9- by 5-inch loaf pan and line with parchment paper.

2. Mix together the honey and coffee in a small saucepan over moderate heat, stirring until combined. Set aside; cool to lukewarm.

3. Sift the flour, baking powder, cinnamon, allspice, baking soda, ginger, salt, and cloves into a medium bowl.

4. Beat the eggs and brown sugar in a large bowl until light and fluffy. Gradually add the oil and continue beating until thoroughly blended. Add the orange zest. Alternate adding the flour mixture with the honey mixture, stirring just until the batter is smooth and blended. Fold in the nuts and the candied orange peel (if using). Spoon the batter into the prepared pan.

5. Bake for 60 to 65 minutes, until a tester inserted into the center of the cake comes out clean.

6. Cool on a wire rack for 10 minutes. Turn the cake out of the pan and cool completely. Wrap the cake in aluminum foil or plastic wrap and let it stand overnight to allow the flavors to intensify. Sprinkle with the confectioners' sugar and cut into very thin slices.

Honey Gathering

IN THE GOOD OLD DAYS, the housewife was not only responsible for making the cake, but she had to extract the honey from the hive as well. Here, then, is "Method of Taking Honey From Bee Hives Without Killing the Bees," from McCall's *Home Cook Book and General Guide,* compiled by Mrs. Jennie Harlan in 1890:

Pour two teaspoonsful of chloroform into a piece of rag, double it twice, and place it on the floor-board of the hive, which must be lifted for the purpose, the entrance-hole being carefully secured. In about two minutes and a half there will be a loud humming, which will soon cease. Let the hive remain in this state for six or seven minutes, making about ten minutes in all. Remove the hive and the greater number of bees will be found lying senseless on the board; there will still be a few clinging to the combs, some of which may be brushed out with a feather. They return to animation in from half an hour to one hour after the operation. This plan possesses a great superiority over the usual mode of brimstoning, the bees being preserved alive; and over the more modern plan of fumigation by puff-ball; it is far less trouble, and the honey does not become tainted with the fumes.

Apple Crumb Cake

Cakes with a sweet, crumbly topping are generally recognized as coffee cakes, and this cake is no exception. The apples impart flavor and moisture, so the cake keeps well.

Serves 8 to 9

CRUMB TOPPING

½ cup sugar
⅓ cup unbleached all-purpose flour
4 tablespoons butter, at room temperature

1 teaspoon ground cinnamon
½ teaspoon freshly grated nutmeg

2 cups unbleached all-purpose flour
1 tablespoon baking powder
1 teaspoon ground cinnamon
½ teaspoon salt
¼ teaspoon freshly grated nutmeg
¾ cup sugar
6 tablespoons butter, at room temperature

1 large egg
½ cup sour cream
¼ cup milk
1 teaspoon vanilla extract
2 large apples, peeled and finely chopped

1. Preheat the oven to 350°F. Grease and flour an 8-inch square baking dish.

2. To make the crumb topping, combine the sugar, flour, butter, cinnamon, and nutmeg in a small bowl. Mix with a fork until the mixture has an uneven, pebbly texture. Set aside.

3. Sift the flour, baking powder, cinnamon, salt, and nutmeg into a medium bowl.

4. Beat the sugar and butter in a large bowl until light and fluffy. Add the egg and beat until well blended. Beat in the sour cream, milk, and vanilla until smooth. Fold in the flour mixture until smooth. Fold in the apples.

5. Spoon the batter into the prepared pan. Sprinkle the crumb topping over the batter.

6. Bake for about 50 minutes, until a tester inserted near the center comes out clean. Serve warm or cooled, directly out of the pan.

Apple-Topped Coffee Cake

This is a very attractive-looking coffee cake, with fanned slices of apples peeping out from the top. It makes a change of pace from the usual crumb-topped coffee cake.

Serves 8 to 10

¾ cup (1½ sticks) butter, at room
     temperature
⅓ cup granulated sugar
⅓ cup firmly packed light brown
     sugar
3 large eggs
1½ cups unbleached all-purpose flour
1 teaspoon baking soda
½ teaspoon baking powder
½ teaspoon salt
¼ teaspoon freshly grated nutmeg
⅓ cup buttermilk

TOPPING

4 small tart apples, peeled, halved,
     and cored
2 teaspoons sugar
     Pinch of ground cinnamon
¼ cup apple jelly, warmed

1. Preheat the oven to 350°F. Grease and flour a 9-inch springform pan.

2. Beat the butter, granulated sugar, and brown sugar in a large bowl with an electric mixer until it is light and creamy. Add the eggs, one at a time, beating well after each addition. Sift the flour, baking soda, baking powder, salt, and nutmeg over the butter mixture and stir in the buttermilk until combined. Spoon the mixture into the pan.

3. To make the topping, partially slice each apple half, starting at the skin side; do not cut through. Fan out the apples and arrange over the top of the cake batter, core-side down. Press the apples into the batter so they are partially submerged; do not allow the batter to cover the apples. Combine the sugar and cinnamon and sprinkle over the apples.

4. Bake for about 50 minutes, until a tester inserted near the center of the cake comes out clean. Remove the cake from the oven and brush the top with the warm jelly.

5. Cool the cake on a wire rack. Remove the sides of the pan and serve.

Caramel Apple Cake

This cake is best served warm — fresh out of the oven if possible. If the timing doesn't work for you, reheat the cake for 6 to 8 minutes at 350°F.

Serves 10 to 12

3 cups sifted unbleached all-purpose flour
2 teaspoons baking powder
¾ teaspoon baking soda
½ teaspoon salt
2 teaspoons ground cinnamon
½ teaspoon freshly grated nutmeg
¼ teaspoon ground allspice
¾ cup (1½ sticks) butter, at room temperature
1 cup granulated sugar

1¼ cups firmly packed dark brown sugar
3 large eggs, at room temperature
1½ cups buttermilk, at room temperature
2 teaspoons vanilla extract
3 cups (3 large) peeled, cored, and diced tart apples (Granny Smith, Pippin)
1 cup coarsely chopped toasted walnuts

CARAMEL TOPPING

½ cup firmly packed dark brown sugar
4 tablespoons butter

¼ cup heavy cream
1 teaspoon vanilla extract

1. Preheat the oven to 350°F. Grease and flour a 10-inch Bundt pan.

2. Sift the flour, baking powder, baking soda, salt, cinnamon, nutmeg, and allspice into a medium bowl.

3. Beat the butter in a large bowl with an electric mixer until creamy. Gradually add the granulated sugar and brown sugar and continue beating for 5 minutes, until the mixture is light and fluffy. Beat in the eggs, one at a time, beating well after each addition. Combine the buttermilk and vanilla. Add one-third of the flour mixture and one-third of the buttermilk. Beat just until well blended. Continue adding the flour mixture and buttermilk in thirds until all is combined. With a large spoon, fold in the apples and walnuts. Spoon the batter into the prepared pan and smooth the top.

4. Bake for 60 to 70 minutes, until a tester inserted into the center of cake comes out clean and the cake pulls away from the sides of the pan.

5. Cool the cake in the pan on a wire rack for 15 minutes while you prepare the caramel topping.

6. To make the topping, combine the brown sugar, butter, and cream in a small, heavy saucepan. Bring just to a boil, then reduce the heat and simmer for 5 minutes, stirring until slightly thickened and smooth. Stir in the vanilla.

7. To remove the cake from the pan, run a thin rubber spatula around the inside edges of the pan to loosen cake. Invert onto a large plate. Let it sit for a minute, then lift off the pan. Pierce the top of the cake with a long skewer in a dozen or so places. Spoon the caramel topping over the warm cake and serve.

Midwestern Hospitality

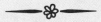

SCANDINAVIAN SETTLERS were perhaps more responsible than anyone else for making the coffee break an America institution — and for perfecting the kind of baked treats that go well with coffee. There was always a pot brewing on the back of the stove in any Scandinavian kitchen, and hospitality and coffee became synonymous. Farmworkers, in the days before fully automated agriculture, could expect a midmorning coffee break with sweet breads or cakes. Some of our favorite recipes hail from this tradition.

Apple Streusel Cake

Apples are available year-round, but they are especially wonderful during the cold-weather baking season, when berries and peaches are just a memory of summer past.

Serves 8 to 12

STREUSEL

¾ cup unbleached all-purpose flour
½ cup firmly packed light brown
    sugar

½ cup finely chopped walnuts
2 teaspoons ground cinnamon
½ cup (1 stick) butter, melted

---

2 cups unbleached all-purpose flour
¾ cup granulated sugar
2 teaspoons baking powder
½ teaspoon salt

2 large eggs
½ cup (1 stick) butter, melted
½ cup milk
2 apples, peeled and diced

1. Preheat the oven to 350°F. Grease a 9- by 5-inch loaf pan and line with parchment paper.

2. To make the streusel, combine the flour, brown sugar, walnuts, and cinnamon in a small bowl. Add the butter and stir with a fork until the mixture is crumbly. Set aside.

3. Whisk the flour, sugar, baking powder, and salt in a large bowl until well blended.

4. Beat the eggs in a medium bowl with a fork just to blend. Stir in the butter and milk to combine. Add to the flour mixture and fold with a rubber spatula just until the dry ingredients are moistened. Fold in the apples.

5. Spoon half the batter into the prepared pan; spread to cover bottom. Sprinkle with half the streusel. Spoon the remaining batter on top, spreading to cover. Sprinkle with the remaining streusel.

6. Bake for about 70 minutes, until a tester inserted near the center of the cake comes out clean.

7. Cool on a wire rack for 10 minutes. Run a knife around the sides and invert the cake onto the rack. Turn the cake streusel-side up and let cool completely.

Apple Tea Cake

This apple cake is simpler than the previous one, but it is still packed with apple goodness. The apple flavor intensifies on the second day.

Serves 8 to 12

2½ cups unbleached all-purpose flour
1 tablespoon baking powder
½ teaspoon baking soda
½ teaspoon salt
¼ teaspoon ground ginger
¼ teaspoon freshly grated nutmeg
2 large apples, peeled, cored, and diced

½ cup (1 stick) butter, at room temperature
¾ cup firmly packed brown sugar
2 large eggs, beaten
1 cup sour cream or yogurt
1 teaspoon vanilla extract

1. Preheat the oven to 350°F. Grease a 9- by 5-inch loaf pan and line with parchment paper.

2. Sift the flour, baking powder, baking soda, salt, ginger, and nutmeg in a large bowl. Add the apples, tossing them to coat with the flour.

3. Beat together the butter, brown sugar, eggs, sour cream, and vanilla in a large bowl. Stir in the flour mixture. Spoon the batter into the prepared pan and smooth the top.

4. Bake for 1 hour, until a tester inserted into the center of the cake comes out clean and the cake has begun to pull away from the sides of the pan.

5. Cool on a wire rack for 15 minutes. Invert the cake onto the rack and finish cooling.

Quick Banana Cake

Do you like your banana cake with nuts or with chocolate? Either way works with this versatile loaf — or choose both. Three medium-size bananas will give you the necessary amount for this cake. Whenever you find bananas going brown on the counter, consider peeling them, popping them in a freezer container, and freezing them for cakes such as this one.

Serves 8 to 12

1½ cups unbleached all-purpose flour
1 teaspoon baking soda
½ teaspoon salt
½ cup (1 stick) butter, at room temperature
1 cup sugar
2 large eggs

1 cup mashed very ripe bananas
½ cup sour cream
1 teaspoon vanilla extract
1 cup mini chocolate morsels or chopped toasted almonds, pecans, or walnuts

1. Preheat the oven to 350°F. Grease a 9- by 5-inch loaf pan and line with parchment paper.

2. Whisk the flour, baking soda, and salt in a medium bowl.

3. Beat the butter and sugar until light and fluffy. Add the eggs and beat until well blended. Add the flour mixture and mix until just combined. Add the bananas, sour cream, and vanilla; mix to combine. Stir in the chocolate chips. Pour into the prepared pan and smooth the top.

4. Bake for 65 to 70 minutes, until a tester inserted into the center of the cake comes out clean.

5. Cool on a wire rack for 10 minutes. Invert the cake onto the rack and finish cooling.

Maple-Pear Tea Cake

The combination of maple syrup and pears is heavenly, and this cake proves it. If fresh pears aren't available, or you want to make this on the spur of the moment, canned pears are perfectly acceptable.

Serves 8 to 12

2½ cups unbleached all-purpose flour	¼ cup firmly packed brown sugar
1 tablespoon baking powder	4 tablespoons butter, melted
½ teaspoon baking soda	1 large egg, beaten
½ teaspoon salt	½ cup sour cream or yogurt
2 large pears, peeled and diced	1 teaspoon vanilla extract
¾ cup pure maple syrup	

1. Preheat the oven to 350°F. Grease a 9- by 5-inch loaf pan and line with parchment paper.

2. Sift the flour, baking powder, baking soda, and salt into a medium bowl. Add the pears, tossing them to coat with the flour.

3. Beat together the maple syrup, brown sugar, melted butter, egg, sour cream, and vanilla in a large bowl. Stir in the flour mixture. Spoon the batter into the prepared pan and smooth the top.

4. Bake for about 1 hour, until a tester inserted into the center comes out clean and the cake has begun to pull away from the sides of the pan.

5. Cool on a wire rack for 15 minutes. Invert the cake onto the rack and finish cooling.

Pineapple Upside-Down Cake

Pineapple upside-down cakes were first mentioned in cookbooks in the 1930s, though they were probably invented much earlier. Some books suggest that the cake evolved from something known as bachelor's bread. This was made by pouring sponge cake batter into a pan lined with thin slices of citron (probably a type of melon, as citrus fruits were rare) and almonds. After the cake was baked, it was turned upside down onto a platter. The cake's name was a sly poke at the upside-down nature of the bachelor's life — and the quality of his baking!

Serves 8

Topping

- 1 (20-ounce) can sliced pineapple
- 4 tablespoons butter
- ⅔ cup firmly packed dark brown sugar
- 16 pecan or walnut halves

Cake

- 1¼ cups sifted unbleached all-purpose flour
- 1½ teaspoons baking powder
- ¼ teaspoon ground ginger
- ¼ teaspoon salt
- 6 tablespoons butter or vegetable shortening, at room temperature
- ⅔ cup granulated sugar
- 1 large egg
- 1 teaspoon vanilla extract
- ⅔ cup pineapple juice, reserved from pineapple for topping

1. Preheat the oven to 350°F.

2. To make the topping, drain the pineapple, reserving ⅔ cup of the juice for the cake. Over low heat, melt the butter in a heavy, ovenproof 9-inch skillet. If you are using a 9-inch glass cake pan or pie pan, melt the butter in the baking pan in the oven. Sprinkle the brown sugar over the melted butter and spread the mixture evenly over the bottom of the pan or skillet. Remove from the heat. Arrange eight pineapple slices over the brown sugar. Fill the centers and spaces between the slices with pecan halves placed flat-side up.

3. To make the cake, sift the flour, baking powder, ginger, and salt into a medium bowl.

4. Beat the butter in a large bowl until creamy. Gradually add the sugar, beating until fluffy. Beat in the egg and vanilla. Add the flour mixture alternately with the pineapple juice, mixing just until the batter is smooth and blended. Spoon the cake batter over the pineapple and pecans.

5. Bake for 40 to 45 minutes, until a tester inserted into the center of the cake comes out clean.

6. Cool for 5 minutes. Loosen the cake around the edges, then invert onto a serving platter. Allow the syrup to drip onto the cake before lifting off the skillet. Serve warm.

Fresh Pineapples

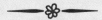

WHILE PINEAPPLE CANNED IN ITS OWN JUICE is an exceptionally fine canned fruit, fresh pineapple often has more texture and a sharper flavor. To judge whether a pineapple is ripe, look for bright green leaves. Try pulling out a leaf; if it yields easily, the fruit is ripe. The flesh should also feel slightly soft, and the pineapple should have a distinctive pineapple-y aroma.

Ginger Pumpkin Tea Cake with Lemon Glaze

We are stuck on using pumpkin for desserts and using winter squash as a savory vegetable. But in truth, there is nothing to distinguish botanically winter squash from pumpkin, so feel free to use them interchangeably. Butternut squash and Hubbard squashes make particularly smooth purées, wonderful in desserts.

Serves 8 to 12

2 cups unbleached all-purpose flour	¾ cup granulated sugar
2½ teaspoons baking powder	½ cup firmly packed light brown sugar
2 teaspoons ground cinnamon	
1 teaspoon ground ginger	1 cup cooked or canned puréed pumpkin
½ teaspoon baking soda	
½ teaspoon freshly grated nutmeg	½ cup sour cream or yogurt, at room temperature
½ teaspoon salt	
½ cup finely chopped crystallized ginger	½ cup vegetable oil
	3 large eggs, at room temperature

LEMON GLAZE

¼ cup confectioners' sugar
1 teaspoon finely grated lemon zest
2 teaspoons fresh lemon juice

1. Preheat the oven to 350°F. Set an oven rack in the lower third of oven. Grease a 9- by 5-inch loaf pan and line with parchment paper.

2. Sift the flour, baking powder, cinnamon, ginger, baking soda, nutmeg, and salt into a large bowl. Toss in the crystallized ginger. Make a well in the center of the flour.

3. In another bowl, combine the granulated sugar and the brown sugar. Beat in the pumpkin, sour cream, and oil. Add the eggs, one at a time, beating well after each addition.

4. Pour the pumpkin mixture into the center of the flour mixture. Using a rubber spatula, fold in the pumpkin mixture, just until the dry ingredients are moistened and the batter is blended. Spoon the batter into the prepared pan.

5. Bake for 55 to 60 minutes, until the cake pulls away from the sides of the pan and a tester inserted near the center of the cake comes out clean.

6. Cool in the pan on a wire rack for 10 minutes. Carefully invert the cake onto the rack and remove the pan. Turn right-side up and cool for about 10 minutes, while you prepare the glaze.

7. To make the glaze, sift the confectioners' sugar into a small bowl. Stir in the lemon zest. Add the lemon juice, 1 teaspoon at a time, mixing until the glaze is a spreading consistency. Brush the top of the still-warm cake with glaze. Let the cake sit for a few hours before serving.

I remember that at one time I saw two of my young mistresses and some lady visitors eating ginger-cakes, in the yard. At that time those cakes seemed to me to be absolutely the most tempting and desirable things I had ever seen and then and there resolved that, if I ever got free, the height of my ambition would be reached if I could get to the point where I could secure and eat ginger-cakes in the way I saw those ladies doing.

— Booker T. Washington, *Up from Slavery*, 1901

Orange Poppy Seed Cake

Poppy seeds are commonly used to top baked goods, particularly ones originally made in Central Europe and Germany. Anyone that finds this cake addictive will be responding to its delicious flavor, not to the poppy seeds themselves.

Serves 8 to 12

2 cups unbleached all-purpose flour	1 cup sugar
1 tablespoon baking powder	1 tablespoon finely grated orange zest
¼ cup poppy seeds (one [1.25-ounce] jar)	2 large eggs
¼ teaspoon salt	½ cup freshly squeezed orange juice
1 cup (2 sticks) butter, at room temperature	1 tablespoon Cointreau or Triple Sec

1. Preheat the oven to 325°F. Grease a 9- by 5-inch loaf pan and line with parchment paper.

2. Whisk the flour, baking powder, poppy seeds, and salt in a medium bowl.

3. Beat the butter and sugar in a large bowl with an electric mixer on medium-high speed until pale and creamy. Add the orange zest and beat in the eggs, one at a time, beating until just blended after each addition. With the mixer on low speed, gradually beat in the flour mixture, alternating with the orange juice and Cointreau. Spoon the batter into the prepared pan and smooth the top.

4. Bake for 60 to 65 minutes, until a tester inserted into the center comes out clean and the cake has begun to pull away from the sides of the pan.

5. Cool on a wire rack for 15 minutes. Invert the cake onto the wire rack and finish cooling.

Rhubarb Tea Cake

By tossing the rhubarb with confectioners' sugar, you avoid the shock of tart rhubarb suspended in a sweet cake. This is an easy cake to make and it freezes nicely, which provides the answer to that perennial question of what to do with all that ripe rhubarb.

Serves 8 to 12

2 cups unbleached all-purpose flour
1 teaspoon baking soda
¼ teaspoon ground cinnamon
¼ teaspoon salt
2 cups rhubarb sliced ½-inch thick
½ cup confectioners' sugar
¾ cup (1½ sticks) butter, at room temperature
1 cup firmly packed light brown sugar
2 large eggs
⅓ cup sour cream, buttermilk, or plain yogurt
1 tablespoon grated lemon zest

1. Preheat the oven to 350°F. Grease a 9- by 5-inch loaf pan and line with parchment paper.

2. Sift the flour, baking soda, cinnamon, and salt into a medium bowl.

3. In another bowl, toss the rhubarb with the confectioners' sugar until each piece is lightly coated.

4. Beat the butter and the brown sugar in a large bowl until fluffy. Add the eggs and beat until the mixture is light and creamy. Beat in the sour cream and lemon zest. Add the flour mixture and beat until just combined. Fold the rhubarb and any loose confectioners' sugar into the cake batter, which will be quite thick. Spoon into the prepared pan and level the top.

5. Bake for about 75 minutes, until a tester inserted near the center of the cake comes out clean. If the cake starts to brown around the edges before the rest of the cake is done, cover the edges with aluminum foil.

6. Cool in the pan on a wire rack for 10 minutes. Carefully invert the cake onto the rack and remove the pan. Turn right-side up and cool completely before serving.

Wonderful Walnuts

THE WORLD'S TWO MOST POPULAR WALNUT VARIETIES are the black walnut and the English walnut. Black walnuts are native to the eastern part of the United States, where they grow on trees that stand more than 100 feet tall. English walnuts originated in Persia, though both walnut varieties are now grown in temperate zones all over the world. Black walnut shells are very strong and more difficult to crack than English walnut shells. Also, black walnuts are much more strongly flavored than English walnuts; in fact, some people prefer to use half English walnuts and half black walnuts in their recipes to subdue the flavor.

Toasting walnuts enhances their flavor. To toast walnuts, place them in a dry skillet over medium heat and toast until fragrant, about 5 minutes, shaking the pan occasionally. Or place them in a shallow pan, such as a pie pan, and toast in the oven at 300°F for 7 to 10 minutes. Store walnuts in a cool, dry place. In their shells, walnuts keep for up to 3 months. Keep shelled walnuts in an airtight container and refrigerate for up to 6 months. Walnuts also can be frozen for up to 1 year.

Walnut-Date Loaf

This tea cake fits the bill as both bread and cake. It is terrific made into tea sandwiches with cream cheese and orange marmalade. If you can, make the cake a day in advance. The flavors will develop more fully if the cake is allowed to sit overnight.

Serves 8 to 12

½ cup water
1½ cups chopped pitted dates (8 ounces)
3 tablespoons butter, cut into chunks
½ cup firmly packed dark brown sugar
1 large egg, lightly beaten

1 cup buttermilk
1 tablespoon finely grated orange zest
2 cups unbleached all-purpose flour
1½ teaspoons baking powder
½ teaspoon baking soda
¼ teaspoon salt
¾ cup chopped toasted walnuts

1. Bring the water to a boil in a small saucepan. Stir in the dates and butter. Set aside for 10 minutes, until the butter is melted and the mixture has cooled. Add the brown sugar, egg, buttermilk, and orange zest, mixing well. Set aside.

2. Preheat the oven to 350°F. Grease a 9- by 5-inch loaf pan and line with parchment paper.

3. Whisk the flour, baking powder, baking soda, and salt in a large bowl. Make a well in the center of the flour mixture. Spoon the cooled liquid ingredients and the walnuts into the center of the well. Stir the whole mixture 12 to 15 times, until the flour is moistened; do not overmix. Spoon the batter into the prepared pan and smooth the top.

4. Bake for 55 to 60 minutes, until the cake pulls away from the sides of the pan and a tester inserted into the center comes out clean.

5. Cool on a wire rack for 10 minutes. Carefully invert the cake onto the rack and remove the pan. Turn right-side up and cool completely before serving.

Zucchini Pecan Cake

All sorts of zucchini confections have been invented over the years to use up gardeners' excess zucchini — which grows prolifically, given half a chance. The best zucchini for a dessert is at least medium-size, and bigger is not undesirable. Very young zucchini are perfect for the skillet but slightly bitter in a dessert.

Serves 12

4 medium zucchini (about 1¼ pounds)	1 cup granulated sugar
2¼ cups unbleached all-purpose flour	½ cup firmly packed brown sugar
2 teaspoon baking powder	3 large eggs, at room temperature
1 teaspoon baking soda	2 tablespoons grated orange zest
½ teaspoon salt	1½ teaspoons vanilla extract
1½ teaspoons ground cinnamon	1 cup toasted chopped pecans
¾ teaspoon freshly grated nutmeg	½ cup dried currants
¼ teaspoon ground allspice	½ cup chocolate chips (optional)
¾ cup vegetable oil	Confectioners' sugar

1. Preheat the oven to 350°F. Grease and flour a 10-inch tube pan.

2. Shred the zucchini with a small- to medium-size grater. Measure out 3 cups (not packed), and then spread out on paper towels to drain off excess moisture.

3. Sift the flour, baking powder, baking soda, salt, cinnamon, nutmeg, and allspice into a medium bowl.

4. Combine the oil, granulated sugar, and brown sugar in a large bowl. Beat until thoroughly combined. Add the eggs, one at a time, beating well after each addition. Beat in the orange zest and vanilla.

5. Gradually add the flour mixture, pecans, and currants. Stir in the zucchini and chocolate chips (if using). Mix just until the batter is smooth and blended. Spoon the batter into the prepared pan.

6. Bake for 60 to 75 minutes, until the cake pulls away from the sides of the pan and a tester inserted into the center comes out clean.

7. Cool in the pan for 10 minutes. Run a knife around the sides and center tube of the pan. Invert onto a wire rack. Use a second rack to turn the cake right-side up and let cool completely.

8. Sprinkle with confectioners' sugar just before serving.

Decorating with Confectioners' Sugar

FOR A SPECIAL PRESENTATION, you can top a plain cake with a design made from confectioners' sugar. To do so, use a triple thickness of decorative paper doilies. Remove any excess uncut paper. Fasten the doilies to the top of the cake with toothpicks or pins. Sift confectioners' sugar over and around the doilies, then remove the toothpicks or pins and lift the doilies straight up. There should remain a lacy snowflake design of powdered sugar.

Moravian Sugar Cake

Ever wonder why many churches serve coffee and cake after Sunday worship service? This tradition of congregants breaking bread together dates back to the Moravian Church, founded some 550 years ago by followers of reformer John Hus of Moravia (a province of Bohemia in his lifetime and now part of the Czech Republic). Moravian immigrants brought their church with them to the New World, beginning in the 1730s. They settled mostly in Pennsylvania and the Carolinas — founding Bethlehem, Pennsylvania, and Salem, North Carolina, which later became part of Winston-Salem. The well-known Moravian sugar cake is a simple yeast-raised cake topped with butter, brown sugar, and cinnamon. The first written recipe for the cake can be traced back to the *Moravian Magazine*, published in Bethlehem, Pennsylvania.

Serves 9 to 12

DOUGH

- 1 (7-ounce) baking potato (Idaho or russet), peeled and cut into ½-inch cubes
- ½ cup warm potato water
- 1 (2¼-ounce) package active dry yeast
- ½ teaspoon plus ½ cup granulated sugar
- ½ cup (1 stick) butter, melted and cooled
- ½ teaspoon salt
- 2 large eggs
- 2½–3 cups unbleached all-purpose flour

TOPPING

- 6 tablespoons butter
- 1 cup firmly packed light brown sugar
- 1½ teaspoons ground cinnamon

1. To prepare the dough, place the cubed potato in a small saucepan and cover with 1 inch of water. Bring to a boil, then cover, reduce the heat, and simmer for about 15 minutes, until the potato is very tender. Reserve ½ cup of the potato liquid and drain the potato.

2. Pour the warm potato-cooking liquid into a small bowl. When the liquid cools to about 110°F on an instant-read thermometer, sprinkle the yeast and the ½ teaspoon granulated sugar over the potato liquid, stirring to combine. Set aside for about 5 minutes, until the yeast bubbles and the mixture is foamy.

3. Using a ricer or potato masher, mash the still-warm potato until very smooth. Put into a large bowl. Mix in the ½ cup granulated sugar, the melted butter, and salt. Add the eggs, one at a time, beating well after each addition. Thoroughly mix in the yeast mixture. Add 2½ cups of the flour, mixing until well combined. If the dough is too sticky to handle, gradually add 2 more tablespoons of flour.

4. Turn out the dough onto a floured surface. Using floured hands, knead the dough for 8 to 10 minutes, and add only as much of the remaining flour as necessary (this is a soft cake dough, not a firm bread dough). When the dough is smooth and elastic, transfer it to a buttered bowl, turning it over to coat the top. Cover the bowl with a towel or plastic wrap.

5. Let the dough rise in a warm place for 1½ to 2 hours, until it is doubled in bulk.

6. Punch down the dough. (The dough may be prepared 1 day ahead and refrigerated. Bring the dough to room temperature before continuing with the next step.)

7. Grease a 9- by 13-inch baking pan. Spread the dough evenly in the pan. Cover with a towel and let rise in a warm place for 30 to 45 minutes, until doubled in bulk and puffy.

8. To make the topping, melt the butter, then set aside to cool. Combine the brown sugar and cinnamon in a small bowl.

9. Preheat the oven to 375°F.

10. Use your fingers to make indentations or holes, 1½ to 2 inches apart, over the top of the dough. Pour the cooled butter all over the surface of the dough, then sprinkle with the brown sugar and cinnamon mixture. Try to get some of the brown sugar into the holes.

11. Bake on the middle rack of the oven for 20 to 25 minutes, until the cake is well browned and cooked through.

12. Cut into squares and serve warm or at room temperature. The cake can be reheated to serve warm.

Applesauce Muffins

Whole wheat, applesauce, raisins — there's good stuff in these muffins. Don't be put off by the long ingredients list. Muffins are quick to whip up, and your house will smell heavenly as they bake.

Makes 12 muffins

1   cup unbleached all-purpose flour
¾   cup whole-wheat flour
2   teaspoons baking powder
½   teaspoon baking soda
¼   teaspoon salt
½   teaspoon ground cinnamon
¼   teaspoon ground allspice
¼   teaspoon freshly grated nutmeg

1   large egg, at room temperature
½   cup firmly packed dark brown sugar
4   tablespoons butter, melted and cooled
1   cup unsweetened applesauce
¾   cup dark or golden raisins

1. Preheat the oven to 400°F. Grease 12 muffin cups or line with paper liners.

2. Whisk the all-purpose flour, whole-wheat flour, baking powder, baking soda, salt, cinnamon, allspice, and nutmeg in a large bowl. Make a well in the center of the flour mixture.

3. Beat the egg in a small bowl. Add the brown sugar, butter, and applesauce and mix well. Pour into the center of the flour mixture. Stir gently a few times, then fold in the raisins. Stir 12 to 15 times, just long enough to moisten the dry ingredients. Do not beat or overmix. Fill the muffin cups three-quarters full.

4. Bake for 20 minutes, until the tops are browned and the muffins pull away from the sides of the pan.

5. Cool on a wire rack for 5 minutes. Then remove the muffins from the pan to finish cooling.

Banana-Nut Muffins

When bananas turn spotted and brown and are too ripe for the cereal bowl, it is time to make these muffins. Three medium to large ripe or overripe bananas should yield enough mashed bananas to make this recipe; but if you fall short, don't worry about it. Compensate with a little more sour cream or yogurt.

Makes 18 muffins

3 cups unbleached all-purpose flour
2 teaspoons baking powder
1 teaspoon baking soda
1 teaspoon salt
⅛ teaspoon freshly grated nutmeg
1 cup toasted nuts, chopped (almonds, pecans, or walnuts)
1 cup sugar

½ cup (1 stick) butter, at room temperature
2 large eggs
1 teaspoon vanilla extract
1¼ cups mashed ripe bananas (about 3 large)
¼ cup sour cream or lemon, vanilla, or plain yogurt

1. Preheat the oven to 350°F. Grease 18 muffin cups or line with paper liners.

2. Sift the flour, baking powder, baking soda, salt, and nutmeg into a medium bowl. Stir in the nuts.

3. Beat the sugar and butter in a large bowl until light and fluffy. Add the eggs, one at a time, and beat until well combined. Beat in the vanilla. Add the bananas and sour cream and beat until smooth. Add the flour mixture and mix until just barely combined. There will still be lumps. Divide the batter among the prepared muffin cups. (Fill any empty muffin cups with water so the muffins bake evenly.)

4. Bake for 20 to 25 minutes, until the muffins are golden brown and a tester inserted into one of the centers comes out clean.

5. Cool on a wire rack for 5 minutes. Then remove the muffins from the pan to finish cooling.

Pumpkin-Pecan Muffins with Cinnamon Topping

These are the perfect Thanksgiving-morning muffins — a hint of the lovely things to come later in the day. They are made with two ingredients native to America: pumpkin and pecans. If you should find yourself with winter squash on hand but no pumpkin, feel free to substitute. Puréed winter squash (particularly butternut or Hubbard squash) and pumpkin can be used interchangeably.

Makes 18 muffins

3 cups unbleached all-purpose flour	1 cup sugar
1 tablespoon baking powder	2 large eggs
1 teaspoon baking soda	1¾ cups cooked and mashed pumpkin
1 teaspoon salt	or winter squash, or canned
¼ teaspoon freshly grated nutmeg	pumpkin purée
1 cup coarsely chopped pecans	1 teaspoon vanilla extract
½ cup (1 stick) butter, at room temperature	¼ cup sour cream

TOPPING

¼ cup sugar
1½ teaspoons ground cinnamon
2 tablespoons butter, melted

1. Preheat the oven to 350°F. Grease 18 muffin cups or line with paper liners.

2. Sift the flour, baking powder, baking soda, salt, and nutmeg into a medium bowl. Stir in the pecans.

3. Beat the butter and sugar in a large bowl until light and fluffy. Add the eggs, one at a time, beating after each addition. Beat in the pumpkin, vanilla, and sour cream. Mix in the flour mixture until moistened.

4. Divide the batter among the prepared muffin cups. The batter will be stiff; a standard, trigger-style ice cream scoop does a great job of distributing it.

5. Bake for 25 to 30 minutes, until the muffins have risen and a tester inserted into the center of one comes out clean.

6. Cool the muffins in the pan on a wire rack for a few minutes.

7. To make the topping, mix together the sugar and cinnamon in a shallow bowl. When the muffins are just cool enough to handle, brush each top with butter, then dip it in the sugar and cinnamon mixture, rolling it around to cover the uneven surface. Serve immediately or when cooled.

The Muffin Man

Do you know the Muffin Man?

The Muffin Man, the Muffin Man.

Do you know the Muffin Man,

Who lives on Drury Lane?

In Victorian England, among the many fresh foods delivered to the door were muffins. They were brought by the muffin man, who rang a bell to signal his arrival. In the 1840s, the muffin man's bell was prohibited by Act of Parliament, though enforcement of the law was reportedly spotty.

Bran Muffins

Bran is a useful source of dietary fiber, and what better way to take your medicine than in the delicious form of a muffin?

Makes 12 muffins

1½ cups All-Bran cereal
1 cup buttermilk or yogurt
½ cup raisins
¼ cup dried currants
½ cup unbleached all-purpose white flour
½ cup whole-wheat flour
2 teaspoons baking powder

1 teaspoon baking soda
¼ teaspoon salt
2 eggs, at room temperature
½ cup firmly packed dark brown sugar
4 tablespoons butter, melted and cooled
¼ cup light or dark molasses

1. Preheat the oven to 400°F. Grease 12 muffin cups or line with paper liners.

2. Combine the All-Bran cereal, buttermilk, raisins, and currants in a large bowl and mix well. Let stand for 5 to 10 minutes, until the cereal is softened.

3. Whisk the all-purpose flour, whole-wheat flour, baking powder, baking soda, and salt in a small bowl. Set aside.

4. In another bowl, lightly beat the eggs. Add the brown sugar, butter, and molasses, mixing until well blended. Add to the cereal mixture, mixing well. Add the flour mixture, stirring together 12 to 15 times, just long enough to moisten the dry ingredients. Do not overmix. Fill the muffin cups about three-quarters full.

5. Bake for 20 minutes, until the muffins spring back when the tops are lightly touched.

6. Cool on a wire rack for 5 minutes. Then remove the muffins from the pan to finish cooling.

Blueberry Cream Scones

Cream gives these scones a rich, soft texture. They are wonderful made with blueberries, but raspberries can be substituted.

Makes 12 scones

2 cups unbleached all-purpose flour
2 tablespoons firmly packed light brown sugar
2 tablespoons granulated sugar
2½ teaspoons baking powder
¼ teaspoon salt
6 tablespoons butter, chilled and diced

2 teaspoons finely grated lemon zest
1 large egg
¾ cup heavy cream plus 1 tablespoon for topping
1 cup fresh blueberries
1 teaspoon fresh lemon juice and 2 tablespoons confectioners' sugar, blended until smooth

1. Preheat the oven to 400°F.

2. Combine the flour, brown sugar, granulated sugar, baking powder, and salt in a large bowl. Cut in the butter with a pastry blender or two knives until the mixture has the consistency of coarse crumbs. Mix in the lemon zest.

3. Beat the egg with the ¾ cup cream in a medium bowl until combined. Make a well in the center of the flour mixture and pour in the egg mixture all at once. Sprinkle the blueberries over all. Stir with a fork, gently mixing in the blueberries, until the dough comes together. Do not overmix.

4. Turn out the dough onto a lightly floured surface. Knead lightly 8 to 10 times, sprinkling with a little flour if the dough is sticky. To avoid crushing the berries, try not to press down too hard on the dough. Divide the dough into two parts. Shape each half into a ball. Roll or pat each ball into a 6-inch-diameter circle about 1 inch thick. With a knife, cut each circle into six wedges. Arrange the scones about ½ inch apart on an ungreased baking sheet. Brush the tops with the remaining 1 tablespoon cream.

5. Bake for 15 to 20 minutes, until the tops of the scones are golden.

6. Cool the scones on a wire rack for 5 minutes. Brush the lemon glaze lightly over the tops of the still-warm scones. Serve warm.

Apricot Buttermilk Scones

With dried fruit, these scones can be made any time of the year. The buttermilk gives them a very tender crumb, without adding fat. Buttermilk is a versatile ingredient that can be used in place of yogurt in many dips, sauces, and salad dressings. But if you don't think you'll use up your buttermilk (it lasts several weeks in the refrigerator), then look for dried buttermilk in the baking section of your supermarket. Mix up just as much as you need at a time.

Makes 12 to 16 scones

2¼ cups unbleached all-purpose flour	1 large egg
5 tablespoons sugar	⅔ cup low-fat buttermilk
2½ teaspoons baking powder	1 teaspoon vanilla extract
½ teaspoon baking soda	½ cup dried currants
¼ teaspoon salt	⅓ cup finely chopped dried apricots
½ cup (1 stick) butter, chilled and diced	

TOPPING

1 tablespoon heavy cream	Whipped cream cheese or crème
2 tablespoons sugar	fraîche, to serve (optional)
½ teaspoon ground cinnamon	

1. Preheat the oven to 400°F.

2. Combine the flour, sugar, baking powder, baking soda, and salt in a food processor and pulse to mix. Add the butter and pulse until the mixture has the consistency of coarse crumbs.

3. Beat the egg with the buttermilk and vanilla in a small bowl, mixing until combined. Stir in the currants and apricots. Add the egg mixture to the flour all at once and process just until the dough comes together. Do not overmix.

4. Turn out the dough onto a lightly floured surface. Knead lightly 8 to 10 times, sprinkling with a little flour if the dough is sticky. Divide the dough into two parts. Shape each half into a ball. Roll or pat each ball into a 6-inch- or 7-inch-diameter

circle ¾ to 1 inch thick. With a knife, cut each circle into six or eight wedges. Arrange the scones about ½ inch apart on an ungreased baking sheet.

5. To make the topping, brush the tops of the scones with the cream. Combine the sugar and cinnamon and sprinkle over the cream.

6. Bake for 15 to 20 minutes, until the tops of the scones are golden.

7. Cool the scones on a wire rack or serve warm. If you like, serve with a soft cream cheese or crème fraîche. Scones are best when eaten the day they are made.

Coffee Break

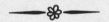

WHEN OLD KING GEORGE made the big mistake of taxing the colonists' favorite beverage — tea — coffee sales increased by 600 percent. When German settlers brought the tradition of the *Kaffeeklatsch* to their frontier communities, the term "coffee klatch" became part of the language. Its original meaning: a moment that combines gossip with coffee drinking. This became the American coffee break (equivalent to England's tea) — a midmorning or midafternoon gathering where coffee and coffee cakes were served, along with a healthy dose of community (or gossip).

Ginger Scones

It is often said that the United States and Great Britain are two nations separated by a common language. This is particularly true when it comes to words that describe foods. What makes a scone different from a biscuit? Very little, except the British are likely to add flavorings — both sweet and savory — to theirs. Also, their shape is generally triangular, while we tend to keep our biscuits plain and round. And the British biscuit? Well, it's a cookie, of course.

Makes 12 scones

2 cups unbleached all-purpose flour	2 large eggs
6 tablespoons sugar	½ cup sour cream (low-fat is fine)
2½ teaspoons baking powder	1 teaspoon freshly grated orange zest
½ teaspoon baking soda	½ cup finely chopped crystallized ginger
½ teaspoon ground ginger	2 tablespoons heavy cream
¼ teaspoon salt	Butter, cream cheese, honey, and jams, to serve
6 tablespoons butter, chilled and diced	

1. Preheat the oven to 400°F.

2. Combine the flour, sugar, baking powder, baking soda, ginger, and salt in a food processor and process briefly to mix. Add the butter and pulse to mix into the flour mixture, until it has the consistency of coarse crumbs.

3. Beat 1 whole egg and 1 egg white (reserve the yolk) with the sour cream and orange zest in a small bowl, mixing until combined. Stir in the crystallized ginger. Add the egg mixture to the flour mixture all at once. Process briefly, just until the dough comes together. Do not overmix

4. Turn out the dough onto a lightly floured surface. Knead lightly 8 to 10 times, sprinkling with a little flour if the dough is sticky. Roll or pat the dough into a 7-inch circle about ¾ inch thick. Using a 2-inch biscuit cutter, cut into about 10 circles. Press together all the cut scraps and pieces of trimmings to make a few more circles. Place the scones about ½ inch apart on an ungreased baking sheet.

5. Make an egg wash by mixing together the reserved egg yolk and the heavy cream with a fork. Brush the tops of the scones with the egg wash.

6. Bake for 15 to 20 minutes, until the tops of the scones are golden.

7. Serve hot, with a choice of butter, cream cheese, honey, and jams.

Baker's Tip

❊ Scones are best on the day they are made, but they can be frozen for up to 2 weeks and reheated before serving.

Pies and Tarts

Can she bake a cherry pie, Billy Boy?" the old song asked. Presumably, a woman wasn't worth much as a wife if she didn't have pie-baking skills. Well, those days are gone, as is the old saying "as easy as pie." Pie making can be challenging, but one advantage modern cooks have is the purchased piecrust. Those who prefer making everything from scratch should know that practice makes perfect.

Ingredients

○ **Chilled pie dough ingredients produce the best results.**

○ **Replace 1 tablespoon of water in a pie dough recipe with 1 tablespoon cider vinegar or lemon juice.** The dough will be easier to roll and will not shrink as much as it bakes. It will not affect flavor or diminish the flaky texture. You will not taste the acid.

○ **Ground spices lose those their pungency and aroma quickly, so buy them in small quantities, label the date of purchase, and discard them after 6 months.**

○ **To avoid making pie pastry from scratch, look for rolled "piecrust" in the refrigerated dairy case.** Conveniently stored in the refrigerator or freezer, it yields surprisingly good results. Most brands contain lard, which contributes to a flaky crust.

○ **Whipped cream sweetened with honey rather than sugar will hold its shape longer.**

Equipment

○ **Always start by preheating the oven and placing a rack in the middle of the oven, unless directed otherwise in the recipe.** Many pie recipes call for baking in the lower third of the oven to encourage the bottom crust to bake more fully.

○ **Make pie dough quickly and easily in the food processor.** But don't overprocess; you want the butter encased in flour, but still in pea-size pieces.

○ **Glass or dull metal pie pans work best.** Avoid shiny metal or disposable aluminum pans, which reflect heat and prevent crusts from browning. Dark pans may cause crusts to brown too much.

Techniques

○ **Once you have added the liquid to the dough, process or mix just until it holds together.** Overworking makes a tough crust.

○ **Flour the work surface very lightly.** Excess flour will toughen pie dough.

○ **To enhance the flavor of the fruit, some recipes call for "dotting" with butter.** This is cookbook-speak for cutting butter into small pieces and sprinkling over the filling.

○ **Place fruit pies on a baking sheet in the oven to catch bubbling juices that will otherwise drip onto the oven floor.**

○ **To keep baked edges from getting too brown, cover them with foil after the first 15 minutes of baking.** Use a 12-inch square piece of foil, cut out a 7-inch circle from the center, and gently fold the foil "ring" around the crust's edge.

○ **To ensure that the filling is set and will not run, allow the baked pie to cool on a rack to room temperature, until barely warm, before slicing.** This will take between 2 to 4 hours, depending on the thickness of the pie.

○ **Custard and cream pies are often served topped with whipped cream.** The whipped cream can be spread over the entire pie or it can be spooned into a pastry bag and piped out to make a decorative edging. If you don't expect to serve the whole pie at once, you might prefer to spoon or pipe the whipped cream onto individual slices.

Fresh Fruit Tart

This is a very easy version of a classic French tart. The pastry is patted into place instead of rolled, and the filling is a no-cook cream cheese mixture instead of the classic custard. This leaves you free to spend time arranging the fruit on top, which you can array with the precision of an artist or with the casual confidence of a baker who knows that fruit is beautiful no matter how it is displayed.

Serves 8

Basic Sweet Pastry (page 267)
4 ounces cream cheese, at room temperature
½ cup confectioners' sugar
1 teaspoon finely grated lemon zest

1 tablespoon fresh lemon juice
2 cups berries or 1–2 pounds fresh fruit
⅓ cup apple or currant jelly

1. Preheat the oven to 400°F.

2. Make the dough and pat it into a 9-inch tart pan with a removable bottom or in a 9-inch pie pan. Make the top edge of the crust level with the rim of the pan. The sides should be about ¼ inch thick. Place a sheet of aluminum foil in the pan on top of the crust and fill with pie weights, dried beans, or rice.

3. Bake the shell for 10 minutes, then reduce the heat to 350°F. Remove the aluminum foil and weights. Prick the crust with a fork to deflate any bubbles that have formed. Bake for 10 to 15 minutes longer, until golden brown. Cool on a wire rack.

4. To make the filling, combine the cream cheese, confectioners' sugar, lemon zest, and lemon juice in a food processor. Process until well blended. Spread over the cooled crust.

5. To prepare the fruit, wash and peel as needed. Slice as desired.

6. Heat the jelly until liquid. Arrange the fruit over the cream cheese filling. Small berries, such as blueberries and raspberries, can be scattered over the filling. Slice any large berries, such as strawberries. Place sliced fruit in concentric circles, each slice resting on the previous one so none of the filling shows through. Brush the fruit with the melted jelly to completely cover the top.

7. Chill the tart for about 30 minutes before serving. Tarts are best on the day they are made.

Fresh Plum Tart

When European colonists first settled the East Coast, they brought with them their favorite plum trees, even though there were plenty of varieties of American plums. Then, in the later 1800s, as California agriculture was taking off, Asian plums were introduced to this country. Now when you go into a supermarket, most of the plums are the Asian types: sweet, juicy, and perfect for eating out of hand. European plums, also known as prune plums, Italian plums, or Stanley plums, are sweet, meaty, and perfect for baking.

Serves 12

TART

- 3 cups unbleached all-purpose flour
- ⅛ cup granulated sugar
- 1 cup (2 sticks) butter, chilled and diced
- 2 large egg yolks, lightly beaten
- 1 teaspoon finely grated lemon zest
- 1 tablespoon fresh lemon juice
- 2 tablespoons water
- 3 pounds fresh plums (preferably an Italian prune plum or other European plum, such as Stanley)

TOPPING

- ⅛ cup granulated sugar
- 1 tablespoon unbleached all-purpose flour
- 1½ teaspoons ground cinnamon
- ⅛ cup butter, melted

TO FINISH

- ½ cup Apricot Glaze (recipe follows)
  Confectioners' sugar

1. Lightly grease a 10- by 15-inch jelly-roll pan.

2. To prepare the tart, combine the flour and sugar in a large bowl. Crumble the butter into the flour mixture with your fingers until the texture is like cornmeal. Stir in the egg yolks with a fork until well blended. Add the lemon zest, lemon juice, and water and mix until blended. Pinch the dough to see if it will clump together. If the dough is too dry, sprinkle in water, a teaspoonful at a time, until it will hold

together. Transfer the dough to the prepared baking pan and press to form an even layer, shaping the dough ½ inch up the sides of the pan. Chill in the refrigerator while you prepare the plums.

3. Preheat the oven to 400°F.

4. Cut the plums into ¼-inch slices. Arrange them over the dough, slightly overlapping them in parallel rows. Place any extra slices between the rows.

5. To prepare the topping, mix together the sugar, flour, cinnamon, and butter. Spoon the mixture over the top of the fruit, spreading it out with the back of the spoon.

6. Bake for 35 minutes, until the fruit is tender and the pastry is golden. Remove from the oven and brush with Apricot Glaze while the fruit is still warm.

7. Cut the pastry between the rows of fruit into 12 rectangles. Just before serving, sprinkle with confectioners' sugar.

Apricot Glaze

This glaze can be used to seal the bottom crust on fruit pies, to top a cake, or to glaze fruit on a tart. If you like, serve a dollop of the glaze on top of baked custard.

Makes 1 cup

....

   1 *cup apricot preserves*
   2 *tablespoons brandy*

....

1. Combine the preserves and brandy in a small saucepan. Stir over low heat until the jam has melted.

2. Strain and cool. Store extra glaze in the refrigerator for up to 1 month.

Linzertorte

Linzertortes have been made for at least 300 years, which we know because written recipes began to appear in cookbooks in the early 1700s. The tart made it to America in 1856, courtesy of an enterprising young Austrian. He came to America with the promise of employment in Milwaukee as conductor of an orchestra. Somewhere between New York and Wisconsin, he lost both his luggage and the letter confirming his job, which, it turned out, was no longer available. Like many immigrants, he turned to the kitchen, producing the specialties of his homeland, which in this case was the linzertorte, made with an almond crust and filled with raspberry jam.

Serves 8

⅔ cup (4 ounces) almonds
1¼ cups unbleached all-purpose flour
1 teaspoon ground cinnamon
¼ teaspoon baking powder
¼ teaspoon salt
⅛ teaspoon ground cloves
6 tablespoons butter, at room temperature
⅓ cup firmly packed light brown sugar

2 teaspoons finely grated lemon zest
1 large egg
½ teaspoon almond extract
1 cup thick red raspberry jam (preferably seedless)
1 tablespoon brandy or raspberry liqueur, such as framboise
Confectioners' sugar, to dust

1. Preheat the oven to 300°F. Butter a 9-inch tart pan with a removable bottom. Set aside.

2. Arrange the almonds in a single layer on a baking sheet and toast for 10 to 12 minutes, until lightly toasted and fragrant. Remove from oven and set aside to cool. Turn off the oven.

3. Combine the almonds and ¼ cup of the flour in a food processor. Process until the almonds are very finely ground.

4. Whisk the remaining 1 cup flour and the cinnamon, baking powder, salt, and cloves in a medium bowl. Set aside.

5. Cream together the butter, brown sugar, and lemon zest in a large bowl, beating until fluffy. Mix in the egg and almond extract, beating until thoroughly combined. Mix in the ground almonds and then add the flour mixture, stirring until blended. Divide the dough into thirds. Wrap one-third of the dough in plastic wrap and chill in the refrigerator.

6. With floured hands and fingers, press the remaining two-thirds of the dough over the bottom and partway up the sides of the prepared pan, creating an edge about ¼ inch below the rim. Cover with plastic wrap and refrigerate the pan for 30 minutes.

7. Preheat the oven to 350°F. Cut the reserved portion of the dough into 10 equal pieces. On a floured surface, with lightly floured hands, roll each piece into a 9-inch rope. If the dough breaks, press it together with a dab of water. Lay the ropes on a plate and chill in the refrigerator for 15 minutes.

8. Remove the tart pan and ropes from the refrigerator. Combine the jam and brandy and spread out over the bottom of the dough in the tart pan. Arrange five of the chilled ropes of dough, evenly spaced, across the top of the torte. Rotate the pan a quarter turn and repeat the pattern, laying the remaining five ropes across the first five ropes to make a lattice. Trim the ends of the ropes even with edge of the tart and press them into the dough around the edge. If there is any dough left over, make it into a rope and arrange it around the rim of the crust. Seal the rope to the edges by pressing it into the bottom crust with a fork.

9. Bake in the middle of the oven for 35 to 40 minutes, until the jam is bubbly and the crust is golden brown.

10. Cool on a wire rack. Remove the sides of the tart pan. Sprinkle the tart with confectioners' sugar. Cut into wedges and serve.

Fresh Strawberry and Chocolate Tart

Chocolate and strawberries makes a wonderful taste combination. This tart is spectacular in both flavor and appearance, but quite simple to make.

Serves 8

Basic Sweet Pastry (page 267)
1 *quart fresh strawberries*
3 *ounces semisweet, dark, or bitter-sweet chocolate, coarsely chopped*

1 *tablespoon butter*
⅓ *cup currant jelly*
1 *tablespoon orange liqueur or brandy*
Whipped cream, to serve

1. Preheat the oven to 400°F.

2. Prepare the dough according to the recipe, then pat it into a 9-inch tart pan with a removable bottom or a 9-inch pie pan. Make the top edge of the crust level with the rim of the pan. The sides should be ¼ inch thick. Place a sheet of aluminum foil in the pan on top of the crust and fill with pie weights or dried beans or rice.

3. Bake the shell for 10 minutes. Reduce the heat to 350°F. Remove the aluminum foil and weights. Prick the crust with a fork to deflate any bubbles that have formed. Bake for 15 minutes longer, until the crust is golden brown. Cool on a wire rack.

4. To prepare the strawberries, rinse and drain well. Leave small strawberries whole; slice large berries in half, reserving one whole berry for the center of the tart. Place the halved berries cut-side down on paper towels until needed.

5. Melt the chocolate and butter in the top of a double boiler over barely simmering water. Stir until melted, then remove pan from the heat and let cool for 2 minutes. With a pastry brush or the back of a teaspoon, paint the chocolate mixture over the bottom and up the sides of the tart shell. Let the chocolate cool and harden.

6. Arrange the berries on the chocolate, starting at the outside edge and working toward the center, packing them together as tightly as possible. Place cut berries pointing outward, starting at the outside and working toward the center overlapping slightly. Put a whole berry in the center.

7. To make a glaze, heat the jelly over low heat until liquid. Stir in the liqueur. Cool slightly. Brush the top of the strawberries with the glaze.

8. Chill the tart for about 30 minutes before serving, garnished with whipped cream. Tarts are best served on the day they are made.

Buttermilk Pie

When fresh fruits were out of season, buttermilk pie was made, particularly in the South, where biscuits and cakes were frequently made with buttermilk. This pie has outstanding flavor — a cross between cheesecake and custard — with a silken texture.

Buttermilk was a staple of rural America, traditionally made from the liquid left after the churning of butter. Today buttermilk is usually a thick cultured milk made from nonfat or low-fat milk. It is used to make pancakes and waffles; tender cakes and biscuits; and creamy salad dressings, soups, and sauces. It can be used as a marinade for both Southern fried chicken and tandoori chicken. If you buy a quart of buttermilk for this outstanding pie, you are sure to find plenty of uses for the leftovers.

Serves 8

Pastry for a 9-inch single-crust pie, homemade (page 261) or purchased	4 large eggs
¾ cup sugar	1⅔ cups buttermilk
3 tablespoons cornstarch	1 cup milk
	1 teaspoon vanilla extract
	¼ teaspoon salt

1. If you are making your own pastry, prepare the pie dough according to recipe directions. Roll out the dough, fit it into a 9-inch pie pan, and crimp the edges. (Fit purchased pastry into the pie pan and crimp the edges.) Partially bake the shell (page 263). Let cool on a rack before filling.

2. Preheat the oven to 375°F.

3. Combine the sugar and cornstarch in a medium bowl. Whisk until no lumps remain. Add the eggs, buttermilk, milk, vanilla, and salt. Whisk until completely smooth. Pour the filling into the prepared pie shell. (Pour any leftover filling into a ramekin or custard cup to bake as a custard.)

4. Bake for 40 to 45 minutes, until it is spotted with gold and set but still slightly wobbly in the center. (Bake individual buttered ramekins for 15 to 20 minutes.) Do not overbake.

5. Cool the pie on a wire rack. Serve warm or cold.

Apple Pie

Apples and apple pie were both well known in the Old World. Indeed, there are indications that apples were known to the people of the Iron Age and were cultivated in Egypt some 4,000 years ago. The Pilgrims brought with them apple seeds and lost no time in getting trees established. Apple orchards were so valuable that by 1648, Governor John Endicott was able to trade 500 apple trees for 250 acres of land. By the end of the nineteenth century, some 8,000 apple varieties were listed with the U.S. Department of Agriculture. Is it any wonder that apple pie became one of America's most popular desserts?

Serves 8

Pastry for a 9-inch double-crust pie, homemade (page 261) or purchased
¾ cup plus 1 tablespoon sugar, or more to taste
2 tablespoons unbleached all-purpose flour
1½ teaspoons ground cinnamon
¼ teaspoon ground allspice
¼ teaspoon freshly grated nutmeg

3½–4 pounds tart, crisp apples, peeled, cored, and sliced ¼ inch thick (about 8 cups)
1 teaspoon finely grated lemon zest
1 tablespoon fresh lemon juice
2 tablespoons butter, cut into small pieces
1 teaspoon milk
Cheddar cheese or vanilla ice cream, to serve

---

1. If you are making your own pastry, prepare the pie dough according to recipe directions and refrigerate.

2. Combine the ¾ cup sugar and the flour, cinnamon, allspice, and nutmeg in a large bowl. Add the apples, and sprinkle with the lemon zest and lemon juice. Toss together to mix thoroughly. If the apples are too tart, add a little extra sugar.

3. Preheat the oven to 425°F with a rack in the lower third of the oven.

4. To prepare the pie shell, lightly flour a work surface. Roll out the larger portion of the chilled dough to a thickness of about ⅛ inch. Fit into a 9-inch pie pan, leaving a 1-inch overhang. (Fit purchased pastry into the pie pan.) Spoon the filling into the pastry, mounding it higher in the center. Dot with butter. Roll out the remain-

ing dough into a circle about 1 inch larger than the pie pan. Moisten the edge of the bottom crust with water. Fold the dough circle in half, lift off the work surface, place the pastry across the center of the filled pie, and unfold. Trim the edge ⅓ inch larger than the pie pan and tuck the overhang under the edge of the bottom crust. Crimp the edges with a fork or make a fluted pattern with your fingers. Make several decorative slits in the top crust to allow steam to escape. Place the pie on a baking sheet to catch any juices that overflow.

5. Bake the pie in the lower third of the oven for 20 minutes. Reduce the heat to 350°F and continue to bake for 30 minutes and then brush the top of the pie with the milk and sprinkle with the 1 tablespoon sugar. Bake for 10 to 15 minutes longer, until the crust is golden and the juices are bubbly.

6. Cool the pie on a wire rack. Serve warm or at room temperature, with slices of cheddar cheese or vanilla ice cream.

But, I, when I undress me

Each night, upon my knees

Will ask the Lord to bless me

With apple-pie and cheese.

— Eugene Field, "Apple-Pie and Cheese"

Cinnamon Streusel Apple Pie

It is heartening to know that Johnny Appleseed is no mere storybook legend. The real Johnny Appleseed, or John Chapman, as he was named in his hometown of Leominster, Massachusetts, was born in 1775. Famously eccentric, he collected vast quantities of apple seeds from cider mills and wandered the countryside, planting apples wherever he went. No wonder there are so many spendid variations on apple pie. This one is particularly delicious served with ice cream or cinnamon-flavored whipped cream.

Serves 8

PIE SHELL AND FILLING

Pastry for a 9-inch single-crust pie, homemade (page 261) or purchased

3½–4 pounds tart apples, peeled, cored, and sliced ¼ inch thick (about 8 cups)

¼ cup granulated sugar

1 tablespoon unbleached all-purpose flour

1 tablespoon finely grated lemon zest

1 tablespoon fresh lemon juice

1 teaspoon ground cinnamon

TOPPING

½ cup unbleached all-purpose flour

½ cup firmly packed dark brown sugar

¼ cup granulated sugar

¼ cup pecan pieces

¼ cup walnut pieces

1 teaspoon ground cinnamon

¼ teaspoon ground ginger

¼ teaspoon freshly grated nutmeg

6 tablespoons butter, at room temperature

1. If you are making your own pastry, prepare the pie dough according to recipe directions. Roll out the dough and fit it into a 9-inch pie pan. (Fit purchased pastry into the pie pan.) Crimp the edges and refrigerate.

2. Preheat the oven to 375°F.

3. Toss the apples with the granulated sugar, flour, lemon zest, lemon juice, and cinnamon in a large bowl. Set aside.

4. To prepare the topping, combine the flour, brown sugar, granulated sugar, pecans, walnuts, cinnamon, ginger, and nutmeg in a food processor. Process until the mixture is combined and the nuts are very finely chopped. Transfer to a bowl. With

your fingertips, rub the butter into the crumb mixture until it resembles coarse meal.

5. Drain off any liquid that has accumulated in the bottom of the apple mixture. Transfer the apples into the prepared pie shell, pressing down on them so that they're level with the top of the dish. Sprinkle the topping over the apples, pressing it down and making sure the edges of the apples are covered.

6. Bake for 50 to 60 minutes, until the top is browned and the apples are tender when tested with a fork.

7. Serve warm.

The friendly cow all red and white,

I love with all my heart:

She gives me cream with all her might,

To eat with apple tart.

— **Robert Louis Stevenson, "The Cow"**

Crumb-Topped Sour Cream-Apple Pie

If an old-fashioned dessert is as rich as it can possibly be, chances are it was developed by the Pennsylvania Dutch, who were not Dutch at all. They were German-speaking religious refugees who settled in Pennsylvania. Although these settlers followed a fairly austere lifestyle, their tables were generously laden with foods of all kinds. Some food historians are convinced that the Pennsylvania Dutch are responsible for the development of American fruit pies (though other historians think fruit pies are of English origin). This apple pie, with its rich filling enhanced with sour cream, and its crumb topping, is Pennsylvania Dutch in origin.

Serves 8

PIE SHELL AND FILLING

Pastry for a 9-inch single-crust pie, homemade (page 261) or purchased
½ cup granulated sugar, or more to taste
2 tablespoons unbleached all-purpose flour
¼ teaspoon freshly grated nutmeg
⅛ teaspoon salt
1 large egg
1 cup sour cream
1 teaspoon vanilla extract
6 large tart, crisp apples, peeled, cored, and sliced ⅛ inch thick

CRUMB TOPPING

½ cup unbleached all-purpose flour
⅓ cup firmly packed dark brown sugar
1 teaspoon ground cinnamon
⅛ teaspoon salt
4 tablespoons butter, at room temperature
½ cup chopped walnuts (optional)

1. If you are making your own pastry, prepare the pie dough according to recipe directions. Roll out the dough and fit it into a 9-inch pie pan. (Fit purchased pastry into the pie pan.) Crimp the edges and refrigerate.

2. Preheat the oven to 400°F with a rack in the lower third of the oven.

3. Combine the granulated sugar, flour, nutmeg, and salt in a large bowl. Add the egg, sour cream, and vanilla and whisk until smooth. Add the apples and toss until the apples are well coated. If the apples are too tart, add a little extra sugar.

4. Spoon the apple mixture into the prepared pie shell. Place the pie on a baking sheet to catch any juices that overflow.

5. Bake in the lower third of the oven for 15 minutes. Reduce the heat to 350°F and cover the pie loosely with aluminum foil (do not let the foil touch the apples). Continue to bake for about 40 minutes, until an apple pierced with a knife is tender.

6. While the pie bakes, prepare the crumb topping. Combine the flour, brown sugar, cinnamon, and salt. With your fingers, rub in the butter until it resembles coarse crumbs. Mix in the walnuts (if using).

7. Remove the foil from the pie. Sprinkle the topping over the pie. Bake for 10 to 15 minutes, until the topping is golden.

8. Cool the pie on a wire rack before serving, warm or at room temperature.

Banana Cream Pie

Americans consume more bananas than any other fruit, but too few of them, in our opinion, wind up in this luscious dessert. Incidentally, bananas were cultivated by the Arabs in the seventh century. Eight centuries later, in 1482, Portuguese explorers found the fruit growing on the west coast of Africa and picked up the name Guinea natives used for it — banana.

Serves 6 to 8

Pastry for a 9-inch single-crust pie, homemade (page 261) or purchased	2 cups milk
⅔ cup sugar	4 large egg yolks, lightly beaten
3 tablespoons cornstarch	2 tablespoons butter, cut into small pieces
2 tablespoons unbleached all-purpose flour	1 tablespoon dark rum
¼ teaspoon salt	1 teaspoon vanilla extract
	1 cup whipping cream
	3 large bananas, sliced

1. If you are making your own pastry, prepare the pie dough according to recipe directions. Roll out the dough, fit it into a 9-inch pie pan, crimp the edges, and fully bake the shell (page 263). (Fit purchased pastry into the pie pan, crimp the edges, and bake according to the package directions.) Let cool on a rack before filling.

2. Make a custard by combining the sugar, cornstarch, flour, and salt in a heavy saucepan. Add the milk gradually, stirring constantly with a wire whisk to remove any lumps. Cook over medium heat, stirring constantly, until the mixture thickens and comes to a boil. Continue stirring and boil for 1 minute. Remove the pan from the heat.

3. Gradually add ½ cup of the custard to the beaten egg yolks, a few teaspoons at a time, mixing constantly until blended. Pour the mixture into the remaining custard in the pan, stirring until combined. Cook the custard, stirring constantly, for 2 minutes, until thick and smooth. Remove the pan from the heat.

4. Gradually add the butter to the custard. Stir in the rum and vanilla. Pour the custard into a bowl. Cover the surface with plastic wrap. Cool completely.

5. Whip the cream until stiff. Fold half of the whipped cream into the cooled custard filling.

6. Spoon a thin layer of custard filling over the bottom of the baked pie shell. Arrange a layer of sliced bananas over the filling. Alternate layers of custard and bananas, ending with custard on top. Pipe or spoon the remaining whipped cream on top of the pie.

7. Refrigerate the pie for 3 to 4 hours, until firm.

Calorie Count

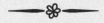

QUESTION: What food yields the most calories per acre?

ANSWER: Bananas. Within six months of planting, the banana plant is twice as tall as a man. Six months later, the fruit begins to form; in another three or four months, the fruit is ready to be harvested. The plant bears only one bunch of fruit, but that bunch will contain about 90 bananas (some have as many as 140). When the one bunch is cut, the whole plant is chopped down and another one planted. Some varieties can yield 600 to 800 bunches a year per acre — some 9 million calories, which means the banana provides more digestible calories per acre than any other major aboveground crop. Still, bananas aren't the answer to world hunger. To subsist entirely on bananas, a person would have to eat 5 pounds a day.

Banoffee Pie

Oh, those Brits! They do like their desserts sweet, and this is a good one for anyone with a sweet tooth. Banoffee Pie is made by combining bananas and toffee (and sometimes coffee). Credit for the pie's invention is claimed by Ian Dowding and Nigel Mackenzie of The Hungry Monk restaurant in East Sussex. This dessert stirs up so much passion, it has its own Web site: www.banoffee.co.uk. Our adaptation of the classic dessert cooks the condensed milk in a saucepan with brown sugar, rather than immersing the unopened can in boiling water and boiling for 3 hours (which is how dulce de leche is made) — and we add almonds. If you like, you can flavor the whipped cream topping with a little instant coffee, as in the original, but we prefer ours plain.

Serves 8

Pastry for a 9-inch single-crust pie, homemade (page 261) or purchased
1 *(14-ounce) can sweetened condensed milk*
⅓ *cup firmly packed brown sugar*
½ *cup flaked almonds*
2 *large bananas*
1 *cup heavy cream*

1. If you are making your own pastry, prepare the pie dough according to recipe directions. Roll out the dough, fit it into a 9-inch pie pan, crimp the edges, and fully bake the shell (page 263). (Fit purchased pastry into the pie pan, crimp the edges, and bake according to the package directions.) Let cool on a rack before filling.

2. Combine the condensed milk and brown sugar in a small, heavy saucepan. Bring to a boil. Reduce the heat and simmer, stirring constantly, for about 20 minutes, until the mixture thickens and the bubbles begin to enlarge. Let cool slightly, then pour into the baked pie shell.

3. Sprinkle the almonds over the filling. Cover and chill if you are not ready to serve.

4. When you are ready to serve, slice the bananas and cover the top of the pie with the slices. Whip the cream until soft peaks form. Spoon over the bananas to cover them completely. Swirl with a spoon to make decorative peaks. Serve at once.

Fresh Blueberry Pie

The deep blue berries glisten under a glaze of blueberries. The fresh flavor of the berries is undiminished in this delicious pie because most of the berries are uncooked.

Serves 8

Pastry for a 9-inch single-crust pie, homemade (page 261) or purchased
4   *cups fresh blueberries*
1   *cup water*
¾   *cup sugar*

2   *teaspoon finely grated lemon zest*
2   *tablespoons fresh lemon juice*
1½ *tablespoons cornstarch*
    Whipped cream or ice cream, to serve

1. If you are making your own pastry, prepare the pie dough according to recipe directions. Roll out the dough, fit it into a 9-inch pie pan, crimp the edges, and fully bake the shell (page 263). (Fit purchased pastry into the pie pan, crimp the edges, and bake according to the package directions.) Let cool on a rack before filling.

2. Rinse and thoroughly drain the blueberries. Spread 3 cups of the berries on a towel to dry while you prepare the glaze. Set aside 1 cup of the berries.

3. Combine ¾ cup of the water and the sugar in a small saucepan. Bring to a boil, reduce the heat to medium, and cook, stirring, until the sugar dissolves. Add the reserved 1 cup blueberries and the lemon zest and lemon juice.

4. Dissolve the cornstarch in the remaining ¼ cup water. Add to the berry mixture and cook, stirring, until the mixture boils; the liquid will thicken and clear, becoming somewhat transparent.

5. Spread the 3 cups of uncooked blueberries in the baked pie shell. Spoon the thickened berry glaze mixture over the fruit.

6. Chill until ready to serve. Serve with whipped cream or ice cream.

Baked Blueberry Pie

Eat in any diner in New England during the summer and you are likely to find blueberry pie on the menu. If you are lucky, the pie will be filled with fresh local berries. Unlucky travelers will be served a pie made with a can of a sweet, blue, gluey concoction that goes by the name of blueberry pie filling. In that case, it's best to go home and bake your own.

Serves 8

Pastry for a 9-inch double-crust pie, homemade (page 261) or purchased
6 cups fresh blueberries
¾ cup sugar
5 tablespoons unbleached all-purpose flour
1 teaspoon ground cinnamon
¼ teaspoon freshly grated nutmeg
Pinch of salt
1 tablespoon fresh lemon juice
1 tablespoon butter, cut into small pieces
1 large egg, beaten
1 tablespoon water

1. If you are making your own pastry, prepare the pie dough according to recipe directions and refrigerate.

2. Rinse and sort the blueberries. Drain thoroughly on paper towels.

3. Combine the sugar, flour, cinnamon, nutmeg, and salt in a large bowl. Add the blueberries. Sprinkle with the lemon juice. Toss lightly to combine. Set aside.

4. Preheat the oven to 425°F with a rack in the lower third of the oven.

5. To prepare the pie shell, lightly flour a work surface. Roll out the larger portion of the refrigerated dough to a thickness of about ⅛ inch. Fit into a 9-inch pie pan, leaving a 1-inch overhang. (Fit purchased pastry into the pie pan.) Spoon the blueberry mixture into the pastry shell and dot with butter. Roll out the remaining dough into a circle about 1 inch larger than the pie pan. Moisten the edge of the bottom crust with water. Fold the dough circle in half, lift off the work surface, place it across the center of the filled pie, and unfold. Trim the edge ½ inch larger than the pie pan and tuck the overhang under the edge of the bottom crust. Crimp the edges with a fork or make a fluted pattern with your fingers. Make several decorative slits in the top crust to allow steam to escape.

6. Make an egg wash by combining the egg and water. Brush the top of the pie with the egg wash. Place the pie on a baking sheet to catch any juices that overflow.

7. Bake in the lower third of the oven for 15 minutes. Reduce the oven temperature to 350°F and bake for 40 to 45 minutes longer, until the crust is golden brown.

8. Cool the pie on a wire rack. Serve warm or at room temperature.

Blueberries

THE HIGHBUSH BLUEBERRY IS CHARMING. It grows, thorn-free, to convenient picking heights. We have picked the plump, dusky berries at pick-your-own farms, stripping a bush and filling buckets in minutes. It was easy — too easy, in fact.

No highbush blueberry can compare to the taste of a wild lowbush blueberry. Picking these tiny berries that grow on ankle-high shrubs is hard labor. Professionals — meaning those seasonal workers who are paid for their efforts with cash, not muffins — use a rake to strip the low-growing shrubs of the berries. But the work is backbreaking and yields are relatively low. Most of the commercial harvest goes into commercial baking, where the small berries are prized for muffins. Still, some of the wild blueberry crops make it to farm stands and fruit markets in New England.

"Wild" is something of a misnomer. The berries are wild only insofar as the fields are not planted by the farmer. But they are managed. After harvest each year, the farmer burns a section of his or her fields to eliminate weeds. Underground, the blueberry rhizomes remain intact, ready to spread to the newly cleared fields. Birds help the process by dropping seeds on the cleared land. By July, new growth is evident. By the second year, blueberries blossom and set tiny, sweet, deliciously fragrant fruits.

Blackberry Pie

Given that there are some 2,000 species of blackberries worldwide, you can expect a variety to be ripening near you at some point each summer — at least if you live in a northern or upland region. Take the time to make a pie this summer. You won't regret it.

Serves 8

Pastry for a 9-inch double-crust pie, homemade (page 261) or purchased
6 cups fresh blackberries
¾ cup granulated sugar
¼ cup firmly packed light brown sugar
5 tablespoons unbleached all-purpose flour

2 teaspoons finely grated lemon zest
Pinch of salt
2 tablespoons butter, cut into small pieces
1 large egg, beaten
1 tablespoon water
1 tablespoon granulated sugar

1. If you are making your own pastry, prepare the pie dough according to recipe directions and refrigerate.

2. Rinse and sort the blackberries. Drain thoroughly on paper towels.

3. Combine the granulated sugar, brown sugar, flour, lemon zest, and salt in a large bowl. Add the blackberries. Toss lightly to combine. Set aside.

4. Preheat the oven to 425°F with a rack in the lower third of the oven.

5. To prepare the pie shell, lightly flour a work surface. Roll out the larger portion of the chilled dough to a thickness of about ⅛ inch. Fit into a 9-inch pie pan, leaving a 1-inch overhang. (Fit purchased pastry into the pie pan.) Spoon the blackberry mixture into the pastry. Dot with butter. Roll out the remaining dough into a circle about 1 inch larger than the pie pan. Moisten the edge of the bottom crust with water. Fold the dough circle in half, lift off the work surface, place the pastry across the center of the filled pie, and unfold. Trim the edge ½ inch larger than the pie pan and tuck the overhang under the edge of the bottom crust. Crimp the edges with a fork or make a fluted pattern with your fingers. Make several decorative slits in the top crust to allow steam to escape.

6. Make an egg wash by combining the egg with the water. Brush the top of the pie with the egg wash. Sprinkle the 1 tablespoon sugar over the top. Place the pie on a baking sheet to catch any juices that overflow.

7. Bake in the lower third of the oven for 15 minutes. Reduce the oven temperature to 350°F and bake for 40 to 45 minutes, until the crust is golden brown.

8. Cool the pie on a wire rack. Serve warm or at room temperature.

Lattice-Top Sour Cherry Pie

It takes a dedicated baker to make a sour cherry pie from scratch. First, you must stake out your tree and harvest the fruits before the birds get them. Then you must pit the cherries, a laborious process that is unrewarding — unless done in the company of kids who enjoy seeing how far a pit can fly when properly popped out of a cherry. A gadget exists for stoning cherries, but a paper clip works just as well. If this kind of labor doesn't sound like your idea of fun, rely on pitted canned cherries.

Serves 8

Pastry for a 9-inch double-crust pie, homemade (page 261) or purchased
2 (16-ounce) cans water-packed pitted sour cherries or 6–7 cups pitted fresh sour cherries
¾ cup plus 1 tablespoon sugar
3 tablespoons cornstarch

Pinch of salt
1 teaspoon fresh lemon juice
¼ teaspoon almond extract
⅛ teaspoon ground cloves
1 tablespoon butter, cut into small pieces
1 teaspoon milk

1. If you are making your own pastry, prepare the pie dough according to recipe directions and refrigerate.

2. If you are using canned cherries, drain the cherries and reserve ⅓ cup of the juice. If you are using fresh cherries, combine the cherries with 3 tablespoons of water in a large saucepan. Heat the mixture to boiling, stirring gently for 1 minute. Remove the saucepan from the heat and drain off the juice to measure ⅓ cup. If there isn't enough liquid, add more water. Cool the juice completely.

3. Combine the ¾ cup sugar, the cornstarch, and salt in a heavy saucepan. Add the cherry juice and stir with a whisk until blended. Cook over medium heat, stirring until the sugar is dissolved. Boil for 2 to 3 minutes, stirring constantly until the mixture is slightly thickened. Remove from the heat. Stir in the lemon juice, almond extract, and cloves. Carefully mix in the cherries. Set aside to cool.

4. Preheat the oven to 425°F with a rack in the lower third of the oven.

5. To prepare the pie shell, roll out the larger portion of the refrigerated dough to a thickness of about ⅛ inch. Fit into a 9-inch pie pan, leaving a 1-inch overhang. (Fit purchased pastry into the pie pan.) Spoon the cooled filling into the pastry shell and dot with butter. Roll out the remaining dough into a rectangle about ⅛ inch thick and 11 inches long. Trim the ragged edges. Using a pastry wheel or sharp knife, cut the rectangle into 10 lengthwise strips, each ½ inch wide. To form the lattice, lay five strips across the filling, each 1 inch apart. Working from the center, interweave the remaining strips, one at a time, over and under the first strips. Trim the ends. Moisten the overhanging edge of the bottom crust and fold up over ends of the strips. Flute the edge of the crust. Brush the lattice strips with milk and sprinkle with the 1 tablespoon sugar. Place the pie on a baking sheet to catch any juices that overflow.

6. Bake in the lower third of the oven for 15 minutes. Reduce the oven temperature to 350°F and bake for 30 minutes longer, until the crust is golden brown and the juices are bubbly.

7. Cool the pie on a wire rack. Serve warm or at room temperature.

Chocolate Cream Pie

What makes a chocolate cream pie so much more wonderful than the chocolate pudding from which it springs? Undoubtedly, it is the contrasts among the crisp crust, the silken chocolate pudding, and the satiny cream topping. This pie speaks of its old-fashioned country origins, of a time when cream and eggs were plentiful and eaten without a sense of sin.

Serves 8

Pastry for a 9-inch single-crust pie, homemade (page 261) or purchased
1 cup granulated sugar
¼ cup unbleached all-purpose flour
1 tablespoon cornstarch
¼ teaspoon salt
3 cups milk
2 ounces semisweet chocolate, chopped, or ⅓ cup semisweet chocolate chips
2 ounces unsweetened chocolate, chopped

4 large egg yolks, lightly beaten
1 tablespoon butter, cut into small pieces
1 tablespoon plus 1 teaspoon dark rum
1 teaspoon vanilla extract
1 cup whipping cream
1 tablespoon sifted confectioners' sugar
Grated chocolate, to garnish

1. If you are making your own pastry, prepare the pie dough according to recipe directions. Roll out the dough, fit it into a 9-inch pie pan, crimp the edges, and fully bake the shell (page 263). (Fit purchased pastry into the pie pan, crimp the edges, and bake according to the package directions.) Let cool on a rack before filling.

2. Combine the granulated sugar, flour, cornstarch, and salt in a heavy saucepan. Add the milk gradually, stirring constantly with a wire whisk to remove any lumps. Add the semisweet and unsweetened chocolates. Cook over medium heat, stirring constantly, until the mixture thickens and comes to a boil; continue stirring and boiling for 1 minute. Remove the pan from the heat.

3. Gradually stir a few teaspoons of the chocolate mixture into the beaten yolks, mixing constantly until blended. When you have added about ½ cup, pour the yolk mixture into the remaining chocolate mixture in the pan, stirring until combined. Cook, stirring constantly, for 2 minutes, until thick and smooth. Remove the pan from the heat.

4. Add the butter gradually. Stir in the 1 tablespoon rum and the vanilla. Pour the filling into the baked piecrust. Cover the surface of the filling with plastic wrap. Let cool.

5. Refrigerate the pie for 3 to 4 hours, until firm. The pie can be refrigerated for up to 24 hours.

6. Just before serving, whip the cream until soft peaks form. Add the confectioners' sugar and the 1 teaspoon rum. Beat until stiff. Pipe the whipped cream on top of the pie. Sprinkle with the grated chocolate.

Cream Pies

CREAM PIES are associated with the rich bounty of the American Midwest. The first cream pie recipe is probably the one found in *The Improved Housewife*, an 1845 edition by Mrs. A. L. Webster. Her recipe called for five eggs, a pint of sweet, thick cream, sugar, raisins, nutmeg, and a pinch of salt.

Black Bottom Pie

This pie is heavenly — a dense chocolate bottom topped by a rum-flavored chiffon. Some black bottom aficionados prefer a gingersnap crust, but we like ours with chocolate.

Serves 8

Chocolate Crumb Crust (page 265) for a 9- or 10-inch pie
1 (¼-ounce) envelope unflavored gelatin
¼ cup cold water
4 large eggs, separated
¾ cup sugar
4 teaspoons cornstarch
2 cups hot (not boiling) milk or half-and-half
3 ounces semisweet chocolate, finely chopped, or ½ cup semisweet chocolate chips

2 ounces unsweetened chocolate, finely chopped
1 teaspoon vanilla extract
2 tablespoons dark rum
¼ teaspoon cream of tartar
¼ teaspoon salt
1 cup whipping cream
Chocolate shavings, to garnish

1. Prepare and bake the piecrust according to the recipe directions. Cool completely.

2. Sprinkle the gelatin over the water in a small bowl. Stir and set aside to soften.

3. In the top of a double boiler, make a custard by beating the egg yolks with a wire whisk until thick and lemon-colored. Mix in ½ cup of the sugar and the cornstarch. Place over simmering water. Gradually add the hot milk and cook, stirring constantly, until the mixture thickens to heavily coat a metal spoon.

4. Remove the top of the double boiler from the heat. Measure 1 cup of the custard and put it into a small bowl. Add the semisweet and unsweetened chocolates. Beat with a fork until smooth. Add the vanilla and pour into the baked piecrust. Set aside.

5. To the remaining hot custard mixture, add the softened gelatin, stirring until dissolved. Mix in the rum. Refrigerate, or place the pan in a bowl of ice water, stirring until the mixture mounds slightly when dropped from a spoon. It should be cold but not set.

6. Beat the egg whites until foamy. Add the cream of tartar and salt and continue beating until soft peaks form. Gradually add the remaining ¼ cup sugar and continue beating until the egg whites are stiff but not dry. The egg whites should hold their shape and remain moist. Gently fold into the custard.

7. Whip the cream until stiff. Fold ½ cup of the whipped cream into the custard mixture. Spread the custard over the chocolate layer.

8. Refrigerate the pie and the remaining whipped cream for 3 to 4 hours, until firm.

9. Pipe dollops of the remaining whipped cream on top of the pie and sprinkle with the chocolate shavings.

Baker's Tip

※ The egg whites in this recipe are not cooked. Please see "Egg Information" on page 388.

Whipped Cream

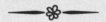

WHIPPED CREAM is the ideal topping for many desserts. It should be whipped to perfection, meaning the texture should be light and billowy, not granular.

For perfect whipped cream, start with cold whipping cream and a chilled bowl and beaters. Start beating slowly, gradually picking up speed. The cream is fully whipped when it forms floppy peaks — they will droop slightly when spooned. You can hold whipped cream in the refrigerator for about 1 hour.

Coconut Cream Pie

The coconut followed the banana as a tropical fruit that met wide acceptance in America. It is native to Malaysia, though coconuts are now grown in many places around the world. The coconut's global propagation was made possible in part by its ability to float long distances. In fact, coconuts have been known to cross entire oceans!

For many people today, packaged coconut is more convenient to buy and use than fresh. Store unopened canned coconut at room temperature for up to 18 months; store coconut purchased in plastic bags up to 6 months.

Serves 8

Pastry for a 9-inch single-crust pie, homemade (page 261) or purchased
1½ cups lightly packed, sweetened flaked coconut
4 large eggs, separated
⅔ cup plus ½ cup sugar
3 tablespoons cornstarch
2 tablespoons unbleached all-purpose flour
¼ teaspoon plus pinch of salt
2 cups milk
2 tablespoons butter, cut into small pieces
2½ teaspoons vanilla extract
1 tablespoon Apricot Glaze (see page 201) or 1 tablespoon melted apple jelly
¼ teaspoon cream of tartar

1. If you are making your own pastry, prepare the pie dough according to recipe directions. Roll out the dough, fit it into a 9-inch pie pan, crimp the edges, and fully bake the shell (page 263). (Fit purchased pastry into the pie pan, crimp the edges, and bake according to the package directions.) Let cool on a rack before filling.

2. Preheat the oven to 300°F.

3. Spread 1 cup of the coconut on a baking sheet. Toast for 5 to 10 minutes, stirring or shaking the pan occasionally, until the coconut is lightly colored. Set aside. Increase the oven temperature to 375°F.

4. To make the custard, beat the egg yolks lightly in a small bowl and set aside.

5. Combine the ⅔ cup sugar, the cornstarch, flour, and the ¼ teaspoon salt in a heavy saucepan. Add the milk gradually, stirring constantly with a wire whisk to remove any lumps. Cook over medium heat, stirring constantly, until the mixture thickens and comes to a boil. Continue stirring and boil for 1 minute. Remove from the heat.

6. Gradually stir a few teaspoons of custard into the beaten egg yolks, mixing constantly until blended. When you have added about ½ cup, pour the yolk mixture into the remaining custard in the pan, stirring until combined. Cook, stirring constantly, for 2 minutes, until thick and smooth. Remove the pan from the heat.

7. Add the butter to the custard gradually. Stir in 1½ teaspoons of the vanilla. Mix in the toasted flaked coconut.

8. Brush the baked piecrust with the Apricot Glaze. Pour in the cream filling.

9. Beat the egg whites in a large bowl with an electric mixer until foamy. Add the cream of tartar and the pinch of salt and beat until soft peaks form. Gradually sprinkle in the ½ cup sugar, 1 tablespoon at a time, beating well after each addition. When all the sugar has been incorporated, add the remaining 1 teaspoon of vanilla and beat well for 3 to 4 minutes longer, until the meringue forms stiff, shiny peaks. The egg whites should hold their shape and remain moist.

10. Spoon about half of the meringue around the edge of the warm filling. Use a rubber spatula to carefully seal it to the piecrust. Pile the remaining meringue in the center and then spread it with the back of a spoon to make decorative swirls. Sprinkle with the remaining ½ cup untoasted coconut.

11. Bake for 7 to 8 minutes, until the meringue and coconut are golden brown.

12. Cool the pie on a wire rack in a draft-free place. Serve at room temperature. This pie tastes best when eaten within 3 hours of cooling. Refrigerate any leftover pie.

Baker's Tip

❋ The egg whites in this recipe are not fully cooked. Please see "Egg Information" on page 388.

Coconut Custard Pie

As anyone who has enjoyed this pie in a diner can attest, it is prone to a soggy crust. Eat this within a few hours of baking, and no one will have any complaints.

Serves 8

Pastry for a 9-inch single-crust pie, homemade (page 261) or purchased
1 cup lightly packed, sweetened flaked coconut
4 large eggs
⅔ cup sugar
1½ teaspoons vanilla extract
¼ teaspoon salt
⅛ teaspoon freshly grated nutmeg, plus more to garnish
2½ cups hot (not boiling) milk or half-and-half
1 tablespoon Apricot Glaze (page 201) or 1 tablespoon apple jelly, melted

1. If you are making your own pastry, prepare the pie dough according to recipe directions. Roll out the dough, fit it into a 9-inch pie pan, and crimp the edges. (Fit purchased pastry into the pie pan and crimp the edges.) Partially bake the shell (page 263). Let cool on a rack before filling.

2. Preheat the oven to 300°F with a rack in the lower third of the oven.

3. Spread the coconut on a baking sheet and toast in the oven for 5 to 10 minutes, stirring frequently, until golden brown. Watch carefully to see that the coconut doesn't burn. Remove from the pan and set aside. Increase the oven temperature to 425°F.

4. In a medium bowl, beat the eggs slightly with a whisk. Stir in the sugar, vanilla, salt, and nutmeg. Gradually add the hot milk stirring constantly. Set aside.

5. Brush the pie shell with the Apricot Glaze, then sprinkle the coconut over the glaze. Place the unfilled pie shell on the rack in the lower third of the oven. Carefully pour or ladle the custard filling into the shell.

6. Bake for 15 minutes. Reduce the oven temperature to 350°F and bake for 20 minutes longer, until a knife inserted 1 inch from the outer edge comes out clean. The center may look a little bit soft but will firm up later. Remove from the oven and sprinkle the top with nutmeg.

7. Cool on a wire rack. Serve warm or at room temperature. Refrigerate leftover pie.

Grasshopper Pie

The great American dessert tradition includes many, many convenience recipes, such as super-moist cakes that contain pudding mixes, or tomato soup, or sauerkraut. Then there are recipes developed in food manufacturers' kitchens to expand the use of their products, such as Jell-O sponge cakes and Ritz Cracker mock apple pies. We don't know who conceived the idea of replacing gelatin with marshmallows in this sweet chiffon pie that was developed in the 1950s, but it works. The filling is a cloud of mellow mint flavor, resting lightly on a crispy chocolate crust. The color of the filling — a bright green — is responsible for the unusual name.

Serves 8

Chocolate Crumb Crust (see page 265) for a 9- or 10-inch pie
30 *large marshmallows (from a 10-ounce package)*
½ *cup milk*

¼ *cup crème de menthe*
3 *tablespoons crème de cacao*
1½ *cups whipping cream*
Chocolate shavings, to garnish

-----

1. Prepare and bake the piecrust according to the recipe directions. Cool completely.

2. Combine the marshmallows and milk in a heavy saucepan over moderate heat. Cook, stirring constantly, until the marshmallows have melted, 5 to 7 minutes. Remove from the heat. Cool to room temperature. (Do not refrigerate; the marshmallows will gel.)

3. Add the crème de menthe and crème de cacao, beating thoroughly until combined.

4. Whip the cream until stiff. Fold in the marshmallow mixture. Spoon the filling into the crumb crust. Garnish with the chocolate shavings.

5. Refrigerate the pie for 3 to 4 hours, until firm. The pie will hold for up to 24 hours in the refrigerator.

Shaker Lemon Pie

Shaker" is the popular name for members of the United Society of Believers in Christ's Second Appearing. The Shakers originated in England in 1774. They were called Shaking Quakers because of the trembling the believers experienced as a result of their religious emotions. Shakers practiced celibacy and lived communally. They grew strong in America under the leadership of Ann Lee, and 18 Shaker communities were founded by 1826. These communities no longer exist, but the Shakers left a legacy of fine furniture designs, handicrafts, and recipes. Interestingly, this lemon pie is said to have been particularly beloved by Shakers because it was made with the one fruit they themselves did not grow.

Serves 8

---

2 large lemons (Meyer lemons, if available)

2 cups sugar
Pastry for a 9-inch double-crust pie, homemade (page 261) or purchased

4 large eggs, lightly beaten
Pinch of salt

---

1. Slice the lemons paper thin. Remove any seeds. Combine the lemon slices and sugar in a medium bowl; toss to mix. Cover and let stand for at least 8 hours, or overnight. Toss occasionally to disperse the sugar.

2. If you are making your own pastry, prepare the pie dough according to recipe directions and refrigerate.

3. Preheat the oven to 450°F.

4. Add the eggs and salt to the lemon mixture. Mix well. Set aside.

5. To prepare the pie shell, lightly flour a work surface. Roll out the larger portion of the refrigerated dough to a thickness of about ⅛ inch. Fit into a 9-inch pie pan, leaving a 1-inch overhang. (Fit purchased pastry into the pie pan.) Spoon the filling into the pastry shell. Roll out the remaining dough into a circle about 1 inch larger than the pie pan. Moisten the edge of the bottom crust with water. Fold the dough circle in half, lift off the board, place the pastry across the center of

the filled pie, and unfold. Trim the edge ½ inch larger than the pie pan and tuck the overhang under the edge of the bottom crust. Crimp the edges with a fork or make a fluted pattern with your fingers. Make several steam vents or slits in the top crust, placing a few near the outer edge.

6. Bake for 15 minutes. Reduce the oven temperature to 350°F and bake for 20 to 25 minutes longer, until the crust is golden and a knife inserted in one of the outer vents comes out clean. If the top of the crust begins to brown too deeply, cover loosely with foil.

7. Cool the pie on a wire rack before serving warm or at room temperature.

Rolling Pins

ROLLING PINS were not always the cylindrical affairs they are today. In Southern plantation kitchens of the 1700s, the rolling pin had a large U-shaped handle that could be grasped in the middle and operated with one hand. This left the other hand free to work the dough — an advantage that was lost with the rolling pin design of today.

Lemon Meringue Pie

Who could fail to sing the praises of a billowy, tall lemon meringue pie? The tangy, silken lemon base is the perfect counterpoint to the airy cloud of sweet meringue. This pie was the epitome of the American-style haute cuisine that was practiced in New York and Philadelphia in the mid- to late 1800s. Part of the appeal in those days was its expense — the excessive number of eggs, the refined sugar, fresh imported lemons, and sweet creamery butter. Incidentally, if you ever find an old recipe for vinegar pie, you will be looking at a poor man's lemon meringue. In that recipe, cider vinegar and the zest of half a lemon replace the fresh lemons. But we accept no substitutes here: This old-fashioned pie tastes as delectable as ever.

Serves 8

Pastry for a 9-inch single-crust pie, homemade (page 261) or purchased
4 large eggs, separated
1¾ cups sugar
6 tablespoons cornstarch
⅛ teaspoon plus 1 pinch salt
1½ cups water
½ cup fresh lemon juice
2 tablespoons butter, cut into small pieces
1 tablespoon plus 2 teaspoons finely grated lemon zest
½ teaspoon cream of tartar

1. If you are making your own pastry, prepare the pie dough according to recipe directions. Roll out the dough, fit it into a 9-inch pie pan, crimp the edges, and fully bake the shell (page 263). (Fit purchased pastry into the pie pan, crimp the edges, and bake according to the package directions.) Let cool on a rack before filling.

2. To prepare the lemon filling, beat the egg yolks lightly in a small bowl. Set aside.

3. In the top of a double boiler, combine 1¼ cups of the sugar, the cornstarch, and the ⅛ teaspoon salt. Gradually stir in the water and lemon juice. Place the double boiler over simmering water. Using a whisk, stir the mixture constantly until the sugar is dissolved and the mixture thickens and just comes to a boil. Remove from the heat.

4. Gradually stir a few teaspoons of the lemon mixture into the beaten egg yolks, mixing constantly until blended. When you have added about ½ cup, pour the yolk mixture into the remaining mixture in the pan, stirring constantly until combined.

5. Place the pan over the simmering water again. Whisk in the butter gradually, then the 1 tablespoon lemon zest. Cook the filling over low heat, stirring constantly, for 10 minutes, until it is thick and smooth. Remove from the heat.

6. Stir the filling to cool slightly, then pour it into the baked piecrust.

7. Preheat the oven to 375°F.

8. Beat the egg whites in a large bowl with an electric mixer until foamy. Add the cream of tartar and the pinch of salt and beat until soft peaks form. Gradually sprinkle in the remaining ½ cup sugar, 1 tablespoon at a time, beating well after each addition. When all the sugar has been incorporated, add the 2 teaspoons lemon zest and beat well for 3 to 4 minutes, until the meringue forms stiff, shiny peaks. The egg whites should hold their shape and remain moist.

9. Spoon about half of the meringue around the edge of the warm filling. Use a rubber spatula to carefully seal it to the piecrust. Pile the remaining meringue in the center and then spread it with the back of a spoon to make decorative swirls.

10. Bake for 7 to 8 minutes, until the meringue is golden brown.

11. Cool the pie on a wire rack in a draft-free place. Serve at room temperature. This pie tastes best when eaten within 3 hours of cooling. Refrigerate any leftover pie.

Baker's Tip

❊ The egg whites in this recipe are not fully cooked. Please see "Egg Information" on page 388.

Lemon Angel Pie

In the 1940s, *McCall's* magazine ran a recipe for lemon angel pie as the "recipe of the month." The pie has since shown up in many community cookbooks. The title contains the word *angel* because the only way to describe this is "heavenly."

Serves 8

MERINGUE PIE SHELL

4 large egg whites, at room
   temperature
1 teaspoon fresh lemon juice
½ teaspoon cream of tartar
¼ teaspoon salt
1 cup sugar

LEMON FILLING

4 large egg yolks, at room
   temperature
¾ cup sugar
1 tablespoon finely grated lemon
   zest
⅓ cup fresh lemon juice
⅛ teaspoon salt
1½ cups whipping cream
6 thin slices lemon, to garnish

1. Preheat the oven to 225°F. Thoroughly grease and flour a 9-inch pie pan.

2. To make the meringue pie shell, beat the egg whites until foamy. Add the lemon juice, cream of tartar, and salt and beat until soft peaks form. Gradually sprinkle in the sugar, 1 tablespoon at a time, beating well after each addition. Continue beating until the meringue is stiff and glossy. Spoon the meringue into the pie pan, building up the sides above the height of the plate to form a bowl. (Don't allow the bowl shape to overhang the lip of the pie pan, however, or the meringue will stick to it.)

3. Bake for 1¼ hours, until the meringue has dried and is light tan in color. Turn off the oven, prop open the oven door with a wooden spoon, and let the pie shell remain in the oven until mostly cool, about 1 hour. The meringue shell should be crisp on the outside and slightly soft in the center. Remove from the oven and finish cooling on a wire rack.

4. While the pie shell cools, prepare the filling. In the top of a double boiler, beat the egg yolks with a wire whisk until thick and lemon-colored. Place the double boiler over simmering water. Gradually whisk in the sugar, lemon zest, lemon juice, and

salt. Using a metal spoon, stir constantly until the mixture coats the back of the spoon and is thickened, 8 to 9 minutes. Immediately remove the pan from the double boiler and cool to room temperature. Place a piece of plastic wrap directly on the filling to avoid having a skin form.

5. Whip the cream until soft peaks form.

6. To assemble the pie, spread half of the whipped cream in the bottom of the meringue shell. Cover with the cooled lemon filling, then top with the remaining whipped cream.

7. Refrigerate for several hours or overnight.

8. Just before serving, garnish the pie with the lemon slices.

Who dares deny the truth,

There's poetry in pie?

— **Henry Wadsworth Longfellow,
American poet, 1807–1882**

Lemon Chiffon Pie

We aren't wearing as much chiffon as we used to (chiffon being a very sheer, delicate fabric, usually made of silk), and we aren't eating fluffy, light chiffon pies as often as we did in the '40s and '50s. That's a shame, because this pie is a delight.

Serves 8

Pastry for a 9-inch single-crust pie, homemade (page 261) or purchased
1 cup whipping cream
1 (¼-ounce) envelope unflavored gelatin
¼ cup cold water
4 large eggs, separated

1 cup sugar
⅛ teaspoon salt
¾ cup hot water
2 tablespoons finely grated lemon zest
⅓ cup fresh lemon juice
6 thin lemon slices and 3 sprigs fresh mint, to garnish

1. If you are making your own pastry, prepare the pie dough according to recipe directions. Roll out the dough, fit it into a 9-inch pie pan, crimp the edges, and fully bake the shell (page 263). (Fit purchased pastry into the pie pan, crimp the edges, and bake according to the package directions.) Let cool on a rack before filling.

2. In a small bowl, beat the cream until it forms stiff peaks. Refrigerate.

3. In another small bowl, sprinkle the gelatin over the cold water. Stir and set aside to soften.

4. Beat the egg yolks with a wire whisk in the top of a double boiler until thick and lemon-colored. Set the double boiler over simmering water. Whisk in ½ cup of the sugar and the salt. Slowly add the hot water, lemon zest, and lemon juice. Stir constantly until the mixture has thickened enough to coat the back of a spoon, 5 to 8 minutes. Add the softened gelatin and stir until the gelatin dissolves.

5. Refrigerate the lemon mixture or place the pan in a bowl of ice water, stirring until it mounds slightly when dropped from a spoon. The center should be cold but not set. Stir frequently and do not allow the mixture to become stiff.

6. In a separate bowl, beat the egg whites until soft peaks form. Add the remaining ⅓ cup sugar, 1 tablespoon at a time, beating well after each addition. Beat until the sugar is dissolved. The egg whites should hold their shape and remain moist.

7. Fold the egg whites into the lemon mixture and then fold in half of the whipped cream. (Refrigerate the remaining whipped cream.)

8. Spoon the filling into the baked piecrust. Refrigerate the pie until firm, about 3 hours. Top with the remaining whipped cream. Garnish the pie with thin slices of lemon and the mint.

Baker's Tip

❋ The eggs in this recipe are not cooked. Please see "Egg Information," page 388.

Key Lime Pie

In 1883, Gail Borden applied for a patent on his process of preserving milk. He boiled off the water in the milk in an airtight vacuum pan, similar to those he had seen Shakers use for condensing sweetened fruit juices. The heat process and the added sugar preserved the milk by inhibiting the activity of bacteria. It took consumers many years to trust Borden's condensed milk, "the milk that would stay sweet." But after the Civil War, it was a godsend to the South, where years of battle and plunder had devastated its agricultural base. In Key West, Florida, sweetened condensed milk was not only a sorely needed food, but it was also the inspiration for the famous Key Lime Pie.

Serves 8

Pastry for a 9-inch single-crust pie, homemade (page 261) or purchased
3 large eggs, separated
1 (14-ounce) can sweetened condensed milk
1 tablespoon finely grated lime zest
½ cup lime juice (preferably Key lime juice, fresh or bottled; if Key lime juice isn't available, use lime juice freshly squeezed from regular limes)

¼ teaspoon cream of tartar
⅛ teaspoon salt
¼ cup sugar
Whipped cream, to garnish

1. If you are making your own pastry, prepare the pie dough according to recipe directions. Roll out the dough, fit it into a 9-inch pie pan, crimp the edges, and fully bake the shell (page 263). (Fit purchased pastry into the pie pan, crimp the edges, and bake according to the package directions.) Let cool on a rack before filling.

2. Preheat the oven to 325°F.

3. Beat the egg yolks in a large bowl with a rotary beater or electric mixer for 3 to 4 minutes, until thick and lemon-colored. Gradually add the condensed milk, beating until blended. Add the lime zest and juice and continue beating until thick and smooth.

4. In another bowl, beat the egg whites until foamy. Add the cream of tartar and salt and beat until soft peaks form. Add the sugar gradually and beat until stiff but not dry. The egg whites should hold their shape and remain moist. Fold the whites into the lime mixture, then spoon the mixture into the baked piecrust.

5. Bake for 20 minutes, until the filling is set and just beginning to turn golden.

6. Cool on a wire rack. Refrigerate the pie for 3 to 4 hours, until firm.

7. Just before serving, pipe whipped cream on top.

Pie Pans
——— ✿ ———

FOR THE BEST RESULTS, select pie pans made of non-shiny darkened metal, anodized aluminum, or heatproof glass. These pans absorb heat well and help to produce evenly browned piecrusts.

Maple Chiffon Pie

Anyone who has ever tasted maple sap knows how much imagination is required to think that such a watery fluid could become sweet syrup. So who thought to boil sap into syrup in the first place? Legend has it that an Iroquois chief by the name of Woksis threw a tomahawk into a maple tree before leaving on a hunt. The weather grew warm that day, and sap flowed from the gash in the tree into a container standing below. The woman who collected the container thought it was filled with plain water and boiled her evening meat in it. The boiling caused the sap to be reduced to syrup, which gave the meat a whole new flavor, and the rest is history.

Serves 8

Pastry for a 9-inch single-crust pie, homemade (page 261) or purchased
1 (¼-ounce) envelope unflavored gelatin
¼ cup cold water
3 large eggs, separated
⅔ cup maple syrup
⅓ cup hot (not boiling) milk or half-and-half

1 teaspoon vanilla extract
⅛ teaspoon cream of tartar
⅛ teaspoon salt
1 cup whipping cream
¼ cup chopped butternuts or walnuts, plus 2 tablespoons finely chopped butternuts or walnuts, to garnish

1. If you are making your own pastry, prepare the pie dough according to recipe directions. Roll out the dough, fit it into a 9-inch pie pan, crimp the edges, and fully bake the shell (page 263). (Fit purchased pastry into the pie pan, crimp the edges, and bake according to the package directions.) Let cool on a rack before filling.

2. In a small bowl, sprinkle the gelatin over the cold water. Stir and set aside to soften.

3. In the top of a double boiler, make a custard by beating the egg yolks with a wire whisk until thick and lemon-colored. Gradually add the maple syrup and hot milk, mixing until combined. Place the pan over simmering water. Stir constantly until the mixture lightly coats a metal spoon. Add the softened gelatin and stir until the gelatin is dissolved. Add the vanilla.

4. Refrigerate the custard or place the pan in a bowl of ice water, stirring the custard until it mounds slightly when dropped from a spoon. The mixture should be cold but not set.

5. Beat the egg whites until foamy. Add the cream of tartar and salt and beat until the egg whites are stiff but not dry. They should hold their shape and remain moist. Gently fold into the cold custard.

6. Whip the cream until stiff. Fold three-quarters of it into the custard, along with the ¼ cup chopped nuts. Spoon the mixture into the baked piecrust. Refrigerate the pie and the remaining whipped cream for 3 to 4 hours, until firm.

7. Just before serving, pipe the remaining whipped cream on top of the pie. Garnish with the 2 tablespoons chopped nuts.

Baker's Tip

❈ The egg whites in this recipe are not cooked. Please see "Egg Information" on page 388.

Maple Season

IN NEW ENGLAND, maple sugaring season generally begins in early March, when the days warm up above freezing but the nights stay cold. This is the optimum weather for a good sap run. Throughout the state, there are open visiting hours at sugarhouses and sugar-on-snow parties, where boiling-hot syrup is poured on snow to harden into a sticky candy.

Maple Walnut Pie

An organization called RAFT (Restoring America's Food Traditions) is a coalition of seven nonprofit food, agriculture, conservation, and educational organizations, including Slow Food USA, the Chefs Collaborative, and Seed Savers Exchange. RAFT is dedicated to rescuing America's diverse foods and food traditions and has divided the country into regions, which it calls "foodsheds." Vermont, of course, is the "maple syrup foodshed." If a foodshed has a signature dish, this may be it.

Serves 8

Pastry for a 9-inch single-crust
    pie, homemade (page 261) or
    purchased
1½ cups walnut halves and pieces,
    toasted
3 large eggs, at room temperature
½ cup loosely packed dark brown
    sugar (see Baker's Tip opposite)
1 tablespoon unbleached all-
    purpose flour

⅛ teaspoon salt
1 cup maple syrup
3 tablespoons butter, melted
1 tablespoon brandy
1 teaspoon vanilla extract
    Whipped cream or vanilla ice
    cream, to serve

1. If you are making your own pastry, prepare the pie dough according to recipe directions. Roll out the dough, fit it into a 9-inch pie pan, and crimp the edges. (Fit purchased pastry into the pie pan and crimp the edges.) Partially bake the shell (page 263). Let cool on a rack before filling.

2. Preheat the oven to 300°F.

3. Arrange the walnuts in a single layer on a baking sheet and toast for 7 to 10 minutes, until lightly toasted and fragrant. Remove from oven and set aside to cool. Increase the oven temperature to 350°F.

4. Lightly beat the eggs with a whisk in a medium bowl. Add the brown sugar, flour, and salt. Mix until thoroughly combined. Whisk in the maple syrup, butter, brandy, and vanilla.

5. Spread the cooled walnuts over the piecrust. Pour the egg filling over the walnuts.

6. Bake for 35 minutes, until a golden crust forms and the center is soft to the touch and almost firm. It will jiggle when touched in the center. Do not overbake; the filling will set and firm up as it cools.

7. Cool the pie on a wire rack. Serve warm or at room temperature with whipped cream or vanilla ice cream.

Baker's Tip

※ When baking with brown sugar, the ingredient list usually calls for the brown sugar to be "firmly packed" in the measuring cup. In this case, we packed the brown sugar loosely because firmly packing would result in an overly sweet pie.

Piecrust Shortcuts

PIECRUSTS AND PASTRY DOUGH CAN BE TRICKY, and preparing them may take more time than a hectic schedule allows. Fortunately, some excellent convenience products are available; an example is ready-to-bake piecrusts in the dairy case.

Frozen piecrusts aren't as high quality as fresh-made ones, and they're prone to breaking while still frozen. Refrigerated pie pastry provides a way around this problem. It is packaged as rolled disks of rolled-out pie dough. You simply unroll the dough, fit it into your pan, crimp the edges, and fill.

Shoofly Pie

There is some question as to who invented the double-crusted American pie — the Pennsylvania Dutch or New Englanders. But there is no question that shoofly pie came from the Pennsylvania Dutch. This pie, really a molasses sponge cake in a crust, should be tried at least once, if only to get a taste of how our ancestors ate. It's awfully sweet, so be prepared to shoo away any flies that are attracted to its sugary aroma.

Serves 8

Pastry for a 9-inch single-crust pie, homemade (page 261) or purchased
1¼ cups unbleached all-purpose flour
½ cup firmly packed light brown sugar
½ teaspoon ground cinnamon
¼ teaspoon freshly grated nutmeg
¼ teaspoon salt
4 tablespoons butter, at room temperature
½ teaspoon baking soda
⅔ cup hot water
⅔ cup dark molasses
Light cream, to serve

1. If you are making your own pastry, prepare the pie dough according to recipe directions. Roll out the dough and fit it into a 9-inch pie pan. (Fit purchased pastry into the pie pan.) Crimp the edges and refrigerate.

2. Preheat the oven to 425°F with a rack in the lower third of the oven.

3. Combine the flour, brown sugar, cinnamon, nutmeg, and salt in a medium bowl. Using your fingers, rub the butter into the flour mixture until the mixture has the consistency of coarse meal.

4. Dissolve the baking soda in the hot water and combine with the molasses. Pour one-third of the molasses mixture into the unbaked pie shell. Sprinkle with one-third of the crumb mixture. Continue layering, ending with the crumb mixture.

5. Bake for 15 minutes. Reduce the oven temperature to 350°F and continue baking for 20 minutes, until the filling is firm when lightly pressed with your fingertip.

6. Cool the pie on a wire rack. Serve warm or cold with the light cream.

Deep-Dish Peach Pie

One has to live in peach country — the Southeast, New Jersey, or the Pacific Northwest — to enjoy a perfect tree-ripened peach these days. For the rest of us, peaches bought a few days in advance and left to ripen in a paper bag with a banana or an apple will do. (The banana or apple produces a gas that hastens ripening.)

Serves 8

Cream Cheese Pastry (page 264)
6 cups fresh peeled, sliced peaches (about 6 medium peaches) (see technique, page 270)
¼ cup firmly packed light brown sugar, or to taste
3 tablespoons unbleached all-purpose flour
¼ teaspoon freshly grated nutmeg
2 tablespoons butter, cut into small pieces
1 large egg yolk
2 teaspoons water
1 teaspoon granulated sugar
Vanilla ice cream or whipped cream, to serve

1. Prepare the pastry dough according to the recipe directions and refrigerate.

2. Preheat the oven to 375°F. Put the peaches in an 8-inch square baking dish or 2-quart casserole.

3. Combine the brown sugar, flour, and nutmeg in a small bowl. Toss with the peaches, mixing gently until they are thoroughly coated. If the peaches lack flavor, add a little more brown sugar. Dot with butter.

4. On a lightly floured work surface, roll out the pastry into a square or circle 1 inch larger than the baking dish. Roll the pastry onto the rolling pin and then gently drape it over the top of the dish. Crimp the edges of the pastry and press around the top of the dish.

5. Make an egg wash by beating the egg yolk with the water and brush it onto the top of the crust. Sprinkle with the granulated sugar. With the tip of a sharp knife, cut three or four slits in the top of the pastry to allow steam to escape.

6. Bake for 35 to 40 minutes, until the crust is golden.

7. Serve warm with vanilla ice cream or whipped cream.

Lattice-Top Mince Pie

Originally, mincemeat pies contained a rich mixture of heavily spiced minced meat and dried fruit, probably as close to medieval cooking as any of us is likely to experience. The meat was dropped in modern times, but beef suet (fat) remains in many recipes, though not this one. Bottled mincemeat is available at holiday times, but homemade is always better.

Serves 8

Pastry for a 9-inch double-crust pie (page 261)
½ small lemon, unpeeled, seeded, and cut into chunks
½ medium navel orange, unpeeled, seeded, and cut into chunks
1½ pounds tart, crisp apples, peeled and cut into chunks
⅔ cup apple juice or apple cider
2 tablespoons cider vinegar
2 tablespoons dark molasses
1 cup dark raisins
½ cup golden raisins
½ cup dried currants

¾ cup firmly packed dark brown sugar
½ teaspoon ground cinnamon
¼ teaspoon ground allspice
¼ teaspoon ground cloves
¼ teaspoon freshly grated nutmeg
⅛ teaspoon salt
½ cup coarsely chopped pecans or walnuts
2 tablespoons bourbon or brandy (optional)
Vanilla ice cream or whipped cream, to serve

1. Prepare the pie dough according to recipe directions and refrigerate.

2. Using a food processor or food chopper, finely chop or grind the lemon and orange. Transfer the fruit mixture to a heavy saucepan. Add the apples to the food processor and finely chop, and then add to the saucepan. Stir in the apple juice, cider vinegar, molasses, dark and golden raisins, currants, brown sugar, cinnamon, allspice, cloves, nutmeg, and salt. Bring to a boil, then reduce the heat and simmer, uncovered, over low heat for 40 to 45 minutes, stirring frequently until the apples are tender and the mixture is thick but still moist. Taste, and add more sugar or spice as needed. Remove from the heat.

3. Add the nuts and bourbon, mixing until combined. Set aside. You can prepare and refrigerate the mince pie filling several days ahead.

4. Preheat the oven to 425°F with a rack in the lower third of the oven.

5. To prepare the pie shell, roll out the larger portion of the refrigerated dough to a thickness of about ⅛ inch. Fit into a 9-ich pie pan, leaving a 1-inch overhang. Spoon the cooled filling into the pastry. Roll out the remaining dough into a rectangle about ⅛ inch thick and 11 inches long. Trim the ragged edges. Using a pastry wheel or sharp knife, cut the rectangle into 10 lengthwise strips, each ½ inch wide. To form the lattice, lay five strips across the filling, each 1 inch apart. Working from the center, interweave the remaining strips, one at a time, over and under the first strips. Trim the ends. Moisten the overhanging edge of the bottom crust and fold up over the ends of the strips. Flute the edge of the crust and place the pie on a baking sheet to catch any juices that overflow.

6. Bake in the lower third of the oven for 15 minutes. Reduce the oven temperature to 350°F and bake for 30 minutes longer, until the crust is golden brown and the juices are bubbly.

7. Cool the pie on a wire rack. Serve warm or at room temperature, with vanilla ice cream or whipped cream.

Sour Cream Raisin Pie

We've eaten many different versions of raisin pie in our days. Raisin pies made in Vermont are likely to be sweetened with maple syrup. Some pies are made without sour cream, in which case they bear a striking resemblance to mince pies. This version has a custard base and is delicately spiced.

Serves 8

Pastry for a 9-inch single-crust
  pie, homemade (page 261) or
  purchased
2 large eggs
¾ cup sugar
1 cup chopped raisins
1 cup sour cream

Zest of 1 lemon, finely grated
1 tablespoon fresh lemon juice
½ teaspoon ground cinnamon
¼ teaspoon freshly grated nutmeg
  Pinch of salt
½ cup chopped walnuts

1. If you are making your own pastry, prepare the pie dough according to recipe directions. Roll out the dough, fit it into a 9-inch pie pan, and crimp the edges. (Fit purchased pastry into the pie pan and crimp the edges.) Partially bake the shell (page 263). Let cool on a rack before filling.

2. Preheat the oven to 425°F with a rack in the lower third of the oven.

3. Beat the eggs and sugar in a medium bowl with a wire whisk until light and fluffy. Add the raisins, sour cream, lemon zest, lemon juice, cinnamon, nutmeg, and salt, whisking until well blended. Pour the mixture into the pie shell. Sprinkle the walnuts over the top.

4. Bake in the lower third of the oven for 10 minutes. Reduce the oven temperature to 350°F and continue baking for 25 to 30 minutes, until a knife inserted 1 inch from the edge comes out clean. (If the crust browns too quickly, cover the edge with a strip of aluminum foil.)

5. Cool the pie on a wire rack. Serve at room temperature or refrigerated. Refrigerate any leftover pie.

Going Nuts

- When buying nuts for baking, buy unsalted nuts, which are usually found in the baking section of the supermarket.
- Generally 4 ounces of shelled nuts yields 1 cup of chopped nuts.
- The oils in nuts cause them to go rancid, which gives the nuts an off flavor (though won't sicken you). Always taste nuts before using to make sure they aren't spoiled.
- Toast nuts for the best flavor and crunch, even if a recipe doesn't call for it. To toast nuts, preheat the oven to 300°F. Spread out the nuts in a thin layer on a baking sheet. Toast for 7 to 10 minutes, until lightly colored and fragrant.
- The best way to chop nuts is with a chef's knife. Spread the nuts on a cutting board. Keeping the tip of the knife stationary against the board, move the handle up and down and from side to side until the nuts are chopped to the desired size.
- The best way to grind nuts is in a food processor with part of the granulated sugar called for in the recipe, to prevent them from turning into a sticky paste.

Pecan Pie

As American as pecan pie" should be the saying. Pecans, like corn and cranberries, are native to North America and were introduced to the early colonists by the Native Americans. The name is derived from a Native American word meaning "hard-shelled nut."

Thomas Jefferson is often credited with the spread of the pecan's popularity. He planted hundreds of trees at Monticello and gave seedlings to George Washington, who planted them at Mount Vernon, where there are still pecan trees today — most likely descendants of the original planting.

Serves 8

....

Pastry for a 9-inch single-crust pie, homemade (page 261) or purchased
1¼ *cups toasted pecan halves*
2 *tablespoons butter, at room temperature*
¾ *cup firmly packed dark brown sugar*
2 *tablespoons unbleached all-purpose flour*

¼ *teaspoon salt*
1 *cup light corn syrup*
3 *large eggs*
1 *tablespoon dark rum*
1 *teaspoon vanilla extract*
Whipped cream flavored with rum or vanilla ice cream, to serve

....

1. If you are making your own pastry, prepare the pie dough according to recipe directions. Roll out the dough, fit it into a 9-inch pie pan, and crimp the edges. (Fit purchased pastry into the pie pan and crimp the edges.) Partially bake the shell (page 263). Let cool on a rack before filling.

2. Preheat the oven to 300°F.

3. Arrange the nuts in a single layer on a baking sheet and toast for 6 to 8 minutes, until lightly colored, stirring once. Set aside to cool. Increase the oven temperature to 350°F.

4. Beat the butter in a medium bowl until creamy. Add the brown sugar, flour, and salt. Mix until thoroughly combined. Blend in the corn syrup. Add the eggs, one at a time, beating well after each addition. Add the rum and vanilla.

5. Spread the cooled pecans over the bottom of the piecrust. Pour the egg mixture over the pecans.

6. Bake for 35 to 40 minutes, until the filling is firm.

7. Cool the pie on a wire rack. Serve warm or at room temperature, with whipped cream or ice cream.

The Pecan: An All-American Nut

THE PECAN — a native American hickory nut (*Carya illinoensis*) — is grown mainly in Georgia and Texas, where some 100 million pounds are harvested each year. Rich and buttery in flavor, the pecan is favored for pies and confections and can be substituted in any recipe calling for walnuts. Pecans are, however, more expensive than walnuts.

Pecans in the shell will keep in an airtight container for 2 to 3 months at room temperature, and up to 6 months in the refrigerator. Shelled nuts will keep for 6 months in the refrigerator and up to 12 months in the freezer.

Figure that 1 pound of pecans in the shell will yield 2¼ cups of shelled pecans. One pound of shelled pecans equals 3½ to 4 cups.

Chocolate Pecan Pie

When trying to decide between a dessert of chocolate cake and pecan pie, the only logical choice is a chocolate pecan pie. This dessert is particularly welcome at Thanksgiving, when it is customary to serve pie. But be warned: This pie is quite rich.

Serves 8

Pastry for a 9-inch single-crust pie, homemade (page 261) or purchased
1½ cups halved or chopped pecans, toasted
3 tablespoons butter
4 ounces bittersweet or dark chocolate, coarsely chopped
¾ cup granulated sugar
3 large eggs
¾ cup dark corn syrup
1 tablespoon bourbon or rum
1 teaspoon vanilla extract
⅛ teaspoon salt

TOPPING

1 cup whipping cream
1 tablespoon confectioners' sugar
1 tablespoon bourbon or rum, or
   1 teaspoon vanilla extract
Chocolate curls, optional

1. If you are making your own pastry, prepare the pie dough according to recipe directions. Roll out the dough, fit it into a 9-inch pie pan, and crimp the edges. (Fit purchased pastry into the pie pan and crimp the edges.) Partially bake the shell (page 263). Let cool on a rack before filling.

2. Preheat the oven to 300°F.

3. Arrange the nuts in a single layer on a baking sheet and toast for 6 to 8 minutes, until lightly colored, stirring once. Set aside to cool. Increase the oven temperature to 350°F.

4. Melt the butter and chocolate in the top of a double boiler set over simmering water. Stir until completely smooth and glossy. Remove the top of the double boiler from the heat and set aside to cool slightly.

5. Whisk the sugar into the cooled chocolate. Add the eggs, one at a time, whisking well after each addition. Mix in the corn syrup, bourbon, vanilla, and salt. Stir in the pecans. Pour the filling into the piecrust.

6. Bake for 45 to 50 minutes, until a dark shiny crust forms and the center is soft to the touch and almost firm. It will jiggle slightly when touched in the center. Do not overbake; the filling will set and firm up as it cools.

7. Cool the pie on a wire rack.

8. To make the flavored whipped cream, beat the cream until soft peaks form. Add the confectioners' sugar and bourbon. Beat until firm but not stiff.

9. Serve warm or at room temperature, topped with the flavored whipped cream and garnished with chocolate curls, if using.

Baker's Tip

❋ If the pie has been refrigerated, you can reheat it in a 350°F oven for 10 to 12 minutes, until warm.

Chess Pie

How did this Southern specialty get its name? A few stories circulate, none of which has anything to do with the ancient board game. Some claim that a chess pie was originally a "chest pie" that would keep in a cupboard without refrigeration. Some say that it is an adaptation of the English cheese pie. Then there is the story of the plantation cook who was asked what she was making. "Jes' pie," she replied. Whatever the origin, today there are many variations. One variation — called a Jefferson Davis Pie — contains spices and dates.

Serves 8

Pastry for a 9-inch single-crust pie, homemade (page 261) or purchased
½ cup firmly packed brown sugar
½ cup granulated sugar
6 tablespoons butter, at room temperature
3 large eggs
1 cup chopped toasted pecans
¼ cup whipping cream
1 tablespoon yellow cornmeal
1 tablespoon unbleached all-purpose flour
1½ teaspoons vanilla extract
⅛ teaspoon salt

1. If you are making your own pastry, prepare the pie dough according to recipe directions. Roll out the dough, fit it into a 9-inch pie pan, and crimp the edges. (Fit purchased pastry into the pie pan and crimp the edges.) Partially bake the shell (page 263). Let cool on a rack before filling.

2. Preheat the oven to 350°F.

3. Beat together the brown sugar, granulated sugar, and butter until creamy. Add the eggs, one at a time, beating well after each addition. Stir in the pecans, cream, cornmeal, flour, vanilla, and salt, blending well. Pour the mixture into the pie shell.

4. Bake for 40 to 45 minutes, until a knife inserted 1 inch from the outer edge comes out clean and the filling is slightly firm.

5. Cool the pie on a wire rack. Serve warm or at room temperature, within 3 hours of cooling.

Sweet Potato Pie

Thought to originate in South America, the sweet potato was cultivated in North America long before Columbus set off from Spain. In the South, sweet potato pies are much more common than pumpkin pies.

Serves 8

Pastry for a 9-inch single-crust pie, homemade (page 261) or purchased
2 large eggs
¾ cup firmly packed dark brown sugar
2 cups mashed, cooked sweet potatoes
1½ cups half-and-half or evaporated milk
3 tablespoons butter, melted and cooled

1 tablespoon bourbon or brandy
1 tablespoon unbleached all-purpose flour
1½ teaspoons ground cinnamon
½ teaspoon ground ginger
½ teaspoon freshly grated nutmeg, plus more to serve
½ teaspoon salt
¼ teaspoon ground allspice or mace
¼ teaspoon ground cloves
Whipped cream sweetened with honey, to serve

1. If you are making your own pastry, prepare the pie dough according to recipe directions. Roll out the dough and fit it into a 9-inch pie pan. (Fit purchased pastry into the pie pan.) Crimp the edges and refrigerate.

2. Preheat the oven to 425°F with a rack in the lower third of the oven.

3. Beat together the eggs and brown sugar in a medium bowl until light. Add the sweet potatoes, half-and-half, butter, bourbon, flour, cinnamon, ginger, nutmeg, salt, allspice, and cloves. Mix thoroughly. Pour the mixture into the unbaked pie shell.

4. Bake in the lower third of the oven for 15 minutes. Reduce the oven temperature to 325°F and continue baking for 35 to 40 minutes, until the filling is firm and a knife inserted 1 inch from the edge comes out almost clean. (A little sweet potato will adhere to the knife.)

5. Cool the pie on a wire rack. Serve at room temperature or refrigerated. Top with the whipped cream and sprinkle with nutmeg. Refrigerate any leftover pie.

Pumpkin Pie

Pumpkin makes an appearance at most Thanksgiving dinners, often in the form of pie. This classic recipe has just a hint of sophistication from the orange liqueur that rounds out the flavors of spice and pumpkin. Ginger-Spiced Whipped Cream is a wonderful accompaniment.

Serves 8

Pastry for a 9-inch single-crust pie, homemade (page 261) or purchased
2 large eggs
¾ cup firmly packed light brown sugar
2 cups cooked or canned puréed pumpkin
1½ cups evaporated milk
2 tablespoons orange liqueur (Grand Marnier)

1 teaspoon ground cinnamon
1 teaspoon ground ginger
½ teaspoon freshly grated nutmeg
½ teaspoon salt
¼ teaspoon ground allspice
¼ teaspoon ground cloves
Whipped cream or Ginger-Spiced Whipped Cream (recipe follows), for serving

1. If you are making your own pastry, prepare the pie dough according to recipe directions. Roll out the dough and fit it into a 9-inch pie pan. (Fit purchased pastry into the pie pan.) Crimp the edges and refrigerate.

2. Preheat the oven to 425°F with a rack in the lower third of the oven.

3. Beat together the eggs and brown sugar in a medium bowl until light. Add the pumpkin, evaporated milk, orange liqueur, cinnamon, ginger, nutmeg, salt, allspice, and cloves. Mix thoroughly. Pour into the unbaked pie shell.

4. Bake in the lower third of the oven for 15 minutes. Reduce the oven temperature to 325°F and bake for 35 to 40 minutes longer, until the filling is firm and a knife inserted 1 inch from the edge comes out clean.

5. Cool the pie on a wire rack. Serve at room temperature or refrigerated, with whipped cream or Ginger-Spiced Whipped Cream. Refrigerate any leftover pie.

Ginger-Spiced Whipped Cream

Serves 8

1 cup whipping cream
2 tablespoons sifted confectioners' sugar
1 tablespoon brandy

2 tablespoons sour cream
2 tablespoons minced crystallized ginger

1. Beat the cream until soft peaks form. Add the sugar and brandy and beat until stiff.

2. Fold in the sour cream and ginger.

Pie Mania

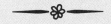

BY A CERTAIN DEFINITION, a Yankee is one who eats pie for breakfast. But the early great pie makers were probably from Dixie. According to food historians, pie making became something of a mania in the South in the nineteenth century. This coincided with the drop in the price of granulated sugar as the cane sugar industry developed in the States. No more did cooks have to depend on strongly flavored honey and sorghum to sweeten their pastries. Instead, they could whip up such blandly sweet delights as Chess Pie, Pecan Pie, and Lemon Meringue Pie.

Lattice-Top Strawberry Rhubarb Pie

Pie plant, as rhubarb is also known, is native to Asia and eastern Europe, where it is valued both for medicinal properties and for eating. You can't do much with rhubarb but cook it with plenty of sugar or honey to make a sauce or a pie. Conveniently, the tart rhubarb matures just as sweet strawberries ripen, allowing for a marriage of great harmony.

Serves 8

Pastry for a 9-inch double-crust pie (page 261)
1¼ cups plus 1 tablespoon sugar
⅓ cup unbleached all-purpose flour
1 teaspoon finely grated orange zest
Pinch of salt
1 pound fresh rhubarb, cut into 1-inch pieces (4 cups)

2 cups halved strawberries
2 tablespoons butter, cut into small pieces
1 teaspoon milk
Whipped cream or vanilla yogurt, to serve

1. Prepare the pie dough according to recipe directions and refrigerate.

2. Combine the 1¼ cups sugar and the flour, orange zest, and salt in a large bowl. Add the rhubarb and strawberries and toss lightly to combine. Set aside.

3. Preheat the oven to 425°F with a rack in the lower third of the oven.

4. To prepare the pie shell, lightly flour a work surface. Roll out the larger portion of the refrigerated dough to a thickness of about ⅛ inch. Fit into a 9-inch pie pan, leaving a 1-inch overhang. Spoon the filling into the pastry shell and dot with butter. Roll out the remaining dough into a rectangle about ⅛ inch thick and 11 inches long. Trim the ragged edges. Using a pastry wheel or sharp knife, cut the rectangle into 10 lengthwise strips, each ½ inch wide. To form the lattice, lay five strips across the filling, each 1 inch apart. Working from the center, interweave the remaining strips, one at a time, over and under the first strips. Trim the ends. Moisten the overhanging edge of the bottom crust and fold up over the ends of the strips. Flute the edge of the crust. Brush the lattice strips with milk and sprinkle with the 1 tablespoon sugar. Place the pie on a baking sheet to catch any juices that overflow.

5. Bake in the lower third of the oven for 15 minutes. Reduce the oven temperature to 350°F and bake for 50 minutes longer, until the filling is bubbly and the crust is golden brown.

6. Cool the pie on a wire rack. Serve warm or at room temperature topped with whipped cream or vanilla yogurt.

To make a light, crisp, and flaky crust, use a good, fine flour and none but the best butter. Have everything, including yourself, cool. A marble slab makes the best pastry board. Use a glass rolling-pin, if convenient; if not, one made from hard wood with movable handles. Always use ice or very cold water in mixing, and keep the paste in a cold place. . . . No matter how light your paste may be, the substance of each stratum is dense and hard of digestion, and should never be eaten by persons of weak digestive powers.

— S. T. Rorer, *Mrs. Rorer's Cook Book, A Manual of Home Economics*, 1866

Fresh Strawberry Pie

This is the ultimate strawberry pie, the quintessential fresh fruit pie that preserves the fresh flavor of uncooked strawberries. The berries glisten like jewels in a thickened sauce that allows you to serve the pie in neat slices. It will be only as good as the strawberries you select, so wait until local berries are ready.

Serves 8

Pastry for a 9-inch single-crust pie, homemade (page 261) or purchased	*2 tablespoons fresh lemon juice*
	1 cup sugar
6 cups (1½ quarts) fresh strawberries, hulled and halved if large	*¼ cup cornstarch*
	⅛ teaspoon salt
2 teaspoons unflavored gelatin	*½ cup water*
	½ cup whipping cream

1. If you are making your own pastry, prepare the pie dough according to recipe directions. Roll out the dough, fit it into a 9-inch pie pan, crimp the edges, and fully bake the shell (page 263). (Fit purchased pastry into the pie pan, crimp the edges, and bake according to the package directions.) Let cool on a rack before filling.

2. Place 2 cups of the berries in a blender or food processor and purée. Set aside.

3. Arrange half of the remaining strawberries in the baked pastry shell and set aside.

4. In a small bowl, sprinkle the gelatin over the lemon juice and let soften.

5. Whisk the sugar, cornstarch, and salt in a heavy saucepan. Whisk in the water and puréed berries. Bring to a boil over medium-high heat, stirring constantly. Boil for 1 minute. Remove from the heat and whisk in the softened gelatin until smooth.

6. Pour half of the strawberry sauce over the strawberries in the pastry shell. Shake the pie pan gently to evenly distribute the sauce. Add the remaining uncooked strawberries. Spoon the remaining strawberry sauce evenly over the berries. Chill for at least 4 hours, up to 8 hours, before serving.

7. Whip the cream in a small bowl until soft peaks form. Serve each slice of pie with a dollop of whipped cream.

Basic Pie Pastry

With a food processor and just a little practice, pie dough is easier to make than you might think. Give it a try before running out to buy the packaged product. This recipe makes enough dough for one double-crust pie or two single-crust pie shells. If you need just one pie shell, you can halve the recipe or make enough dough for two pie shells and freeze the extra dough, wrapped in plastic wrap and heavy-duty aluminum foil. Use within 3 to 4 weeks.

1 double crust for an 8- or 9-inch pie or two 9-inch single crusts

....

2½ cups unbleached all-purpose flour
½ teaspoon salt
½ cup (1 stick) butter, cut into small
     pieces
6 tablespoons vegetable shortening
     (refrigerate the shortening if
     you are using a food processor)
6 tablespoons ice water, or more if
     needed

....

TO MIX THE DOUGH

If you are mixing by hand:

1. Combine the flour and salt in a large bowl.

2. With a pastry blender or two knives, cut in the butter.

3. Add the shortening and combine until the particles are the size of small peas.

4. While stirring lightly and quickly with a fork, sprinkle with the water, 1 tablespoon at a time, just until all the flour is moistened.

5. If the dough doesn't hold together when squeezed, sprinkle with additional water until it holds together and does not crumble. If the dough is sticky, sprinkle with a little more flour.

6. Using the heel of your hand, press portions of the dough flat against your work surface. This will help distribute the fat and make the dough easier to roll out.

If you are mixing in a food processor:

1. Combine the flour and salt in a food processor fitted with a metal blade.

2. Add the butter and shortening and process with on-and-off pulses until the mixture has the consistency of coarse meal.

3. Add 1 tablespoon of ice water through the feed tube, then pulse for 3 seconds. Repeat this start-and-stop procedure with additional tablespoons of water.

4. Process this mixture until it just begins to stick together, but do not allow it to form a ball.

5. Turn out the dough onto a sheet of plastic wrap and pull up on the corners to form a ball.

TO REFRIGERATE THE DOUGH

1. Reshape the dough and flatten it into two disks (if you are making a double-crust pie, make one disk slightly larger than the other) and dust with flour. Wrap separately in plastic wrap. Refrigerate for at least 30 minutes, or up to 4 days.

2. If the dough has been refrigerated for several hours, remove it from the refrigerator and leave at room temperature for 15 minutes so it will be easier to handle.

TO ROLL OUT THE DOUGH

On a lightly floured work surface, roll out the dough into a circle, rolling from the center to the edges in even, light strokes. (For a double-crust pie shell, roll out the larger disk first.) Work quickly to handle the dough as little as possible. Roll the dough to a thickness of a little less than ⅛ inch and a diameter 2 inches larger than the inverted pie pan. Fold the circle in half, lift up, and lay the fold across the center of the pie pan. Unfold and loosely ease the dough into place without stretching it.

TO FIT THE DOUGH INTO THE PIE PAN

For a single-crust pie:

Trim the overhanging edge ½ inch larger than the outside rim of the plate. Fold it under, even with the rim of the pie pan, and crimp or flute the edge. Refrigerate the pie shell for 15 minutes, then fill and bake as directed in a recipe or bake unfilled. (See instructions for fully and partially baked pie shells below.)

For a double-crust pie:

Trim the overhanging edge even with the rim of the pie pan. Fill the pie shell with the desired filling. To make the top crust, roll out the remaining dough into a circle about 1 inch larger than the pie pan. Moisten the edge of the bottom crust with water. Fold the dough circle in half, lift off the board, place it across the center of the filled pie, and unfold. Trim the edge ½ inch larger than the pie pan. Tuck the overhang under the edge of the bottom crust. Crimp the edges with a fork or make a fluted pattern with your fingers. Make several decorative slits in the top crust to allow steam to escape. Refrigerate the pie for 15 minutes. Bake as directed in the recipe used.

TO PREPARE THE DOUGH FOR FILLING

Fully baked pie shell:

1. Preheat the oven to 425°F with a rack in the lower third of the oven. Remove the unbaked pie shell from the refrigerator and prick the bottom and sides of the dough with a fork at ½-inch intervals. Fit a large circle of foil into the bottom and up the sides of the pie dough. Fill it with dried beans or baker's pellets to provide weight and to prevent the crust from buckling.

2. Bake in the lower third of the oven for 10 minutes, then remove the foil and weights. Prick the bottom of the crust with a fork again to keep it from puffing up. Return the pie shell to the oven for 10 to 12 minutes, until it is golden. Cool on a rack before filling.

Partially baked pie shell:

1. Preheat the oven to 425°F with a rack in the lower third of the oven. Remove the unbaked pie shell from the refrigerator. Do not prick the crust. Line the pie shell with a circle of foil and weight it with dried beans or baker's pellets to prevent buckling.

2. Bake in the lower third of the oven for 10 minutes, until the pastry is set. Remove the foil and weights and bake for 3 to 4 minutes longer, until the pie shell just begins to set. Cool on a rack before filling.

Cream Cheese Pastry

Here's a rich pastry that makes a wonderful single-crust pie shell. Double the recipe if you want a double-crust pie.

Makes one 9-inch pie shell

1 cup unbleached all-purpose flour
⅛ teaspoon salt
3 ounces cream cheese
½ cup (1 stick) butter, cut into small
pieces

1. Combine the flour and salt by hand or in a food processor fitted with a steel blade. Add the cream cheese and butter and process — or use a pastry blender to cut in the cream cheese and butter — until the mixture has the consistency of coarse meal.

2. Turn out the dough onto a floured board and knead lightly, just until the dough holds together. Shape the dough into a ball and then flatten into a disk. Dust with flour. Wrap in plastic wrap and refrigerate while you prepare the filling.

3. If the dough has been refrigerated for several hours, remove it from the refrigerator and leave at room temperature for 15 minutes so it will be easier to handle.

4. On a lightly floured work surface, roll out the dough into a circle, rolling from center to edge in even, light strokes. Work quickly to handle the dough as little as possible. Roll the dough to a thickness of a little less than ⅛ inch and to a diameter 2 inches larger than the inverted pie pan. Fold the circle in half, lift off the board, and lay the fold across the center of the pie pan or tart pan. Unfold and ease the dough loosely into place without stretching it.

5. Trim the overhanging edge ½ inch larger than the outside rim of the pan. Fold it under, even with the rim of the pie pan, and crimp or flute the edge. Refrigerate the pie shell for 15 minutes.

6. Fill and bake as directed in a recipe or bake unfilled.

7. Follow instructions on page 263 for a fully or partially baked pie shell.

Graham Cracker Crust

To save time, some people don't bother to bake crumb crusts. But we find that baking results in a pie that is less soggy, cuts better, and has a nice toasty flavor.

Makes one 9-inch pie shell

- 1½ cups finely ground graham cracker crumbs
- 3 tablespoons sugar
- 6 tablespoons butter, melted
- ¼ teaspoon ground cinnamon

1. Preheat the oven to 350°F. Lightly grease a 9-inch pie pan or springform pan.

2. Combine the graham cracker crumbs, sugar, butter, and cinnamon. Press firmly onto the bottom and up the sides of the pan.

3. Bake for 8 minutes, then set aside on a rack to cool before filling.

Baker's Tip

※ It takes about 10½ sheets of graham crackers (each sheet has 4 crackers) to make 1½ cups of crumbs. Make them quickly in a food processor.

Chocolate Crumb Crust

Makes one 9-inch pie shell

- 1¾ cups finely ground chocolate wafer crumbs (about 35 wafers)
- 5 tablespoons butter, melted

1. Preheat the oven to 350°F. Lightly grease a 9-inch pie pan or springform pan.

2. Combine the crumbs and melted butter. Press firmly onto the bottom and up the sides of the pan.

3. Bake for 8 minutes, then set aside on a rack to cool before filling.

Nut Crust

Use in any recipe where you might use a graham cracker crust. Pecans, almonds, or hazelnuts can replace the walnuts.

Makes one 9-inch pie shell

¾ cup walnuts	⅛ teaspoon freshly grated nutmeg
⅓ cup butter, at room temperature	1 large egg yolk
¼ cup sugar	1 teaspoon vanilla extract
1 cup unbleached all-purpose flour	A few drops water, if needed

1. Finely grind the walnuts in a food processor. Add the butter and sugar and process just until combined. Add the flour and nutmeg and process for 3 to 5 seconds, until well mixed. Add the egg yolk and vanilla and mix until blended, about 5 seconds. Remove the dough and place on a sheet of plastic wrap. Using the plastic wrapped around the dough, compress the dough into a ball. Add a few droplets of water if needed to hold the dough together. Flatten the dough into a thick disk. Chill the dough for 1 hour in the refrigerator or for 20 minutes in the freezer.

2. Butter a 9-inch pie pan. Press the dough over the bottom and up sides of the pan. Refrigerate for 15 minutes, until firm.

3. Preheat the oven to 350°F.

4. Place the pie pan on a baking sheet and bake for about 20 minutes, until golden.

5. Cool on a wire rack. The pie shell can be prepared several days ahead or frozen.

Basic Sweet Pastry

The French call this pastry *pâte brisée sucrée* — a rich, sweet dough used for tart shells. It is a strong dough that will hold its shape when you remove the sides of the tart pan.

Makes pastry for 1 tart shell

....

    1¼ cups sifted unbleached
          all-purpose flour
    3 tablespoons sugar
    ⅛ teaspoon salt

½ cup (1 stick) butter, chilled and cut
   into ½-inch chunks
1 egg yolk combined with
   1 tablespoon cold water

....

To mix the dough by hand:

1. Combine the flour, sugar, and salt in a large bowl.

2. With your fingers, a pastry blender, or a fork, work the butter into the flour mixture until it has the consistency of coarse meal.

3. Make a well in the center of the flour mixture and pour in the egg yolk and water mixture. Mix well with a fork.

4. Continue mixing with your hands and mold the dough into a thick disk shape. If the dough is too dry to hold together, add water a few drops at a time, until the dough can be molded into a disk shape.

5. Wrap in plastic wrap and refrigerate for 1 hour.

To mix the dough in a food processor:

1. Combine the flour, sugar, and salt in the processor.

2. With the motor running, add the butter, one chunk at a time. Process until the mixture resembles coarse meal.

3. Add the egg yolk and water and pulse rapidly for 5 seconds.

4. Continue pulsing just until the dough begins to hold together; it will look crumbly.

5. Transfer the dough to a sheet of plastic wrap. Shape into a ball, then flatten it into a 1-inch-thick disk.

6. Wrap in plastic wrap and refrigerate for 1 hour.

Fruit and Nut Desserts

The most skilled pastry chef in the world can do nothing to improve upon a perfect peach. Or a ripe strawberry. Or a juicy orange, crisp apple, perfumed mango, or custardy banana. Well, you get the idea.

For most occasions, a bowl of fruit and a bowl of nuts in their shells make a perfect dessert. In the height of summer, a bowl of berries and another of whipped cream is exceptionally fine. A platter of melon slices is the perfect way to finish a spicy meal. A platter of sliced tropical fruits in the winter is a grand finale.

And for those times when you want to bake a crisp, make a shortcake, or create a fool, the classic recipes gathered here should fit the bill.

Ingredients

✪ **Wash all fruit under cold running water before using.**

✪ **Overripe fruit that is soft but still tastes good can be puréed, sweetened with sugar, and frozen.** Use it as a topping for ice cream or pancakes, or as a filling for crepes. You can also purée fruit, punch up the flavor with fruit liqueur, and serve it as a sauce.

✪ **Buy local fruits whenever possible, and try to buy them in season.** Overtraveled, underripe, out-of-season fruits can dull the palate and erase the memory of how good fruit actually tastes.

✪ **Ground spices lose their pungency and aroma quickly, so buy them in small quantities, label the date of purchase, and discard them after 6 months.**

Techniques

✪ **To ripen fruit such as peaches, nectarines, and pears, place them in a paper bag with a ripe apple for 2 to 3 days.** The ripening process will stop when the fruit is refrigerated.

✪ **To prevent apples, pears, and other fruits from turning dark after peeling, dip them in a bowl of cold water mixed with lemon juice.** Use 2 cups of water to 1 tablespoon of lemon juice.

✪ **To peel peaches, bring a large pot of water to a boil.** Add the peaches and blanch for 30 seconds. Remove with a slotted spoon and immerse them in a bowl of cold water. The skins will then slip off easily.

✪ **For an easier time cutting up dates and other sticky fruits, chill them in the freezer** for about an hour beforehand. Scissors sometimes work better than knives.

✪ **To peel an orange or grapefruit when you need the sections in a salad, immerse the whole fruit in a pot of boiling water and let it stand 4 minutes.** Remove the fruit from the water and allow it to cool until it's easy to handle. When you peel away the skin, the pith should come with it. Any remnants can be pulled off with a grapefruit knife.

✪ **Before juicing citrus fruit, microwave it for 15 to 45 seconds, until slightly warm to the touch.** Then it will yield more juice. Another trick is to roll the fruit on the counter for a few seconds to help break the cell walls.

✪ **Zest is the colored part of the rind on a citrus fruit.** It does not include the white membranes, which are often bitter. Zest contains essential oils that add a great deal of flavor to a dessert. If a recipe calls for both fresh juice and zest, grate the zest first, then juice the fruit. To finely grate zest, use a zester, the fine-holed side of a box grater, or a Microplane. Or strip the zest from the fruit with a zester or swivel-bladed peeler and finely mince.

✪ **One of the easiest and most effective ways to cut butter into flour is to grate refrigerated or frozen butter into the flour and then briefly work it in with your fingers.** The resulting biscuit or pastry should be very flaky.

✪ **For an elegant presentation, serve fruit desserts in wine goblets, oversized martini glasses, brandy snifters, and old-fashioned glasses.**

Fruit Fritters

Everything tastes better fried, and fruits are no exception — at least sometimes. Choose fruits that are firm and ripe, not mushy. Cut the fruit as uniformly as possible so slices or chunks are about ½ inch thick. Be sure that the outside of the fruit is dry before dipping the pieces so the extra moisture doesn't thin the batter. Also, batter will not stick to wet fruit.

Serves 4 to 6

¾ cup unbleached all-purpose flour
1 tablespoon cornstarch
1 tablespoon granulated sugar
1 teaspoon baking powder
⅛ teaspoon salt
1 large egg, at room temperature
⅔ cup milk, at room temperature
1 teaspoon Kirsch or vanilla extract

1 teaspoon vegetable oil
5–6 cups vegetable oil, for frying
3–4 apples or pears, cut into medium slices (about 1½ pounds)
Confectioners' sugar or cinnamon-sugar (¼ cup granulated sugar mixed with 1½ teaspoons ground cinnamon), to serve

1. Sift the flour, cornstarch, sugar, baking powder, and salt into a large bowl. Make a well in the center.

2. Beat the egg lightly in a medium bowl. Add the milk, Kirsch, and vegetable oil, mixing until combined. Pour into the flour mixture. Mix together until just combined.

3. Heat 3 to 4 inches of vegetable oil in a deep kettle, heavy saucepan, or deep-fryer to 370°F to 375°F. If you don't have a thermometer, test the oil by sprinkling in a few drops of batter. If they immediately rise to the surface, the oil is ready.

4. Pat dry the pieces of fruit with paper towels. Dip the fruit, one piece at a time, into the batter, turning to coat thoroughly. Slide the fruit into the oil, no more than five or six pieces at a time, and fry until golden and crisp on both sides. Remove with a slotted spoon and drain on paper towels. Continue until all the fruit has been fried, making sure the oil temperature remains constant.

5. Serve immediately, dusted with confectioners' sugar or cinnamon-sugar. If you prefer, keep the finished fried pieces on a baking sheet in a 250°F oven for 10 to 15 minutes, until all the pieces are fried.

Ambrosia

For a very attractive presentation, serve this ambrosia in a glass dish to display the colorful layers of fruit.

4 to 6 servings

....

4 large navel or seedless oranges
½ cup freshly squeezed orange juice
    or pineapple juice (see Baker's
    Tip opposite)
    Confectioners' sugar
2 cups diced fresh or canned
    pineapple

1 tablespoon chopped fresh mint
    (optional)
¾ cup lightly packed, sweetened
    flaked coconut
2 tablespoons orange liqueur
    (Grand Marnier) or brandy
    (optional)

....

1. With a vegetable peeler, remove the zest of one of the oranges. Cut it into very fine julienne. Slice off the white membrane of that orange. Peel the remaining three oranges, removing all the white membrane.

2. Over a bowl to catch the juice, section the oranges or cut them into ½-inch wedges and set them in a separate dish. Place the juice caught in the bowl into a measuring cup and add juice until you have ½ cup. Mix ¼ cup of the juice, the julienned orange zest, and a little confectioners' sugar to sweeten the fruit, if needed. Pour it over the cut oranges.

3. In another bowl, combine the pineapple with the mint (if using) and the remaining ¼ cup juice. Sweeten to taste with confectioners' sugar.

4. Set aside 2 tablespoons of the coconut. In a serving bowl, alternate layers of oranges and pineapple, sprinkling each layer with coconut. Drizzle in the orange liqueur (if using) and the juice in which the fruits have macerated. Refrigerate for several hours.

5. Sprinkle with the reserved coconut and serve.

Baker's Tip

❉ If you are using canned pineapple packed in pineapple juice, you can use that juice instead of the orange juice. This recipe has tremendous flexibility and need not be followed to the letter.

Variations

Substitute mandarin oranges for the navel oranges. You can also add sliced bananas, but they should be mixed in just before serving because they brown easily.

Food of the Gods

MANY OF OUR FRUIT DESSERTS originated in colonial America. Cobblers and crisps were most often made from apples and berries, which were homegrown or gathered in the wild. Not so with ambrosia, a dessert that originated in the South in the nineteenth century, when coconut and oranges could be purchased in stores. The recipe made its first appearance in print in an 1879 cookbook of recipes from Virginia, where it was a simple combination of oranges, sugar, and coconut. More-elaborate versions soon evolved, incorporating pineapple and bananas and sometimes even sour cream, marshmallows, and dates. Today, it is acceptable to include any fruit you choose; just be sure to top the dessert with coconut if you want to call it ambrosia.

Dried Fruit Compote

Slow cooking ensures that each piece of fruit retains its shape and flavor. This is an old-fashioned dessert from a time when it was unthinkable to serve out-of-season fresh fruits from halfway around the world. A dollop of crème fraîche makes a lovely accompaniment.

Serves 4 to 6

1 lemon
1 large orange
2 cups (13 ounces) pitted prunes
4 cinnamon sticks, each about 2 inches long
12 whole cloves
1¾ cups (10 ounces) dried apricots
1 cup (4 ounces) pitted dried cherries
2 cups (8 ounces) coarsely chopped dried pears

2 cups apple juice, plus more as needed
2 cups port wine, plus more as needed
1 cup firmly packed dark brown sugar
2 tablespoons butter, cut into small pieces
2 tablespoons toasted slivered almonds, to garnish

1. Preheat the oven to 350°F. Lightly grease a deep 2-quart baking dish or casserole.

2. Remove half the zest from the lemon and cut it into thin strips. Squeeze the juice from the lemon. Cut the orange crosswise into thin slices.

3. Put half of the prunes on the bottom of the baking dish. Toss one-quarter of the lemon strips, orange slices, cinnamon sticks, and cloves over them. Cover with a layer of apricots, then cherries, then pears, sprinkling each layer with one-quarter of the lemon strips, orange slices, and spices. Put the remaining prunes on top.

4. Mix together the lemon juice, apple juice, port wine, and brown sugar. Pour over the fruit. Dot with butter. Loosely cover the baking dish with aluminum foil.

5. Bake for 1 hour. Remove the aluminum foil and check the liquid level. If it is below the fruit, add more apple juice and port. Bake for 30 minutes longer, basting two or three times with the fruit juices in the pan during the last 30 minutes.

6. Remove the spices, if desired. Serve warm or chilled, sprinkled with almonds.

Apple Brown Betty

This is one of the simplest of the fruit desserts, and we have no idea how the name originated. The walnuts add extra flavor and texture.

Serves 6

- 1 cup dry unseasoned breadcrumbs
- ¼ cup granulated sugar
- ⅓ cup butter, melted
- 5–6 medium apples, peeled, cored, and sliced (about 5 cups)
- ½ cup firmly packed light or dark brown sugar
- ½ cup chopped walnuts
- 1 teaspoon ground cinnamon
- ½ teaspoon freshly grated nutmeg
- Zest and juice of 1 lemon
- Cream, whipped cream, or ice cream, to serve

1. Preheat the oven to 350°F. Lightly butter a 1½-quart baking dish.

2. Combine the breadcrumbs, granulated sugar, and butter in a medium bowl. Pat half of the mixture into the bottom of the baking dish.

3. In another bowl, combine the apples, brown sugar, walnuts, cinnamon, nutmeg, and lemon zest and juice. Spread over the crumb mixture in the baking dish. Top with the remaining crumb mixture.

4. Cover with aluminum foil and bake for 40 minutes. Remove the cover, increase the heat to 400°F, and bake for 10 minutes longer.

5. Serve warm with cream.

Apple Crisp

Apple crisp, apple crunch, apple delight — there are many names for (and variations of) this dessert, which has an apple pie filling and a crunchy topping. This sort of dessert was widespread in early American kitchens because it was the perfect way to make use of the less-than-perfect apples that were stored in bins in the root cellar. After all the wormholes and bruises were cut away, baked apples were out of the question, but apple crisp, crunch, or delight was just the thing.

6 servings

FILLING

- 3 *pounds tart apples, peeled, cored, and sliced (about 7 cups)*
- ¼ *cup granulated sugar*
- 1 *tablespoon finely grated lemon zest*
- 1 *tablespoon fresh lemon juice*
- 1 *teaspoon ground cinnamon*
- ½ *teaspoon freshly grated nutmeg*

TOPPING

- ½ *cup firmly packed dark brown sugar*
- ½ *cup ground cookie or graham cracker crumbs (see Baker's Tip opposite)*
- ½ *cup unbleached all-purpose flour*
- ½ *cup (1 stick) butter, at room temperature*
- ⅓ *cup chopped almonds*
  Cream, whipped cream, or ice cream, to serve

1. Preheat the oven to 350°F. Lightly grease a 9-inch square baking dish or a deep 9-inch pie pan.

2. To make the filling, combine the apples in a large bowl with the granulated sugar, lemon zest, lemon juice, cinnamon, and nutmeg. Toss to mix. Transfer the apples to the baking dish, pressing down on them so that they're level with the top of the dish.

3. To make the topping, in the same bowl that held the apples combine the brown sugar, cookie crumbs, and flour. With your fingers, rub the butter into the crumb mixture until it resembles coarse meal. Mix in the almonds. Sprinkle the topping over the apples, pressing it down and making sure the edges of the apples are covered.

4. Bake for 45 minutes, until the top is browned and the apples are tender when tested with a fork.

5. Serve warm or chilled with cream.

Baker's Tip

❋ For ½ cup of ground cookie crumbs, you will need approximately 8 gingersnaps or 11 vanilla wafers. For ½ cup of graham cracker crumbs, use about 3½ sheets, or 14 individual crackers.

Brandy Vanilla Sauce

This sauce couldn't be easier to make — it requires no cooking whatsoever. It is best made with a high-quality vanilla ice cream. Serve it over fruit desserts, including any crisp, cobbler, or crumble. It is the perfect finish for baked apples and poached pears.

Makes about 1 cup

1 cup softened vanilla ice cream
2 tablespoons brandy

Stir together the softened ice cream and brandy until the sauce has a good pouring consistency. Serve at once.

A Is for Apple

FROM A COOK'S POINT OF VIEW, it would be nice if the best eating apples were also the best cooking apples. Then you could conduct your own taste test, stock up on your favorite eating apple, and know that whenever the mood strikes for apple pie or crisp, you've got the right ingredients.

When new apple varieties are developed, they are rigorously tested for cooking characteristics because there are no hard-and-fast rules for which varieties cook best. Juicy apples don't necessarily become watery when cooked, though some, like McIntosh, do. Sweet apples don't necessarily stay sweet when cooked, though some, like Newton Pippins, do. Some, like Red Delicious, become bland and flat-tasting. Apples that make a great sauce, like Braeburns, may be a poor choice for making pie.

For making pies and crisps, nothing beats a Northern Spy, which is one of those formerly popular, now disappearing varieties. Jonagolds, Jonathans, and Rhode Island Greenings make great pies. Golden Delicious, paired with a tart variety, such as Granny Smith or McIntosh, is terrific in pies and crisps. For sauce, most people use a mix of what hasn't been used in baking or eating fresh, and will make up with sugar and cinnamon whatever the apples don't provide. Sauce makers, as a rule, recommend Braeburn, Gala, Golden Delicious, Granny Smith, Jonagold, Jonathan, Newtown Pippin, and Winesap. Cortlands are an excellent choice for salads because of their remarkably white flesh. Golden Delicious apples hold their color well, too. Cortlands dry well, as do Galas and Winesaps. When in doubt, choose Golden Delicious or Jonagold. Both are excellent, all-purpose apples.

Baked Apples

Consider this a crustless apple pie — very easy to make. We stuff ours with almonds, but any nut, or even cookie crumbs, can be used instead.

Serves 6

6 large Rome Beauty or other baking apples	1 tablespoon finely grated lemon zest
¼ cup firmly packed light brown sugar	1 teaspoon ground cinnamon
2 tablespoons toasted slivered almonds (optional)	½ teaspoon freshly grated nutmeg
	2 tablespoons butter, cut into pieces
2 tablespoons dried currants	1½ cups apple juice or cider, heated
2 tablespoons golden raisins	2 teaspoons granulated sugar
	Light or heavy cream, to serve

1. Preheat the oven to 375°F.

2. Core the apples to ½ inch from the bottom. Remove a 1-inch strip of skin around the top of each apple. Stand the apples upright in a shallow baking dish that will hold them compactly but without crowding.

3. Mix the brown sugar, almonds (if using), currants, raisins, and lemon zest. Fill the apple centers evenly with the mixture. Sprinkle with cinnamon and nutmeg. Dot with butter. Pour the hot apple juice around the apples to a depth of ½ inch.

4. Bake for 45 to 60 minutes, basting frequently, until the apples are tender when pierced with a fork. Sprinkle the granulated sugar over the apples during the last 5 minutes of baking. (The baking time will depend upon the variety and size of the apples.)

5. Serve warm or at room temperature in dessert dishes, with the juices remaining in the baking dish spooned over the apples. Top with the cream.

Baker's Tip

※ The currants and raisins can be plumped in apple brandy or sherry for several hours before you fill the apples.

Apple Charlotte

This dessert, something of a fancy variation on Apple Brown Betty, has French origins. One theory suggests it was named after one Charlotte Buff, on whom Johann Wolfgang von Goethe based the heroine of *Die Leiden des Jungens Werthers*, a very popular novel in its day (1774). Some think that the original charlotte was invented in England as early as 1796 and was probably named after Queen Charlotte, wife of George III, said to be the patron of apple growers. The first published recipe for apple charlotte might be the one that appeared in *American Domestic Cookery*, by Maria Eliza Rundell, in 1823.

Serves 8 to 10

CHARLOTTE

¾ cup (1½ sticks) butter
3½–4 pounds tart apples, peeled, cored, and sliced ¼ inch thick (about 8 cups)
2 tablespoons water
¾–1 cup firmly packed light brown sugar
1 tablespoon finely grated lemon zest

2 tablespoons fresh lemon juice
2 teaspoons ground cinnamon
¼ teaspoon freshly grated nutmeg
12–14 thin slices firm white bread, crusts removed
Whipped cream, to serve

RUM APRICOT SAUCE

1 cup apricot jam
1 tablespoon water
3 tablespoons dark rum

1. Lightly grease a 2-quart charlotte mold, soufflé dish, or straight-sided glass baking dish.

2. Melt ¼ cup of the butter in a large skillet over medium heat. Add the apples and water and cook, covered, stirring occasionally, until the liquid just begins to boil, 5 to 8 minutes. Stir in ¾ cup of the brown sugar and the lemon zest and lemon

juice. Cook, uncovered, until the apples are softened and glazed, 5 to 10 minutes. All the liquid should be absorbed. Mix in the cinnamon and nutmeg. Taste and add more brown sugar if needed. Set aside.

3. Preheat the oven to 375°F.

4. Melt the remaining ½ cup butter. Cut three or more slices of bread into narrow triangles (like slices of pie) to fit the bottom of the mold. Brush both sides of the bread with the melted butter and arrange in the bottom of the mold. The points should meet in the center and fan out like the spokes of a wheel. Cut six or more slices of the remaining bread in half lengthwise. Brush both sides of each rectangle with butter and then line the sides of the mold with the bread, standing the slices upright and overlapping them slightly.

5. With a slotted spoon, transfer the apple mixture to the prepared baking dish. Brush the remaining bread with butter and trim to fit over the apples. Tap the mold on the work surface and gently press down the bread. Trim excess bread from around the edge until it is flush with the top of the apple charlotte.

6. Bake for 30 minutes. Press down the apples and bake for 15 minutes longer, until the top is golden brown. Trim the bread again from around the top edge, if necessary.

7. Cool on a rack for 15 minutes while you prepare the sauce.

8. To prepare the sauce, combine the apricot jam and water in a small saucepan. Stir over low heat until the jam is melted. Simmer, stirring occasionally, for 3 minutes. Remove from the heat and strain. Blend in the rum. Let cool slightly.

9. To serve, carefully loosen the charlotte by running a knife around the inside of the mold. Invert it onto a serving dish and brush with warm apricot sauce. Pour some of the sauce around the base of the charlotte. Serve warm with the whipped cream.

Apple Pandowdy

A pandowdy is a cross between a pie and a pudding. It starts with a crust that is chopped up until it disappears into the fruit — a step that is called "dowdying." With a filling that includes butter and a little cream, a pandowdy is richer than your average pie. This old-fashioned dessert is obviously for those of us with old-fashioned work habits. Serve after a hard day of gardening, chopping wood, or running a marathon.

Serves 6

PASTRY

- 1¼ cups unbleached all-purpose flour
- ⅛ cup cornmeal, preferably stone-ground
- 2 tablespoons sugar
- ¼ teaspoon salt
- 6 tablespoons butter, chilled
- ¼ cup vegetable shortening
  About ¼ cup ice water

APPLE FILLING

- 6–8 apples, peeled, cored, and sliced (about 6 cups)
- 1½ teaspoons ground cinnamon
- ½ teaspoon ground mace
- ⅓ cup plus 2 tablespoons maple syrup
- 6 tablespoons butter, melted
- ¼ cup apple cider or juice
- ¼ cup light cream

1. To make the pastry, combine the flour, cornmeal, sugar, and salt in a medium bowl or in a food processor. Cut in the butter and shortening until the mixture resembles coarse crumbs. Add just enough ice water to allow the mixture to hold together. Divide into two balls and flatten into disks. Refrigerate while you prepare the filling.

2. Preheat the oven to 400°F. Lightly butter a 1½-quart baking dish.

3. To prepare the filling, combine the apples, cinnamon, mace, the ⅓ cup maple syrup, and 4 tablespoons of the butter in a large bowl.

4. On a lightly floured work surface, roll out one piece of pastry about ⅛ inch thick to fit into the baking dish. Transfer the dough to the dish and trim the uneven edges. The dough should fit up the sides of the baking dish, but don't worry if it doesn't. Spoon the apples into the baking dish, scraping out the syrup and butter from the bottom of the bowl. Roll out the second piece of dough and fit it over the apples. Seal against the sides of the dish.

5. Bake for about 10 minutes. Remove the pandowdy from the oven and reduce the heat to 325°F. Using a sharp knife or a chopper, cut the crust into the fruit until the crust has almost disappeared into the filling. Combine the apple cider, cream, the 2 tablespoons maple syrup, and the remaining 2 tablespoons melted butter. Pour over the top. Return the pandowdy to the oven and continue to bake for 45 to 50 minutes, until the fruit is tender.

6. Serve warm.

Comfort me with apples: for I am sick of love.

— **The Song of Solomon 2:5**

Apple Dumplings

Apple dumplings take a little more time than some of the other desserts in this chapter, but they can be assembled hours ahead and kept in the refrigerator until baking time. The baked dumplings don't keep well, so make only as many as you plan to serve, and bake just before serving.

Serves 6

PASTRY

- 2 cups unbleached all-purpose flour
- 2 tablespoons sugar
- ½ teaspoon salt
- ½ cup (1 stick) butter, chilled, cut into small pieces
- ¼ cup vegetable shortening
- 4–6 tablespoons ice water
- 1 egg white, slightly beaten with 1 teaspoon water

FILLING

- 6 large baking apples
- 4 tablespoons butter, at room temperature
- ¼ cup raspberry or blackberry preserves
- ¼ cup chopped almonds
- 2 teaspoons finely grated orange zest
- Whipped cream or ice cream, to serve

1. Preheat the oven to 400°F. Lightly butter a large, shallow baking dish.

2. To make the pastry, combine the flour, sugar, and salt in a medium bowl or in a food processor. Cut in the butter and shortening until the mixture resembles coarse crumbs. Add just enough of the ice water, 1 tablespoon at a time, until the mixture holds together. Divide the pastry dough into six cubes and flatten into square disks. Refrigerate them while you prepare the filling.

3. To prepare the filling, peel the apples and core about three-quarters of the way down. Trim the bottoms, if necessary, to enable the apples to stand.

4. Beat together the butter and preserves. Mix in the almonds and orange zest. Stuff into the apple centers.

5. On a lightly floured work surface, roll out each pastry disk to a square of approximately 6 inches. Brush with the egg white and center an apple on each square. Bring up the dough over each apple and press the edges of the dough together,

using the egg white mixture if needed to make them stick. If you want to get fancy, use scraps of dough to make apple leaves and affix them on top of the dumplings with the egg white mixture. Place in the prepared baking dish.

6. Chill for 3 to 5 minutes in the freezer (or for several hours in the refrigerator).

7. Bake for 45 minutes, until the pastry tops are golden brown.

8. Serve warm with the whipped cream or ice cream.

In one word, Queequeg, said I, rather digressively; hell is an idea first born on an undigested apple dumpling; and since then perpetrated through the hereditary dyspepsias nurtured by Ramadans.
— **Herman Melville,** *Moby-Dick* **(1851)**

Apple Strudel

Filo dough, which is used in a host of Middle Eastern pastries, is virtually the same dough that is used to make strudel, which is found throughout Germany, Austria, Hungary, and the former Yugoslavia. Clarified butter is brushed on the filo, ensuring a crispy pastry. Clarifying removes the water from butter. You could use unclarified butter, but the results will not be nearly as good. For tart apples, Granny Smith or Newton Pippins are your best bet.

Serves 12 to 18

FILLING

- 4–5 large tart apples, peeled, cored, and finely diced (about 3 cups)
- 2 teaspoons finely grated lemon zest
- 2 teaspoons fresh lemon juice
- ½ cup granulated sugar
- ¾ cup chopped walnuts
- ¼ cup currants
- ½ cup golden raisins
- 2 teaspoons ground cinnamon

PASTRY

- ¾ cup (1½ sticks) butter
- 9 sheets filo dough
- ¾ cup dry cookie crumbs (vanilla wafers are recommended) or dry bread crumbs
- Confectioners' sugar

1. To make the apple filing, combine the apples, lemon zest, and lemon juice in a medium bowl, and toss to mix. Mix in the sugar, walnuts, currants, raisins, and cinnamon. Set aside in a colander to drain off any excess liquid while you clarify the butter.

2. To clarify the butter, melt the butter over medium heat in a small saucepan. With a spoon, skim off and discard the bubbly foam that rises to the top. Let the butter settle for a few minutes, then spoon off the clear butter, avoiding the milky solids on the bottom of the pan.

3. Preheat the oven to 375°F. Grease a large baking sheet or half sheet pan with some of the butter.

4. Place a dry kitchen towel on a work surface with the long side facing you. Put the first sheet of filo on the towel. Place another dry towel on the work surface and lay out eight sheets of filo. Cover with plastic wrap and a damp towel to keep them from drying. Brush the first sheet of filo with the melted butter and sprinkle with 1 rounded tablespoon of crumbs. Take a sheet of filo from under the damp towel and place it on top of the crumbs. Repeat the process with more crumbs and a third sheet of filo. Cover the remaining filo to keep it from drying out.

5. Using a slotted spoon, spread one-third of the apple filling in a lengthwise strip (or log) about 1 inch from the bottom edge of the filo, extending to within 1 inch of both ends. Tuck in the ends and, using the towel to help you, lift up the bottom of the pastry so it covers the filling. Continue rolling up the filo in jelly-roll fashion. Place the rolled strudel seam-side down on a greased baking sheet and brush the top with butter.

6. Make two more strudels in the same way, using three sheets of filo and one-third of the filling mixture for each roll. For ease of serving, score the top of the unbaked strudel with a sharp knife to indicate the diagonal cuts you will make to serve.

7. Bake for 35 minutes, until the pastry is golden brown.

8. Cool on a wire rack. Sprinkle with confectioners' sugar. Slice on the diagonal while warm or at room temperature.

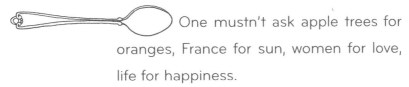 One mustn't ask apple trees for oranges, France for sun, women for love, life for happiness.

— Gustave Flaubert,
French novelist (1821–1880)

Fresh Apple Roll

For people with fear of filo, or of handling any thin dough, this is a strudel-like pastry made with convenient and easy-to-handle puff pastry, which is found in the freezer section of most supermarkets.

Serves 6 to 8

FILLING

⅓ cup raisins
1 tablespoon dry sherry
3 large tart green apples, peeled, cored, and thinly sliced (about 3 cups)
¼ cup granulated sugar, or more to taste

1 tablespoon unbleached all-purpose flour
1 teaspoon finely grated lemon zest
1 teaspoon fresh lemon juice
½ teaspoon ground cinnamon
⅓ cup chopped toasted walnuts

PASTRY

½ (17-ounce) package frozen puff pastry, thawed
1 large egg
1 tablespoon water
Confectioners' sugar

1. Preheat the oven to 375°F. Lightly grease a baking sheet or half sheet pan.

2. To make the filling, put the raisins in a small cup or ramekin. Sprinkle with the sherry. Microwave for 30 seconds or steam for 1 minute. The raisins will absorb most of the sherry. Drain off excess liquid. Set aside to cool.

3. Combine the apples, sugar, flour, lemon zest, lemon juice, and cinnamon in a medium bowl. Add the raisins and walnuts and toss until well mixed.

4. On a lightly floured surface, roll out the puff pastry to form a 12- by 16-inch rectangle. Place the pastry on a sheet of waxed paper a little larger than the pastry. Drain off the excess juice from the apple filling. With the short side of the pastry closer to you, spoon the apple mixture onto the lower third of the pastry to

within 1 inch of the edges. Using the waxed paper to help you, lift up the bottom of the pastry so it covers the filling; continue rolling up the strudel in jelly-roll fashion. Place the roll seam-side down onto the prepared baking sheet. Tuck in the ends to seal.

5. Make an egg wash by mixing the egg with the water. Brush over the pastry. Cut several slits, 2 inches apart, along the top of the pastry.

6. Bake for 35 minutes, until the pastry is golden brown. Remove from the oven and cool on the baking sheet on a wire rack for 30 minutes.

7. Sprinkle the top of the warm strudel with confectioners' sugar. Slice on the diagonal and serve. If there are any leftovers, heat in a 300°F oven for 5 to 8 minutes before serving.

I know the look of an apple that is roasting and sizzling on the hearth on a winter's evening, and I know the comfort that comes of eating it hot, along with some sugar and a drench of cream . . . I know how the nuts, taken in conjunction with winter apples, cider, and doughnuts, make old people's tales and old jokes sound fresh and crisp and enchanting.

— Mark Twain (Samuel Langhorne Clemens), American writer (1835–1910)

Apple Turnovers

Just about every culture has its handheld pies, consisting of some sort of chopped fruit or savory mixture of meats and vegetables wrapped in dough. Everything from Chinese eggrolls to the empanadas of Central America qualify under this broad definition. A specific form of handheld pie is made when the dough is rolled out and the filling is placed on half; the remaining dough is folded over the filling, creating the classic "turnover" shape. These turnovers are filled with a delicious mix of apples and spices. Granny Smith or Newton Pippins are the recommended apples here.

Makes 18 turnovers

Pastry for a 9-inch double-crust pie (page 261)
6–7 tart green apples, peeled, cored, and chopped (3½–4 cups); see Baker's Tip opposite
½ cup golden raisins
⅓ cup sugar
1 tablespoon unbleached all-purpose flour

1 teaspoon finely grated lemon zest
2 teaspoons fresh lemon juice
1 teaspoon ground cinnamon
¼ teaspoon freshly grated nutmeg
1 egg yolk
1 tablespoon water

1. Prepare the pastry dough according to the recipe directions. Divide the dough in half and shape each piece into a flattened square about 1 inch thick. Lightly dust each square with a little flour, then wrap separately in plastic wrap and chill for 1 hour or up to 3 days.

2. To prepare the filling, combine the apples in a large bowl with the raisins, sugar, flour, lemon zest, lemon juice, cinnamon, and nutmeg. Mix well. Set aside in a colander to drain off any excess liquid while you prepare the dough.

3. Remove one of the squares of dough from the refrigerator. On a lightly floured board or between sheets of waxed paper, roll out one square of dough at a time. Roll into a 9-inch square with a thickness of ⅛ inch. Cut the large square into nine 3-inch squares. Repeat with the second square of dough. When you are done you will have eighteen 3-inch squares.

4. Lightly grease two baking sheets and set aside.

5. Moisten the edges of a 3-inch square with a little water. Keeping in mind that the dough will be folded diagonally to form a triangle, spoon a rounded tablespoon of the drained apple mixture on half of the square to within ¼ inch of the edges. Fold the other half of the dough over the apple mixture and press the edges together with a fork to enclose the filling and seal them. Prick the top with a fork.

6. Carefully transfer the filled turnover to one of the prepared baking sheets. Form a crescent by pulling together the ends on the folded side of the turnover. Make more turnovers with the remaining dough and filling, shaping each one on the baking sheet. Place in the refrigerator and chill for 30 minutes.

7. Preheat the oven to 350°F.

8. Prepare an egg wash by mixing together the egg yolk and water. Brush the chilled turnovers with some of the egg wash. Bake for 15 minutes. Brush again with egg wash and continue to bake for 10 to 15 minutes more, until golden brown.

9. The turnovers are at their best when served at once. Store leftover turnovers in an airtight container in the refrigerator or freezer. Reheat them for 5 minutes in a 300°F oven before serving.

Baker's Tip

❋ The apples can be chopped in a food processor, but don't chop them too fine. You want chunks of apples, not applesauce.

Cornish Pasties

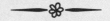

WHEN WELSH MINERS SETTLED in Michigan in the late 1700s and early 1800s, they brought with them handheld pies known as Cornish pasties. These pies contained a meat filling on one end and a sweet fruit filling on the other end — main course and dessert, all in one convenient package. It didn't take long for their neighbors to notice these turnovers and adapt them with their own fillings, most often made with apples.

Applesauce

Applesauce is a wonderful food to have on hand — perfect for a simple dessert, not to mention feeding babies or serving with savory dishes. Extra can be frozen or canned. The apples used can be any type at all, including the older apples in the back of the fruit drawer that just aren't going to be eaten out of hand anymore. If you make applesauce with peeled apples, it will be a lovely pale yellow, like the kind you buy at the store, and you can mash the apples by hand for a chunky texture. If you leave the apples with the skins on, the applesauce will be pink and must be run through a food mill to get rid of the skins. A food mill will also remove cores, pits, and stems, so you can leave those in as well. The recipe can be halved, doubled, tripled, even quadrupled.

Makes 5 cups

  4 pounds apples
  ¼ cup light-colored fruit juice, such as
        white grape, orange, pineapple,
        or mango (or use water)
     Sweetener, such as white or brown
        sugar, maple syrup, or honey

1. Peel, core, and quarter the apples or simply quarter the apples and put in a large pot. Add the fruit juice.

2. Cook over medium heat, stirring occasionally, until the apples are falling apart and very soft, about 45 minutes.

3. For chunky applesauce with peeled and cored apples, simply mash the apples with a potato masher until you have achieved the desired consistency. For a smooth applesauce made with unpeeled apples, run the apples and any liquid through a food mill, discarding the skins and pits.

4. Sample the applesauce. It may be sweet enough. If not, add the sweetener of your choice to taste. Serve warm or chilled.

Apricot Soufflé

Soufflé dishes have straight sides that facilitate the rising of the soufflé. You can make this one in a large dish or in individual soufflé cups or custard cups.

Serve 6 to 8

1½ cups coarsely chopped dried apricots (about 8 ounces)
⅓ cup granulated sugar, plus more as needed
1 teaspoon finely grated lemon zest
1 teaspoon fresh lemon juice
¼ teaspoon ground allspice
5 large egg whites, at room temperature
¼ teaspoon cream of tartar
⅛ teaspoon salt
Confectioners' sugar, to garnish

1. Lightly butter the inside of a 6- to 8-cup soufflé dish or six to eight custard cups. Sprinkle a little sugar over the butter to coat the dish. Turn upside down to shake out excess sugar. Set aside.

2. Put the apricots in a small saucepan and add just enough water to cover. Bring to a boil over medium-high heat. Cover, reduce the heat, and simmer until the apricots are tender and all the liquid is absorbed, about 15 minutes. Add the sugar, lemon zest, lemon juice, and allspice. Stir over the heat for 1 minute longer. Taste for sweetness and add more sugar if the mixture is too tart.

3. Transfer the apricot mixture to a blender or food processor and process until the apricots are finely chopped but not puréed. Transfer the apricot mixture to a bowl and let cool to room temperature.

4. Preheat the oven to 325°F with a rack in the lower third of the oven.

5. Beat the egg whites until foamy. Add the cream of tartar and salt and continue beating until the egg whites are stiff but not dry. Stir one-quarter of the egg whites into the apricot mixture, then gently fold in the rest. Spoon into prepared soufflé dish or custard cups. The mixture should almost reach the top of the dish(es).

6. Bake in the lower third of the oven, for 40 to 45 minutes in a soufflé dish or for 20 to 25 minutes in the custard cups, until the soufflé is golden brown and has risen above the dish.

7. Remove from the oven, dust with a sprinkling of sifted confectioners' sugar, and serve immediately.

Bananas Foster

Sometime in the 1950s, Bananas Foster was created for a Richard Foster, owner of the Foster Awning Company at Brennan's Restaurant in New Orleans. This was part of a "Breakfast at Brennan's" advertising campaign. The dish became so popular that it has been claimed by the city of New Orleans as a traditional dessert.

Serves 4

1 pint vanilla ice cream
4 firm ripe bananas
4 tablespoons butter
½ cup firmly packed brown sugar

2 tablespoons freshly squeezed orange juice
¾ cup dark or light rum (dark has more flavor)

1. Place a scoop of ice cream on each of four dessert plates. If you prefer, scoop the ice cream ahead of time and put the plates in the freezer. Keep frozen until 5 to 10 minutes before serving.

2. Peel the bananas. Cut them into halves lengthwise, then into halves again cutting crosswise.

3. To make the sauce, melt the butter over medium heat in a large skillet. Add the sugar and orange juice and cook, stirring, until the sauce is bubbly and smooth. Add the bananas and sauté for 3 to 5 minutes, basting the bananas with the sauce until they are nicely coated. Remove from the heat and keep warm.

4. Heat the rum in a small saucepan just until warm. Ignite with a match and pour the flaming liquor over the bananas. Rotate the pan back and forth until the flames subside. (If you have a fan over the stove, make sure it is off before you attempt to do this.)

5. Spoon the bananas and sauce over the ice cream and serve at once.

Berry Fool

So easy even a fool can make this? Or a variation on the French word *feuillet*, which means layer? This dessert is an easily prepared blending of fruit and whipped cream. Simple and sublime.

Serves 6

2 cups sliced fresh or frozen strawberries, whole raspberries, or gooseberries	1 cup whipping cream
¼ cup sugar	1 tablespoon Kirsch, fraise des bois, or cherry brandy
3 tablespoons water	⅓ cup toasted macaroon crumbs, to garnish
2 teaspoons fresh lemon juice	

1. Combine the berries, sugar, and water in a small saucepan. Bring to a boil, reduce the heat, and simmer for 4 to 5 minutes, until the juices become syrupy.

2. Pour the berries into a bowl, cover, and refrigerate for 2 hours, until the berries are very cold.

3. Purée the berries and the lemon juice in a food processor or blender. If you are using raspberries, press the berries through a sieve, collecting as much pulp and juice as possible and discarding the seeds.

4. Whip the cream until soft peaks form, then add the liqueur and beat until stiff. Fold the cream into the berry purée.

5. To serve, spoon the berry mixture into six dessert dishes or a 1-quart serving dish. Sprinkle with the macaroon crumbs. Serve immediately or cover with plastic and refrigerate for several hours.

Baker's Tip

❋ If you are using frozen sweetened fruit, thaw, and reserve the juice. Heat the juice to boiling and cook until the syrup is reduced to 3 tablespoons. Use the reduced juice in place of the water and eliminate the sugar.

Berry Cobbler

The term "cobbler" is probably derived from an old Middle English word that means "to lump together." It also means, according to Webster, "to make or do clumsily or unhandily." Well, this lumped-together dish of biscuit and fruit tastes lovely no matter what its name and despite its homely appearance. The rough, uneven surface of the biscuit topping is also similar in appearance to cobblestones.

Serves 6

BERRY FILLING

- 6 cups fresh blackberries, boysenberries, raspberries, blueberries, or a combination of berries
- ½ cup sugar, or to taste
- 3 tablespoons unbleached all-purpose flour
- 2 teaspoons finely grated orange zest
- 1 tablespoon freshly squeezed orange juice
- 2 tablespoons butter, cut into small pieces

BISCUIT DOUGH TOPPING

- 1 cup unbleached all-purpose flour
- 3 tablespoons sugar
- 1½ teaspoons baking powder
- ¼ teaspoon salt
- 3 tablespoons butter, chilled and cut into small pieces, plus 1 tablespoon
- 1 tablespoon vegetable shortening
- ¼–⅛ cup milk or half-and-half
  Cream, to serve

1. To make the berry filling, stem and gently rinse the berries. Drain on paper towels. Transfer to an 8-inch square baking dish or 1½-quart casserole.

2. Combine the sugar, flour, orange zest, and orange juice in a small bowl. Toss with the berries, mixing gently until they are thoroughly coated. If the berries are particularly tart, add more sugar to taste. Dot with butter.

3. Set aside the filling for 30 minutes or refrigerate for several hours. Bring to room temperature before baking.

4. Preheat the oven to 400°F.

5. To make the biscuit dough, sift the flour, 2 tablespoons of the sugar, the baking powder, and salt into a bowl or food processor. Cut the 3 tablespoons butter and the shortening into the flour mixture until it has the consistency of coarse crumbs. Add ¼ cup of the milk all at once and stir with a fork or pulse the machine briefly just until the dough comes together, adding more milk if necessary.

6. Turn out the dough onto a lightly floured work surface. Knead lightly 12 to 15 times, sprinkling with a little flour if the dough is sticky. (Biscuit dough can be refrigerated for up to 2 hours before baking.)

7. Press out the dough gently into a shape that will be large enough to cover the berries. Transfer the dough carefully to the baking dish, crimping the edges around the dish.

8. Melt the 1 tablespoon butter. Brush the top of the dough with the melted butter. Sprinkle with the remaining 1 tablespoon sugar. With the tip of a sharp knife, cut three or four vents in the top of the dough to allow steam to escape.

9. Bake for 35 to 40 minutes, until the biscuit topping is golden.

10. Serve warm with a spoonful of cream topping each serving.

Blueberry Grunt

One can easily imagine how this recipe came about. On a hot August day in Maine, a cook, planning to make a blueberry shortcake, decided it was just too hot to fire up the woodstove oven for the shortcake biscuits. Instead, she put the blueberries in a pot with some sugar and water and steamed the biscuit dough like dumplings, hoping for the best.

You may also hope for the best when you see the gluey-looking biscuits. But this dessert is an absolute favorite. Serve it up in the kitchen in dessert bowls and cover with a slosh of unsweetened cream. The flavor, the contrast of textures — it's divine.

Serves 6

- 6 *cups fresh or unsweetened frozen blueberries*
- 1½ *cups sugar*
- 1 *cup water*
- ½ *teaspoon ground cinnamon*
- 1¾ *cups unbleached all-purpose flour*
- 1 *tablespoon baking powder*
- ½ *teaspoon salt*
- 6 *tablespoons butter, chilled and cut into small pieces*
- *Approximately ¾ cup milk*
- *Cream, to serve*

1. In a 9- or 10-inch nonreactive skillet, combine the berries, sugar, water, and cinnamon. Bring to a boil, reduce the heat, and simmer for 10 minutes. Remove from the heat while you prepare the biscuit dough.

2. Sift the flour, baking powder, and salt into a medium bowl or food processor. Cut in the butter until the mixture resembles coarse crumbs. Add the milk and mix just enough to combine. The dough will be lumpy.

3. Drop the dough by the spoonful over the berries.

4. Cover tightly and steam for 15 to 20 minutes, keeping the heat just high enough to allow the berries to bubble.

5. Serve warm in bowls, with a little cream poured over each serving.

Many Berry Crisp

If you were raised in England, you might call this a crunch. But in America, our crunchy crumb-topped fruit desserts are crisps. This dessert is perfect with any type of berry or any combination of berries.

Serves 6 to 9

FRUIT

6 cups assorted fresh berries
   (blueberries, blackberries,
   strawberries, raspberries)
2–4 tablespoons granulated sugar
   Finely grated zest of 1 orange
   (about 1 tablespoon)
2 tablespoons fresh orange juice

TOPPING

½ cup unbleached all-purpose flour
⅓ cup firmly packed dark brown sugar
⅓ cup granulated sugar
½ cup crushed almond macaroons, vanilla
   wafers, or almond cookies
½ teaspoon ground cinnamon
¼ teaspoon freshly grated nutmeg
½ cup (1 stick) butter, at room temperature
½ cup slivered almonds
   Cream, whipped cream, crème fraîche,
   or vanilla ice cream, to serve

1. Preheat the oven to 350°F. Lightly grease a 9-inch square baking dish or a deep 9-inch pie pan.

2. Combine the berries in a large bowl with 2 tablespoons of the granulated sugar, orange zest, and orange juice. Toss gently to mix. Taste, then add more sugar if the berries are too tart. Transfer the berries to the baking dish, pressing down lightly on them to form an even layer.

3. To make the topping, combine the flour, brown sugar, granulated sugar, cookie crumbs, cinnamon, and nutmeg in the same bowl that held the berries. With your fingers, rub the butter into the crumb mixture until it resembles coarse meal. Mix in the almonds. Sprinkle the topping evenly over the berries, pressing it down and making sure the edges of the fruit are covered.

4. Bake for 50 to 60 minutes, until the topping is browned.

5. Serve warm or chilled with cream, whipped cream, or ice cream.

Summer Pudding

The fact that this dessert is a called a pudding speaks to its British origins. In England, any sort of dessert may be called a pudding — even ones that aren't smooth and creamy like our American puddings. Summer pudding is a "thrifty-housewife" sort of dish, made of berries, white bread, and cream. These ingredients were close at hand in rural England, where this dish was created. Red currants and raspberries were the fruit of choice. In the United States, a mix of blueberries, strawberries, and raspberries is ideal, though any fruits can be used. You will need a total of 3 pounds of fruit, and the dish must be prepared a day in advance to give the fruit juices time to soften, color, and flavor the bread.

Serves 6 to 8

1   (1-pound) loaf stale white bread, sliced
1   pound fresh or unsweetened frozen and thawed blueberries
1   pound fresh or unsweetened frozen and thawed strawberries, halved
1   pound fresh raspberries or a combination of raspberries, cherries, and pitted plums (do not use frozen raspberries)

½–1 cup sugar
¼   cup water
    Fresh raspberries, to garnish
    Fresh mint leaves, to garnish
    Whipped cream, to serve

1. Remove the crusts from the bread. Line a 6-cup bowl or soufflé dish with plastic wrap, allowing it to hang over the outside. Using as many slices as needed, completely line the bottom and sides of the dish with one layer of bread. You can cut a circular shape for the bottom and wedges for the sides. They should fit closely together without any gaps (like putting together a jigsaw puzzle). Reserve some of the slices for the top.

2. Wash and rinse the berries and remove stems. Combine the blueberries and strawberries in a large saucepan with ½ cup of the sugar and the water. Bring to a boil, then reduce the heat and simmer for 4 to 5 minutes, stirring occasionally until the sugar is dissolved and the juices begin to run. Taste and add as much of

the remaining ⅓ cup sugar as needed. Add the raspberries and cook over low heat for 2 minutes longer. Remove from the heat and cool slightly.

3. Using a slotted spoon, fill the bread-lined bowl with the fruit. Reserve the remaining cooking juices. Top the berries with the remaining bread slices so that the fruit is completely covered. Brush the bread with some of the reserved fruit juice and cover with plastic wrap. Put a plate that fits inside the bowl on top of the pudding and weight it down with a heavy can.

4. Let the pudding sit for at least 8 hours or overnight in the refrigerator.

5. To serve, remove the weights and plastic wrap. Unmold the pudding by turning it upside down onto a serving plate. Spoon the remaining fruit juices over the top and along the sides of the pudding. Garnish with a few raspberries and mint leaves. Cut into wedges and serve with a dollop of whipped cream.

Baker's Tip

❋ The white bread should be a firm type, not squishy Wonder Bread.

A table, a chair, a bowl of fruit and a violin;

what else does a man need to be happy?

— Albert Einstein,
American physicist (1879–1955)

Cherry Crunch

The cherries in this dish are sandwiched between two coarse-textured, brown sugar pastry layers. After baking, the cherries appear as bumps pressing up on the crust.

6 servings

- 2 cups drained and pitted canned cherries (reserve ½ cup cherry juice) or 2 cups thawed frozen cherries, drained (reserve juice and add enough grape or orange juice to make ½ cup)
- 1½ tablespoons quick-cooking tapioca
- 1 cup firmly packed light brown sugar
- 1 cup unbleached all-purpose flour
- ¼ teaspoon baking powder
- ¼ teaspoon baking soda
- ¼ teaspoon salt
- 1 cup rolled oats (not quick-cooking)
- ½ cup (1 stick) butter, at room temperature
- ½ cup chopped walnuts
- ¼ teaspoon almond extract
- Cream, whipped cream, or vanilla ice cream, to serve

1. Mix the cherry juice with the tapioca in a small bowl, stirring to combine. Set aside for 15 minutes.

2. Preheat the oven to 350°F. Lightly grease a 9-inch square baking dish.

3. Combine the brown sugar, flour, baking powder, baking soda, and salt in a medium bowl. Stir in the oats. With your fingertips, rub the butter into the flour mixture until it resembles coarse meal. Stir in the walnuts.

4. Press half of the crumb mixture into the bottom of the baking dish. Arrange the cherries over it. Add the almond extract to the tapioca mixture and spoon it over the cherries. Cover the fruit with the remaining crumb mixture.

5. Bake for 35 to 40 minutes, until the top is golden brown.

6. Serve warm or chilled with cream.

Cherry Clafouti

This dessert is a French country classic, the sort of dessert that a thrifty housewife near Limousin, France, would whip up with ingredients on hand when cherries were in season. The dish, once a regional favorite, became a national favorite and then crossed borders. Although cherries are traditional in a clafouti, almost any flavorful fruit can be substituted, including grapes, or sliced plums, apricots, nectarines, or peaches.

Serves 6 to 8

3 cups fresh dark sweet pitted cherries or pitted canned Bing cherries, drained
1¼ cups milk, at room temperature
½ cup sifted unbleached all-purpose flour

⅓ cup granulated sugar
3 large eggs, at room temperature
1 tablespoon Kirsch
⅛ teaspoon salt
Sifted confectioners' sugar, to dust

1. Preheat the oven to 375°F. Grease a 10-inch round baking dish or ovenproof skillet.

2. Cover the bottom of the baking dish with the cherries.

3. Combine the milk, flour, sugar, eggs, Kirsch, and salt in a blender. Blend for about 30 seconds. Scrape down the mixture on the inside of the blender and then blend for 30 seconds longer. Pour the batter over the cherries.

4. Bake for 45 to 50 minutes, until the clafouti is puffed and brown and a knife inserted near the center comes out clean. Serve hot or warm. Dust with the confectioners' sugar just before serving.

Peach Slump

Many of our heritage fruit dessert recipes are variations on a single theme — fruit and biscuit dough — and this slump is no exception. Here, peaches are baked under a biscuit topping, but then the dessert is inverted onto a serving plate so the fruit can "slump" into the pastry. You can further the slumping process by whacking the fruit with a spoon, as some recipes recommend, but we prefer to skip that step. Serve this as soon as possible after you remove it from the oven. (After sitting around for a couple of hours, the biscuit dough becomes pasty.) Nectarines or apples can be substituted for the peaches.

Serves 4 to 6

8 cups thinly sliced peeled peaches (about 8 medium peaches)	2 teaspoons baking powder
2 tablespoons light brown sugar	6 tablespoons butter, chilled and cut into small pieces
½ teaspoon almond extract	½ cup milk
½ teaspoon ground cinnamon	¼ cup buttermilk or plain yogurt
1½ cups unbleached all-purpose flour	1 egg, well beaten
2 tablespoons granulated sugar	

1. Preheat the oven to 400°F. Lightly grease a 1½-quart baking dish.

2. Toss together the peaches, brown sugar, almond extract, and cinnamon in a medium bowl. Spread in the bottom of the baking dish.

3. Sift the flour, granulated sugar, and baking powder into a medium bowl or food processor. Cut in the butter with two knives or by pulsating the food processor until the mixture has the consistency of coarse crumbs. Combine the milk, buttermilk, and egg. Add to the flour mixture and mix briefly. Do not knead; the dough will be sticky, stiff, and lumpy.

4. Drop the dough by the spoonful over the peaches. Try to get even coverage, but don't worry about a few bare spots.

5. Bake for about 25 minutes, until the top is golden and the juices are bubbling.

6. Cool on a wire rack for about 5 minutes. Loosen the biscuit from the sides of the pan with a spatula and invert onto a serving platter. Serve warm.

Peach Crumble

A crumble is nothing more than a crisp with a British accent. For the best texture, crush the cookies in the topping so that the cookies are crumbled, not ground.

Serves 4 to 6

FILLING

- 6–7 fresh ripe peaches, peeled and sliced ½ inch thick (about 6 cups)
- 2 tablespoons granulated sugar
- 1 tablespoon cornstarch
- 1 tablespoon fresh lemon juice
- ¼ teaspoon freshly grated nutmeg

TOPPING

- ½ cup unbleached all-purpose flour
- ⅓ cup firmly packed light brown sugar
- ½ cup crushed almond macaroons, vanilla wafers, or almond cookies
- ⅓ cup finely chopped almonds
- ⅛ teaspoon ground ginger
- 6 tablespoons butter, at room temperature
- ⅓ cup sliced almonds, to garnish

1. Preheat the oven to 375°F. Lightly grease a 1½-quart casserole.

2. To make the peach filling, put the peaches into the prepared baking dish. Add the granulated sugar, cornstarch, lemon juice, and nutmeg. Toss to mix, and arrange the peaches so the filling is level. Place the baking dish on a baking sheet. Set aside.

3. To prepare the topping, combine the flour, brown sugar, crushed cookies, chopped almonds, and ginger in a medium bowl. With your fingers, rub the butter into the crumb mixture until it resembles coarse meal.

4. Sprinkle the topping over the peaches, making sure the edges of the peaches are covered. Sprinkle the sliced almonds over the top.

5. Bake for 35 to 40 minutes, until the peaches are tender and bubbling and the topping is golden brown.

6. Serve warm or at room temperature.

Peach Cobbler

Poets from China (where wild peach trees still grow) and throughout the Western world have celebrated the peach. T. S. Elliot wrote, "I grow old . . . I grow old / I shall wear the bottoms of my trousers rolled. / Shall I part my hair behind? Do I dare to eat a peach? / I shall wear white flannel trousers, and walk upon the beach. / I have heard the mermaids singing, each to each." Here's a humble dessert worth singing about.

Serves 6

PEACH FILLING

6–7 ripe yellow peaches, peeled and sliced ⅓ inch thick (about 6 cups)	2 tablespoons fresh orange juice
6 tablespoons sugar, or to taste	1 tablespoon fresh lemon juice
2 tablespoons cornstarch	2 tablespoons butter, chilled and diced
½ teaspoon freshly grated nutmeg	

BISCUIT DOUGH TOPPING

1 cup unbleached all-purpose flour	4 tablespoons butter, chilled and diced
3 tablespoons sugar	5–6 tablespoons milk or cream
1 tablespoon finely grated orange zest	
1 teaspoon baking powder	
¼ teaspoon salt	

SUGAR TOPPING

1 tablespoon milk or cream
1 tablespoon sugar

1. Grease an 8-inch square baking dish or 1½ quart casserole.

2. To make the peach filling, put the peaches in the prepared baking dish. Combine the sugar, cornstarch, and nutmeg in a small bowl and mix well. Sprinkle over the peaches. Drizzle in the orange juice and lemon juice. Toss the peaches, mixing gently until they are thoroughly coated. If the peaches are particularly tart, add more sugar to taste. Dot with butter.

3. Set the filling aside for 30 minutes or refrigerate for several hours. Bring to room temperature before baking.

4. Preheat the oven to 400°F.

5. To make the topping, combine the flour, sugar, orange zest, baking powder, and salt in a food processor. Pulse briefly to mix. Add the butter and process until the mixture has the consistency of coarse crumbs. (Alternatively, you can mix the ingredients in the bowl and cut in the butter with two knives or a pastry blender.) Add 5 tablespoons of the milk or cream, all at once, and pulse the machine briefly just until the dough comes together, adding more milk if necessary. (If mixing by hand, stir in with a fork.)

6. Turn out the dough onto a lightly floured surface. Knead lightly 12 to 15 times, sprinkling with a little flour if the dough is sticky. (Biscuit dough can be refrigerated for up to 2 hours before baking.) Press or roll out the dough gently into a shape that will be large enough to cover the peaches. Transfer the dough carefully to the baking dish, crimping the edges around the dish.

7. To prepare the sugar topping, brush the top of the dough with milk and then sprinkle with sugar. With the tip of a sharp knife, cut three or four vents in the top of the dough to allow steam to escape.

8. Bake for 35 to 40 minutes, until the biscuit topping is golden.

9. Serve warm with a dish of vanilla ice cream.

Peach History

THE PEACH has made a very successful journey from China to the New World. Actually, it went from China to Persia to Rome and then spread throughout Europe. The fruit bore the name Persian apple, which in Middle English became *peche*. The Spanish brought the peach to the New World in the seventeenth century.

Pears Poached in Red Wine

Ralph Waldo Emerson was exaggerating when he said, "There are only ten minutes in the life of a pear when it is perfect to eat," but not by much. For best results with this recipe, select a pear that is just barely ripe. You can select any variety you like, but you may have to adjust the timing, which is based on using a Bartlett pear.

Serves 4 to 6

POACHING LIQUID

- 3 cups red wine, such as Merlot, Zinfandel, or Burgundy
- 1 cup water
- 1 cup freshly squeezed orange juice
- 1 cup sugar
- 2 tablespoons grated lemon zest
- 2 tablespoons fresh lemon juice
- 2 cinnamon sticks
- ¼ teaspoon ground allspice
- 2 tablespoons pear liqueur or brandy

FRUIT AND GARNISH

- 5–6 medium-size firm ripe pears
- 20–24 fresh pitted cherries or 1 (16-ounce can) pitted Bing cherries
  Sprigs of fresh mint, to garnish
  Brandy Vanilla Sauce (page 277) (optional)

1. To prepare the poaching liquid, combine the red wine, water, orange juice, sugar, lemon zest, lemon juice, cinnamon sticks, and allspice in a large skillet or Dutch oven. Bring to a boil, stirring occasionally until the sugar dissolves.

2. To prepare the fruit, peel and cut the pears in half lengthwise. Using a spoon or melon baller, remove the cores and cut out the stems. When the poaching liquid comes to a boil, place the pears, cut-side down, in the liquid. Reduce the heat, cover the pan, and simmer for 8 to 10 minutes, until a pear shows light resistance when pierced with a sharp knife or skewer.

3. Turn the pears over and add half of the cherries, reserving the other half for a garnish. Bring to a boil, then reduce the heat and simmer, basting occasionally, until the pears are just tender when pierced, about 5 minutes. The exact time depends on the variety of pear and the ripeness of the individual fruits; do not overcook.

Lift the pears and cherries out of the liquid with a slotted spoon and transfer to a bowl to cool.

4. Bring the poaching liquid to a boil over medium-high heat and cook until the liquid is reduced by half and becomes slightly syrupy. Remove the pan from the heat and discard the cinnamon sticks. Stir in the pear liqueur.

5. To serve, place the pears in individual serving dishes or in a bowl, with some of the syrup poured over them. Garnish with the reserved cherries and a sprig of mint. Accompany with Brandy Vanilla Sauce (if using).

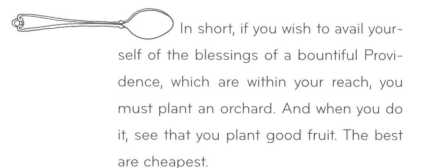

In short, if you wish to avail yourself of the blessings of a bountiful Providence, which are within your reach, you must plant an orchard. And when you do it, see that you plant good fruit. The best are cheapest.

— Jennie Harlan, *McCall's Home Cook Book and General Guide*, 1890

Prune Whip

Honey beaten into whipping cream is the secret to this old-fashioned fruit dessert. Honey is hygroscopic, meaning it readily absorbs moisture. By adding honey to the whipped cream, you keep it from weeping, enabling it to sit in the refrigerator for a few hours without becoming runny. Indeed, whenever you want to hold whipped cream for a few hours — say, on top of a cream pie — sweeten the cream with honey to stabilize it.

Serves 4 to 6

1½ cups coarsely chopped, pitted dried prunes	⅓ cup sugar
1½ cups water	1 cup whipping cream
2 teaspoons freshly grated lemon zest	1 teaspoon honey
2 tablespoons fresh lemon juice	⅓ cup finely chopped toasted almonds, to garnish

1. Combine the prunes, water, lemon zest, lemon juice, and sugar in a small saucepan. Bring to a boil, then cover and simmer for 10 to 15 minutes, until prunes are soft and almost all of the liquid is absorbed. Let cool.

2. Finely chop the prunes by hand or in a food processor. Transfer to a medium bowl.

3. In another bowl, beat the cream until soft peaks form. Add the honey and beat until stiff. Stir a few tablespoons of whipped cream into the prunes and then gradually fold in the remainder, gently mixing until combined.

4. Spoon the prune whip into four to six custard cups or sherbet dishes. Sprinkle the tops with chopped almonds. Cover with plastic wrap and refrigerate for 2 to 3 hours, until slightly set and chilled.

Variation

Apricot Whip. Substitute 1½ cups chopped dried apricots for the prunes and make the recipe as instructed above.

Rhubarb Compote

In some areas of the country, rhubarb is ready for harvest a full month before the local strawberries are ripe. But why wait? Rhubarb is delicious on its own, especially when made with brown sugar (the "secret" ingredient). Serve this compote warm or cold over vanilla ice cream for a wonderful spring treat. The recipe is easily doubled and extra can be frozen for up to 6 months.

Serves 4

3½ cups fresh rhubarb, cut into
    ½-inch pieces (about 1 pound)
1 cup firmly packed brown sugar
2 tablespoons water
    Pinch of freshly grated nutmeg

1. Combine the rhubarb, brown sugar, water, and nutmeg in a heavy saucepan. Stir over medium heat until the sugar dissolves. Reduce the heat to medium-low, cover, and simmer until the rhubarb is tender, stirring occasionally, about 15 minutes.

2. Transfer the rhubarb mixture to a bowl. Cover and chill until cold, about 2 hours. The compote can be made 1 or 2 days before using. Keep refrigerated.

Rhubarb Rolypoly

Here is an old-fashioned dessert that wraps rhubarb in a tender biscuit dough and bakes it in a sweet, spicy syrup. It is best served warm with a dollop of cream. It makes a fine dish for brunch or dessert. Thinly sliced apples are often used instead of rhubarb.

Serves 12

SYRUP

1½ cups sugar
1½ cups water

1½ teaspoons ground cinnamon
⅛ grated teaspoon nutmeg

FILLING

2 pounds fresh rhubarb or 6 cups thawed frozen unsweetened rhubarb

¼ cup sugar
1 teaspoon finely grated orange zest

BISCUIT DOUGH

2 cups unbleached all-purpose flour
¼ cup sugar
2 teaspoons baking powder
2 teaspoons finely grated orange zest
½ teaspoon salt

6 tablespoons butter, chilled and cut into small pieces
1 large egg
Milk
1 tablespoon butter, melted

1. Preheat the oven to 400°F. Grease a 9- by 13-inch baking dish.

2. To make the syrup, combine the sugar, water, cinnamon, and nutmeg in a heavy saucepan. Bring to a boil. Reduce the heat and simmer for 5 minutes. Measure out ½ cup of the syrup and set it aside. Pour the rest of the syrup into the prepared baking dish.

3. To make the filling, with a swivel-bladed peeler or paring knife, remove any fibrous strings from the rhubarb stems. Dice the rhubarb into ¼-inch pieces. Toss with the sugar and orange zest. Set aside.

4. To make the biscuit dough, combine the flour, sugar, baking powder, orange zest, and salt in a bowl or a food processor. Mix well or process briefly to mix. Cut in the butter with two knives or by pulsing the food processor, until the mixture resembles coarse crumbs. Break the egg into a measuring cup and beat slightly. Add enough milk to make ⅔ cup. Add it to the flour mixture and stir with a fork or process until the dough comes together as a ball. Refrigerate the dough for 10 minutes to make it easier to handle.

5. Turn out the dough onto a lightly floured board and knead lightly 10 to 12 times. Roll out the dough to form a 9- by 12-inch rectangle. Brush the dough with the melted butter. Thoroughly drain the rhubarb (you should have about 5 cups left). Spread the rhubarb over the dough, leaving 1 inch of bare dough all the way around the edges. Roll up the dough, as for a jelly roll, starting with the long edge. Pinch the edges of the roll to seal.

6. Cut into 12 slices and place the slices in the syrup, cut-side down.

7. Bake for 35 minutes. Drizzle with the reserved syrup and bake for 10 minutes longer.

8. Serve warm.

Raspberry Buckle

In buckles, the fruit is covered by a cake layer, which has a tendency to buckle and crack as it bakes. No problem: The crumb topping hides all while the cake layer becomes permeated with the flavor of raspberries. This is a casual sort of dessert, good to serve at brunch or whenever you might serve a coffee cake.

Serves 10 to 12

BERRIES

6 cups fresh or frozen unsweetened raspberries

½ cup granulated sugar
1 tablespoon fresh lemon juice

CAKE

2½ cups sifted unbleached all-purpose flour
1½ teaspoons baking powder
½ teaspoon baking soda
¼ teaspoon freshly grated nutmeg
¼ teaspoon salt
10 tablespoons (1¼ sticks) butter, at room temperature

1⅓ cups granulated sugar
3 large eggs
1 cup buttermilk or ½ cup plain yogurt and ½ cup milk, at room temperature
1 teaspoon almond extract

TOPPING

⅓ cup unbleached all-purpose flour
⅓ cup firmly packed brown sugar
½ teaspoon ground cinnamon

4 tablespoons butter, at room temperature
¾ cup sliced almonds

1. Preheat the oven to 350°F. Grease a 9-inch by 13-inch baking dish.

2. To prepare the berries, combine them with the sugar and lemon juice in a saucepan. Heat over low heat until the sugar dissolves. Spoon into the prepared baking dish.

3. To make the cake, sift together the flour, baking powder, baking soda, nutmeg, and salt. Sift two more times, set aside.

4. Cream the butter and sugar with an electric mixer in a large bowl until light and fluffy. Add the eggs, one at a time, beating well after each addition. Add one-third of the buttermilk alternately with one-third of the flour mixture, beating well after each addition. Continue adding the buttermilk and flour in thirds until the batter is smooth. Stir in the almond extract. Pour the batter over the raspberries.

5. Bake for 25 to 30 minutes, until the center of the cake is set but still soft.

6. While the cake bakes, make the topping by combining the flour, brown sugar, and cinnamon. With your fingers, rub the butter into the crumb mixture until it resembles coarse meal. Toss in the almonds. Sprinkle the mixture on top of the partially baked cake.

7. Continue baking for 15 to 20 minutes, until a tester inserted into the cake layer comes out clean.

8. Serve warm or cool, directly out of the pan.

Raspberry Trifle

Did this taste any better when it was known as Tipsy Parson? This English dessert is a favorite no matter where it's served, no matter what it's called.

Serves 16

CUSTARD

4 large egg yolks	2½ cups hot (not boiling) milk
¼ cup granulated sugar	2 tablespoons brandy
2 tablespoons cornstarch	1 cup whipping cream
Pinch of salt	

CAKE AND FRUIT

1 pound cake or sponge cake, homemade (pages 161 and 118) or purchased	2 (10-ounce) packages frozen, thawed raspberries, drained, or 2 cups fresh raspberries, sweetened with sugar to taste and drained
½ cup raspberry jam	
½–⅔ cup cream sherry	

GARNISH

1 cup whipping cream	¼ teaspoon almond extract
2 tablespoons sifted confectioners' sugar	½ cup toasted slivered almonds
	¼ cup fresh raspberries

1. To make the custard, in the top part of a double boiler, beat the egg yolks with a wire whisk until thick and lemon-colored. Mix in the sugar, cornstarch, and salt. Place over simmering water. Gradually add the hot milk and cook, stirring constantly, until the mixture thickens and coats a metal spoon.

2. Remove the custard from the heat. Stir in 1 tablespoon of the brandy. Cover the surface of the custard with plastic wrap and set the bowl in a pan of ice water, stirring occasionally, until the custard mounds on a spoon and begins to thicken.

3. Whip the cream until stiff. Stir in the remaining 1 tablespoon of brandy and then fold into the cold custard.

4. To assemble the trifle, cut the cake into ¼-inch slices (18 to 20 slices). Spread a layer of jam on half the cake slices and then sandwich the slices together. Using a pastry brush, soak both sides of the cake sandwiches with the sherry and then cut them into four equal pieces. Arrange half of the cake sandwiches over the bottom and partway up the sides of a large glass trifle bowl or other clear glass bowl. Spoon half of the berries into the bowl. Spread half of the custard over the berries. Repeat the layers with the remaining cake pieces, berries, and custard.

5. Cover the trifle with plastic wrap and refrigerate for several hours or for up to 2 days.

6. Before serving, whip the cream for the garnish until soft peaks form. Add the confectioners' sugar and almond extract and beat until stiff. Pipe the whipped cream on top of the trifle. Sprinkle the toasted almonds over the top and garnish with the fresh raspberries. Serve in dessert dishes.

Strawberries Marinated in Balsamic Vinegar with Fresh Basil

This is a wonderful way to serve fresh, local strawberries. The combination of flavors has to be experienced to be described. You could serve these berries instead of the expected sugar-and-strawberry mixture over biscuits or pound cake. Or you could top it with Greek-style yogurt drizzled with honey. But served plain in wine goblets, these strawberries make an elegant, light ending to any summer meal.

Serves 4 to 6

1 quart fresh strawberries
3 tablespoons balsamic vinegar
3 tablespoons water
3 tablespoons firmly packed dark
   brown sugar
⅓ cup slivered fresh basil leaves

1. Rinse and drain the strawberries. Remove the hulls and cut the berries in half. Put into a bowl and refrigerate until 1 to 2 hours before serving.

2. Combine the vinegar, water, and brown sugar in a small bowl or jar with a lid. Shake or mix well and then taste with a strawberry. If it's too sweet or too tart, add vinegar or sugar to taste. Pour over the strawberries, add half of the basil, and mix gently. Refrigerate for 1 to 2 hours.

3. Spoon into wine glasses and garnish with the remaining basil.

Strawberries Romanoff

Plenty of people claim to have invented this dish, including a Hollywood restaurateur who called himself Prince Michael Romanoff (but was no prince, by all accounts). Most likely Antonin Carême, when he was chef to Czar Alexander I, invented the dish around 1820. Romanoff was the house name of the Russian rulers, and this dish is fit for royalty — but simple enough for anyone to make.

Serves 6

5 cups fresh strawberries, hulled
6 tablespoons superfine sugar, plus more as needed
2 tablespoons plus 2 teaspoons orange liqueur
2 tablespoons vodka
2 teaspoons finely grated orange zest
1 cup whipping cream
¼ cup confectioners' sugar
1 pint vanilla ice cream, softened to room temperature
6 sprigs mint leaves, to garnish

1. Slice 4 cups of the strawberries. Combine the sliced strawberries, 5 tablespoons of the superfine sugar, the 2 tablespoons orange liqueur, and the vodka and orange zest. Toss together lightly. Cover and refrigerate for 2 hours to allow the flavors to blend. Taste the strawberries for sweetness and add another tablespoon of superfine sugar if needed.

2. Finely chop the remaining 1 cup strawberries. Toss with the remaining 1 tablespoon superfine sugar. Set aside.

3. Beat the cream until soft peaks form. Add the confectioners' sugar and the 2 teaspoons orange liqueur. Beat just until stiff. Fold in the softened ice cream and the chopped strawberries.

4. Set aside 1 cup of the sliced strawberries for a garnish. Divide the remaining sliced strawberries among six dessert dishes or glasses. Cover the strawberry layer with the whipped cream mixture. Freeze for 30 minutes.

5. To serve, spoon the reserved sliced strawberries over the top of each serving. Garnish with the mint and serve immediately.

Strawberry Shortcake

There was a time, not so long ago, when strawberry season marked the beginning of summer, when fresh strawberries could be had for the briefest of seasons, and the idea of strawberries in February was unthinkable. The Cello-packed berries shipped from who-knows-where are as tasteless as last summer's dried flowers. Strawberry shortcake, that quintessential summer dessert, can be enjoyed only when berries are fresh and local. And if there are pink stains on your hands from picking the strawberries yourself and the berries are still warm from the sun, so much the better.

Serves 6

STRAWBERRIES

- 6 cups fresh strawberries
- 3 tablespoons granulated sugar, or to taste
- 1 tablespoon framboise or crème de cassis

SHORTCAKE BISCUITS

- 2 cups unbleached all-purpose flour
- 3 tablespoons granulated sugar
- 1 tablespoon baking powder
- ½ teaspoon salt
- ½ cup (1 stick) butter, chilled and cut into small pieces, or 4 tablespoons butter and 4 tablespoons vegetable shortening
- ⅔ cup milk or half-and-half
- 1–2 tablespoons butter, at room temperature

TOPPING

- 1 cup whipping cream
- 2 tablespoons sifted confectioners' sugar
- ⅛ teaspoon freshly grated nutmeg

1. Set aside six strawberries for a garnish. Slice the remaining berries, place them in a bowl, and sprinkle them with 3 tablespoons of sugar and the strawberry liqueur. Toss until thoroughly combined. Cover and refrigerate for several hours, stirring occasionally.

2. To make the biscuits, preheat the oven to 425°F. Lightly grease a baking sheet.

3. Sift together the flour, granulated sugar, baking powder, and salt. Process or cut or rub the butter into the flour mixture in a food processor, with a pastry blender, or with your fingertips until it has the consistency of coarse crumbs. Add the milk all at once. Process or stir with a fork just until the dough comes together.

4. Turn out the dough onto a lightly floured work surface. Knead lightly 12 to 15 times, sprinkling with a little flour if the dough is sticky. Roll out or pat the dough into a rectangle ½ inch thick. Cut into six rounds with a floured 3-inch biscuit cutter or use a knife to cut into squares. Place the biscuits close together on the baking sheet. (The biscuits can be refrigerated for up to 2 hours before baking.)

5. Bake for 15 to 18 minutes, until the biscuits are golden.

6. Cool the biscuits briefly on the baking sheet before transferring them to a wire rack until cool enough to handle.

7. Split each biscuit in half. Coat the bottom layers with a little soft butter and transfer to individual serving plates.

8. To make the topping, whip the cream until stiff, gradually adding the confectioners' sugar and nutmeg as you beat.

9. To assemble the dessert, spoon some of the berries over each buttered biscuit half. Cover the berries with some of the whipped cream. Gently press on the top biscuit half. Spoon the remaining strawberries over the top biscuit half. Finish with another spoonful of whipped cream. Garnish each with a whole strawberry.

Charlotte Russe with Strawberry Sauce

In the early 1800s, the famous French chef Carême adapted the apple charlotte, an apple dessert dish, and gave it the name charlotte russe, perhaps in honor of Czar Alexander I. New Yorkers who grew up in the '20s and '30s remember charlotte russe as a special treat that came in individual servings in a special cardboard carton with a hole in the bottom, so you could push the dessert up (like push-up ice cream). On the top was a bit of custard, a lot of whipped cream, and a maraschino cherry, and it was said to be heavenly — like this dessert.

Serves 6 to 8

1 (7-ounce) package ladyfingers (you will not need the entire package)

1–2 tablespoons orange liqueur (Triple Sec, Cointreau, or Grand Marnier)

CREAM FILLING

3 tablespoons water
1 (¼-ounce) envelope or 1 tablespoon unflavored gelatin
1 cup milk
4 large egg yolks
⅓ cup granulated sugar
Finely grated zest of 1 orange

2 tablespoons freshly squeezed orange juice
1 tablespoon orange liqueur (Triple Sec, Cointreau, or Grand Marnier)
½ cup vanilla ice cream
¾ cup whipping cream, chilled

STRAWBERRY SAUCE

1 (16-ounce) package frozen sweetened or unsweetened strawberries
Superfine sugar (optional)

2 tablespoons orange liqueur (Triple Sec, Cointreau, or Grand Marnier)
1 pint fresh strawberries, for garnish

1. Open the ladyfingers and brush the flat insides lightly with orange liqueur. Line the bottom and sides of a charlotte mold, or a 6-cup bowl, with ladyfingers. Arrange them standing up, side by side, around the inside of the mold, with the curved sides facing out. Some may need to be cut to fit in. If there are any open spaces between them, fill with small pieces of ladyfingers.

2. To make the cream filling, pour the water into a small bowl and sprinkle with gelatin. Stir together and set aside to soften.

3. Warm the milk in a small saucepan over low to medium heat, until bubbles begin to appear around the edge of the pan. The milk should be hot but not boiling.

4. Beat the egg yolks in a medium bowl until smooth. Continue to beat, gradually adding the granulated sugar, until the mixture is thick and lemon-colored. Very slowly pour the hot milk into the eggs while continuing to stir. Pour the mixture into the remaining milk in the saucepan and cook over low to medium heat, stirring constantly for 6 to 7 minutes, until the mixture thickens and coats the back of a metal spoon. Do not let it boil or it will curdle.

5. Remove the saucepan from heat. Add the softened gelatin mixture, stirring until it has dissolved. Pour the custard mixture through a sieve into a large bowl. Stir in the orange zest, juice, and liqueur. Stir in the ice cream, mixing until it has softened.

6. Beat the whipping cream in a medium bowl until soft peaks form. Set aside.

7. Place the bowl of custard into a larger bowl, filled halfway with ice and water. Watch carefully and stir until the mixture mounds slightly when dropped from a spoon. It should be cold but not set. This will only take a few minutes. Fold in the whipped cream.

8. Immediately spoon the custard into the ladyfinger-lined mold. Smooth the top, cover with plastic wrap, and refrigerate for 4 to 5 hours.

9. To prepare the strawberry sauce, process the strawberries in a blender or food processor until puréed. If the berries are unsweetened, add superfine sugar to taste. Stir in the orange liqueur.

10. To serve, invert a large serving plate on top of the mold and, holding the plate and mold firmly together, turn them over. Gently tap the mold around the top and sides and remove the mold. Spoon a little of the sauce over the top of the dessert and arrange fresh berries around the bottom. Serve with the remaining sauce.

Crepes with Strawberry Sauce

If you master the art of making crepes, you will always have a fallback dessert, easy to make with common ingredients. The filling in this recipe is a sauce made with fresh strawberries, but feel free to substitute any other fruit. Or spread the crepes with Nutella or a chocolate ganache. The crepes can be made in advance, layered between sheets of waxed paper, and refrigerated overnight or frozen for up to a month. If you've never made crepes before, consider making a double batch of batter, to have extra for throwing away any crepes that don't come out right. The most common mistake is making them too thick.

Serves 4 to 8

½ cup unbleached all-purpose flour	½ teaspoon salt
½ cup milk	Strawberry Sauce (page 386)
¼ cup lukewarm water	Whipped cream, to serve
2 large eggs	Mint sprigs or chocolate syrup,
2 tablespoons butter, melted	to garnish

1. To prepare the crepe batter, combine the flour, milk, water, eggs, butter, and salt in a blender and process until smooth. Set aside at room temperature for 30 minutes or refrigerate for up to 2 days.

2. To make the crepes, melt a little butter (about ½ teaspoon) in a nonstick or well-seasoned crepe pan over medium heat. Swirl the pan to distribute the butter. When the butter foams, stir the batter and ladle in about 2 tablespoons, lifting the pan off the heat and swirling the pan until the batter forms a very thin, even layer. Place the pan over the heat and cook until the top is set and the bottom is browned, about 1½ minutes. Turn the crepe over using tongs, your fingers, or a spatula and cook until the second side is lightly browned, about 30 seconds. Transfer the crepe to a piece of waxed paper. Continue cooking crepes, adding a little butter and stirring the batter before starting each one. You should be able to make at least eight crepes from this batter.

3. Prepare the Strawberry Sauce and whip the cream.

4. To serve, spoon about ¼ cup of the strawberry sauce on each crepe and roll up. Place one or two crepes on each dessert plate, seam-side down. Top with a dollop of whipped cream. Garnish with a sprig of mint or a drizzle of chocolate syrup.

Chocolate-Dipped Nut and Cranberry Clusters

Sometimes the best dessert of all is a small nibble of a sweet served with coffee. You can't go wrong with chocolate. These candy clusters are also a lovely addition to a dessert table.

Makes about 28 pieces

½ cup pecan halves
½ cup hazelnuts
8 ounces dark or bittersweet
chocolate, coarsely chopped
½ cup dried cranberries

1. Preheat the oven to 325°F.

2. Arrange the pecans in a single layer on a baking sheet and toast for 8 to 10 minutes, until lightly colored and fragrant, stirring them once or twice. Test for doneness by breaking a nut. The inside should be light golden brown. Shake off any loose flakes of skin. Let cool, then coarsely chop, keeping the pieces fairly large.

3. Increase the oven temperature to 350°F. Spread out the hazelnuts on a baking sheet and toast for 8 to 10 minutes, until browned, stirring once or twice, until the nuts turn brown. Cool a few minutes, then rub the nuts back and forth with a dish towel to remove the skins. Shake off the loose skins. Then coarsely chop, keeping the pieces fairly large.

4. Line a baking sheet with waxed paper or parchment paper.

5. Melt the chocolate in the top of a double boiler set over barely simmering water. Stir until smooth. Stir in the pecans, hazelnuts, and cranberries. Immediately drop by level teaspoonfuls onto the prepared baking sheet. Refrigerate until the chocolate is set, about 30 minutes.

6. Put each cluster into a small, candy-size paper or foil cup. Store in a covered container. The clusters will keep in the refrigerator for up to 5 days.

Baklava

Between 1820 and 1920, about 360,000 Greek immigrants entered the country, bringing many new foods to America. Baklava, a treat found throughout the Middle East, is one of the most famous of all the Greek dishes brought in at this time. It is made by layering sheets of paper-thin filo dough with melted butter and nuts — walnuts, almonds, or pistachios, or some combination of the three — and then drenching the pastry with a luscious sweet syrup made of lemon and honey.

Makes about 36 pieces

FILLING

4 cups walnuts	1 cup blanched almonds, toasted
¼ cup sugar	1½ teaspoons ground cinnamon

SYRUP

¾ cup sugar	1 tablespoon fresh lemon juice
1½ cups water	2-inch-long stick cinnamon
1 tablespoon finely grated lemon zest	½ cup honey

PASTRY

1½ cups (3 sticks) butter
1 (1-pound) package filo dough, thawed overnight in the refrigerator, if frozen

1. To make the filling, combine half of the walnuts and 1 tablespoon of the sugar in a food processor. Process until finely chopped but not pasty. Remove from processor and repeat with remaining walnuts and another 1 tablespoon of the sugar. Finely chop the almonds in the same way. Combine the chopped walnuts and almonds and mix with the cinnamon in a medium bowl. Set aside.

2. To make the syrup, combine the sugar, water, lemon zest, lemon juice, and cinnamon stick in a heavy saucepan. Bring to a boil, stirring until the sugar dissolves,

then reduce the heat and simmer for 15 minutes. Add the honey and simmer for 2 minutes longer. Remove from the heat and let cool.

3. To clarify the butter, melt it over medium heat in a small saucepan. With a spoon, skim off and discard the bubbly foam that rises to the top. Let the butter settle for a few minutes, then spoon off the clear butter, avoiding the milky solids on the bottom.

4. Preheat the oven to 325°F. Grease a 9- by 13-inch baking pan with some of the clarified butter.

5. To assemble the baklava, unroll the filo dough on a large sheet of plastic wrap and lay it flat. Remove one sheet of filo. Cover the remaining sheets with plastic wrap and a damp towel to keep the dough from drying out. Brush half of the first sheet with clarified butter, then fold it in half crosswise. Place in the baking pan, folding it to fit the pan. Brush the top surface with the butter. Remove another sheet of filo and brush half of it with butter, as before. Fold in half and place it on top of the first and brush with the butter. Repeat until four sheets have been used, making eight layers.

6. Sprinkle the filo surface with one-quarter of the nut mixture. Drizzle over a little of the butter and 2 tablespoons of the syrup. Cover this with two more sheets of filo, brushing each with the butter and folding, making four layers. Sprinkle with one-quarter of the nuts, then drizzle with additional butter and 2 more table-spoons syrup. Repeat this two more times, finishing with a layer of nuts, butter, and syrup. (Do not use all of the syrup.) Top with four sheets of filo, brushed with the butter and folded (eight layers). Firmly press down on the filo. Trim the edges if necessary and brush the top with the remaining butter.

7. With a sharp knife, score the top of the dough in a diamond pattern. Score length-wise into four equal sections, then diagonally at 1½-inch intervals to form diamond shapes. To keep the top of the filo from curling, brush the top layer with a little water.

8. Bake for 50 to 60 minutes, until the pastry is puffed and golden brown.

9. Place on a rack to cool for 5 minutes. Cut the scored pieces all the way through. Spoon the remaining cool syrup over the hot pastry, a little bit at a time until the liquid has been absorbed. Let stand at room temperature for several hours before serving.

Puddings and Custards

Taste one spoonful of a homemade pudding and you'll never return to pudding mixes, which, it turns out, aren't that wonderful after all.

These thick, creamy desserts have a long and varied history. In the old days, a pudding was often steamed for hours inside a pudding mold or cloth-lined basin. Those puddings were heavy affairs not at all like the luxurious French mousse or Spain's creamy flan (also known as caramel custard), one of the most legendary and popular desserts the world over.

Ingredients

✪ **Cornstarch easily forms lumps.** Combining it with sugar before adding liquids reduces lumps. So does mixing it with a small amount of cold liquid to form a runny paste before you add the rest of the liquid.

✪ **To "temper eggs" before adding them to hot milk, slowly stir a few tablespoons of the hot milk into the beaten egg yolks, mixing constantly until blended.** When you have added about ¼ cup, slowly pour the yolk mixture back into the pan, stirring until combined. This gradual heating prevents curdling.

✪ **The fluffy texture of mousses is a result of using uncooked beaten egg whites.** Eating egg whites that are not completely cooked carries the risk of salmonella food poisoning. The risk is greatest for pregnant women, the elderly and very young, and people with an impaired immune system. If you are concerned about salmonella, use reconstituted powdered egg whites or pasteurized egg whites.

✪ **Use a scrupulously clean bowl and beaters to beat egg whites.** Wipe out the bowl and beaters with a cloth dipped in white vinegar to be sure every trace of fat is removed.

✪ **Adding a small amount of acid, such as cream of tartar, stabilizes egg whites and allows them to reach their full volume.** If you don't have cream of tartar, you can substitute lemon juice or vinegar (substitute 1 tablespoon of lemon juice or vinegar for every 1 teaspoon of cream of tartar.)

✪ **Substituting low-fat or skim milk for whole milk in a pudding recipe is acceptable but will result in a dessert that tastes less rich and creamy.**

Techniques

✪ **Stir constantly as you bring your cornstarch pudding to a boil.** Cook for as long as the recipe directs but no longer. Cornstarch mixtures will thin if overcooked.

✪ **Custards must be cooked at low temperatures to prevent the eggs from curdling and the milk from scorching.** Cook custards slowly on top of the stove in a double boiler or a heavy saucepan. Custards can also be cooked in a water bath in the oven.

✪ **Stir constantly as you cook the custard.**

✪ **To make a water bath for your custard, place a roasting pan in the oven.** Set the custard-filled baking dish in the roasting pan. Using a kettle with a spout, carefully pour hot water into the roasting pan until the water comes about halfway up the sides of the baking dish holding the custard.

✪ **A stirred custard is done when it is thick enough to coat the back of a spoon.** Run your finger across the custard on the spoon, and it should leave a definite track.

✪ **Avoid beating a custard mixture that is going to be baked, or the surface of the baked custard will appear pockmarked.**

✪ **To test a baked custard for doneness, insert a thin knife halfway between the edge of the custard and the center.** If the knife comes out clean, the custard is done. The center will set as the custard cools. If the center is set, the custard is overbaked and may "weep" as it cools.

✪ **All puddings, custards, and mousses should be covered and stored in the refrigerator until you are ready to serve them.**

Old-Fashioned Vanilla Cornstarch Pudding

This is the pudding that Americans have been led to believe should come out of a box. It is the original, creamy, easily made vanilla pudding minus the artificial ingredients. It may be a little shocking to see a vanilla pudding that is white, not yellow (no eggs), but one taste will convince you that this is a mighty fine pudding.

Serves 4 to 6

....

    ½ cup sugar
    ¼ cup cornstarch
    ¼ teaspoon salt
 2¾ cups whole milk or a combination
         of half-and-half and whole milk
    1 tablespoon vanilla extract

....

1. Combine the sugar, cornstarch, and salt in a heavy saucepan. Stir in ¼ cup of the milk to form a smooth, runny paste. Make sure you dissolve any lumps that form.

2. Whisk in the remaining 2½ cups milk, whisking until no lumps remain. Turn on the heat to medium and, stirring with a heatproof spatula or wooden spoon, cook until the mixture begins to thicken and just barely comes to a boil.

3. Remove from the heat and stir in the vanilla. Transfer to a bowl or individual serving cups. Cover with plastic wrap, pressing the wrap onto the surface if you want to prevent a skin from forming.

4. Chill for at least 2 hours, up to 12 hours, before serving.

Updated Chocolate Cornstarch Pudding

As easily made as a box pudding, this chocolate pudding has old-fashioned flavor with a slight update. Two ounces of dark chocolate give the pudding a depth of goodness that will delight chocolate lovers.

Serves 4 to 6

½ cup sugar
6 tablespoons unsweetened cocoa powder
¼ cup cornstarch

¼ teaspoon salt
2½ cups whole milk
2 ounces dark or bittersweet chocolate, coarsely chopped

1. Combine the sugar, cocoa, cornstarch, and salt in a heavy saucepan. Stir in ½ cup of the milk to form a smooth, runny paste. Make sure you dissolve any lumps that form.

2. Whisk in the remaining 2 cups milk, whisking until no lumps remain. Turn on the heat to medium and, stirring with a heatproof spatula or wooden spoon, cook until the mixture begins to thicken and comes to a boil.

3. Remove from the heat and stir in the dark chocolate. Continue to stir until the chocolate is completely melted. Transfer to a bowl or individual serving cups. Cover with plastic wrap, pressing the wrap onto the surface if you want to prevent a skin from forming.

4. Chill for at least 2 hours, up to 12 hours, before serving.

Custard Trickery

CUSTARDS CAN BE TRICKY. If you take them off the heat too soon, they will never firm up. If you leave them on the heat too long or cook over too high a temperature, they will curdle. How do you identify that magic moment of perfection?

First, a definition. A custard is a sweetened mixture of milk and eggs that is baked (a baked custard) or stirred on a stovetop (a stirred custard). Adding cornstarch or gelatin will help the custard stiffen.

A stirred custard should be cooked in a double boiler or a heavy saucepan to prevent the milk from scorching and the custard from curdling. A stirred custard is done when it leaves a velvety coating on the back of a metal spoon. If you run your finger across a custard-dipped spoon, it will leave a definite track. If you have an *accurate* candy thermometer or instant-read thermometer, it will register 170°F when the custard is done.

If you are baking the custard, the baking dish should be immersed in a hot-water bath to prevent overcooking. A baked custard is done when a knife inserted halfway between the edge of the pan and the center of the custard comes out clean, even though the center is still jiggly. It will become firm as it cools.

Take your time with custards. Bake custards long and slow. Cook stirred custards over medium heat, stirring constantly. It should take about 10 minutes for a stirred custard to reach the right consistency.

Rich Chocolate Pudding

American cooks have always been enamored of kitchen gadgets. When cornstarch manufacturers started giving away pudding molds in the nineteenth century, cornstarch sales soared, and cornstarch puddings became very popular. Americans are also fond of convenience foods. Ever since Jell-O started manufacturing its pudding mix, far too few children have had the opportunity to taste creamy, flavorful, made-from-scratch cornstarch puddings, like this one.

Serves 6

PUDDING

2 ounces semisweet chocolate, coarsely chopped

2 ounces unsweetened chocolate, coarsely chopped

2 cups whole milk

½ cup granulated sugar

⅛ teaspoon salt

2 tablespoons cornstarch

2 large egg yolks, lightly beaten

1 tablespoon butter, at room temperature

1 teaspoon vanilla extract

TOPPING

1 cup whipping cream

2 tablespoons sifted confectioners' sugar

1 tablespoon vanilla extract, dark rum or rum extract

1. To make the pudding, in a heavy saucepan over very low heat, melt the semisweet and unsweetened chocolates. Stir in 1¾ cups of the milk, the sugar, and the salt. Heat almost to boiling, stirring frequently. Flecks of chocolate will remain until the pudding has finished cooking.

2. Combine the cornstarch and the remaining ¼ cup milk in a small bowl. Add it to the hot chocolate mixture. Cook over medium heat, stirring until the mixture thickens and comes to a boil. Reduce the heat slightly and boil gently for 1 minute. Remove from the heat.

3. Gradually stir a few teaspoons of the pudding mixture into the egg yolks, mixing constantly until blended. Continue adding the pudding gradually until you have added about ⅓ cup. Pour the yolk mixture into the remaining pudding mixture in the pan, stirring until combined. Cook over low heat for 2 minutes, stirring constantly, until the mixture is thick and smooth. Remove from the heat.

4. Stir in small bits of butter at a time, mixing until the butter is melted. Stir in the vanilla.

5. Immediately pour into six dessert dishes and cover the surface of the puddings with plastic wrap to prevent a skin from forming. Cool on a wire rack, then refrigerate.

6. Just before serving, make the topping. Beat the cream until soft peaks form. Add the sugar and vanilla and beat until stiff. Pipe a portion of whipped cream on top of each serving.

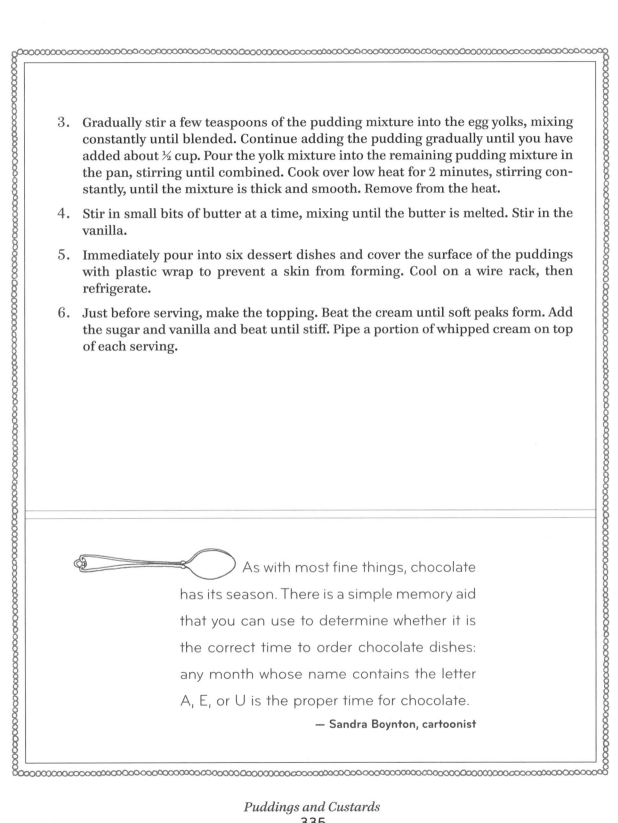 As with most fine things, chocolate has its season. There is a simple memory aid that you can use to determine whether it is the correct time to order chocolate dishes: any month whose name contains the letter A, E, or U is the proper time for chocolate.

— **Sandra Boynton, cartoonist**

Butterscotch Pudding

Butterscotch is a rich flavor derived from butter, brown sugar, and lemon juice. It is not clear whether there is a true connection to Scotland. The flavor first appeared in print in 1885 as *butterscot*, a flavor originally found only in a candy. American cooks adopted the flavor of cooked sugar and butter and turned it into a sauce for ice cream and a pudding flavor.

Serves 6

PUDDING

- ½ cup granulated sugar
- ⅓ cup water
- 2½ cups whole milk
- 3 tablespoons butter
- ¾ cup firmly packed dark brown sugar
- 3 tablespoons cornstarch
- 2 tablespoons unbleached all-purpose flour
- ⅛ teaspoon salt
- 4 large egg yolks, lightly beaten
- 1 teaspoon vanilla extract

TOPPING

- 1 cup whipping cream
- 2 tablespoons sifted confectioners' sugar
- ¼ teaspoon freshly grated nutmeg

1. Cook the granulated sugar in a small heavy saucepan or skillet over medium heat without stirring until the sugar melts and is golden brown. Remove from the heat. Slowly and carefully pour in the water. (The water will steam and boil up as it hits the caramelized sugar.) Cook without stirring until the sugar dissolves in the water. Add 2 cups of the milk and heat almost to boiling. Remove from the heat and stir in the butter. Set aside.

2. In another heavy saucepan, combine the brown sugar, cornstarch, flour, and salt. Add the remaining ½ cup milk gradually, stirring with a wire whisk to remove any lumps. Slowly add the hot caramel–milk mixture. Cook over medium heat, stirring, until the mixture thickens and comes to a boil. Continue stirring and boil for 1 minute. Remove from the heat.

3. Gradually stir a few teaspoons of the pudding mixture into the beaten egg yolks, mixing constantly until blended. When you have added about ½ cup, pour the yolk mixture into the remaining pudding mixture in the pan, stirring until combined. Cook, stirring constantly, for 2 minutes, until the mixture is thick and smooth. Remove from the heat. Stir in the vanilla.

4. Pour the pudding into six dessert dishes. Cool on a rack, then refrigerate.

5. Just before serving, make the topping. Beat the cream until stiff and add the confectioners' sugar and nutmeg. Pipe the whipped cream on top of each serving.

A Word about Pudding

THE VERY WORD *PUDDING* has inspired wits and pundits throughout the ages. Pudding doesn't always mean, well, pudding. Here are some examples:

• If someone tells you "not a word of pudding!" then say nothing about it (late seventeenth century, early eighteenth century).

• "I beg your pudding!" means "I beg your pardon!" (circa 1890).

• 'Join the Pudding Club!" refers to pregnancy (twentieth century).

• A pudding-sleeves is a clergyman (eighteenth to nineteenth century).

• A piece of pudding is a piece of good luck (circa 1870).

• Shakespeare seemed to have been quite inspired by pudding, having one character threaten, "I'll let out your puddings," meaning "I'll spill your guts." Another character says, "He'll yield the crow a pudding one of these days," which is a rather colorful way to talk about death.

Creamy Rice Pudding

Rice pudding, like bread pudding, is often regarded as a way to use up leftovers. But stop right there. The creamiest, most delectable rice puddings start with short-grain or medium-grain rice simmered to a creamy consistency in milk. The rice is then folded into a stirred custard and the result is ambrosial.

Serves 4 to 6

3¾ cups whole milk
½ cup uncooked short-grain or medium-grain rice, such as Arborio
Pinch of salt
3 large eggs
½ cup sugar

½–¾ cup raisins, plumped in hot water and drained
1 teaspoon vanilla extract
½ teaspoon ground cinnamon
Milk, light cream, or whipped cream, to serve

1. In the top of a double boiler set over simmering water, combine 2¼ cups of the milk, the rice, and the salt. Simmer, covered, until the milk is mostly absorbed and the rice is tender, about 60 minutes. Stir frequently. Transfer the rice to a serving bowl and let cool.

2. Heat the remaining 1½ cups milk in a heavy saucepan until very hot but not boiling. Beat the eggs in a small bowl. Gradually stir a few teaspoons of the hot milk into the beaten eggs, mixing constantly until blended. When you have added about ½ cup, pour the egg mixture into the pan with the remaining hot milk. Stir in the sugar. Cook over low to medium heat, stirring constantly, until the custard is slightly thickened and coats the back of a spoon, 10 to 12 minutes.

3. Stir the custard into the rice. Stir in the raisins, vanilla, and cinnamon until thoroughly blended. Cover and refrigerate until completely cooled.

4. Serve with a pitcher of milk or cream passed at the table or top each serving with a dollop of whipped cream.

Baked Rice Pudding

It has always been a mystery why the best-tasting rice puddings are served at diners, particularly Greek-run diners on the East Coast. But then again, diners often serve the best pies, too. What it comes down to is this: If you want good old-fashioned desserts, a good old-fashioned diner may be as good as Grandmother's house.

Serves 6 to 8

2 egg yolks	1 teaspoon vanilla extract
½ cup sugar	1½ cups cooked short- or medium-
2 teaspoons cornstarch	grain rice
½ teaspoon ground cinnamon	½ cup raisins
¼ teaspoon freshly grated nutmeg	Freshly grated nutmeg, to garnish
⅛ teaspoon salt	Milk or cream, to serve
2½ cups whole milk, warmed	

1. Preheat the oven to 325°F. Lightly grease a 1½-quart baking dish. Set it into a slightly larger pan that is at least 2 inches deep.

2. Combine the egg yolks, sugar, cornstarch, cinnamon, nutmeg, salt, and a few tablespoons of the milk in a large bowl. Whisk until blended. Add the remaining milk gradually, along with the vanilla. Fold in the cooked rice and the raisins.

3. Spoon the pudding into the baking dish. Pour 1 inch of hot water around the dish.

4. Bake, uncovered, for 1 hour and 30 minutes, stirring with a fork every 15 minutes during the first hour. This will prevent the rice from settling and will keep the custard creamy. Do not stir during the last 30 minutes. The pudding is done when the rice looks creamy and almost all of the milk is absorbed.

5. Remove the pudding from the water bath and let it cool on a rack.

6. Sprinkle with the nutmeg. Serve warm or cold with milk or cream passed in a pitcher at the table.

Baker's Tip

❋ The raisins can be plumped in sherry for several hours for extra flavor. Drain before using.

Tropical Rice Pudding

Rich, creamy, and studded with fruit, this rice pudding is irresistible. You can dress it up (and extend the number of servings) with more tropical fruit, such as sliced banana, diced papaya, or pineapple chunks.

Serves 6

2 cups whole milk or low-fat milk
1 (14-ounce) can coconut milk
¾ cup uncooked Arborio rice
¼ teaspoon salt
2 tablespoons dark rum or Cointreau

1 teaspoon unflavored powdered gelatin
½ cup firmly packed light brown sugar
2 cups diced mangoes
Toasted coconut flakes, to garnish

1. In the top of a double boiler set over simmering water, combine the milk, coconut milk, rice, and salt. Cover and simmer until the rice is tender and most of the milk is absorbed, about 1 hour and 15 minutes.

2. Pour the rum into a small cup. Sprinkle the gelatin over the rum and let soften for 5 minutes.

3. Stir the gelatin mixture into the hot rice mixture along with the brown sugar. Cook, stirring, until the gelatin is completely dissolved, about 3 minutes.

4. Refrigerate until well chilled, at least 2 hours.

5. Just before serving, stir in the mangoes. Garnish with coconut.

Forbidden Rice Pudding

Although rice pudding is regarded as "nursery food" in England — and pudding, in general, is considered kids stuff — this pudding comes with a whiff of sin. Forbidden rice is a short-grain black heirloom variety that originated in China. Some say its name suggests that it was reserved for the emperor's table, and that it was sometimes enjoyed as an aphrodisiac. Legends aside, this rice is higher in fiber and iron than most rice, and has a very pleasant, nutty flavor. It is indeed black and turns the cooking liquid a deep purple. This pudding makes a fine ending to an Asian meal.

Serves 8

1 cup uncooked black or forbidden rice (available at natural-food stores and Asain markets)	4 cardamom pods (optional)
	1 (14-ounce) can coconut milk
	½ cup firmly packed light brown sugar
3 cups plus 2 tablespoons water	
¼ teaspoon salt	2 tablespoons cornstarch

1. Combine the rice, the 3 cups water, and the salt and cardamom in a heavy saucepan. Cover and bring to a boil. Reduce the heat and simmer for 45 minutes, until the rice is tender. Remove the cardamom.

2. Stir in the coconut milk and brown sugar. Bring to a boil, uncovered. Simmer gently for 20 to 30 minutes, until the rice grains have swelled and the pudding is somewhat thickened.

3. Mix the cornstarch with the 2 tablespoons water and stir until smooth. Stir into the pudding. Bring to a boil and boil for 1 minute.

4. Chill before serving.

Dulce de Leche Rice Pudding

Dulce de leche, a caramelized sugar and milk syrup, can be bought as a spreadable sauce (like caramel sauce) wherever there is a large Hispanic population, though it is also easy to make your own (see box).

Serves 4

2¼ cups whole milk
½ cup uncooked short-grain or
    medium-grain rice, such as
    Arborio
1 cinnamon stick

Pinch of salt
1 teaspoon unflavored gelatin powder
2 tablespoons water
½ cup dulce de leche
1 teaspoon vanilla extract

1. In the top of a double boiler set over simmering water, combine the milk, rice, cinnamon stick, and salt. Simmer, uncovered, until the milk is mostly absorbed and the rice is tender, 60 to 75 minutes. Stir occasionally.

2. Sprinkle the gelatin over the water in a small bowl. Let stand for 5 minutes, then stir into the hot rice. Stir in the dulce de leche and vanilla until thoroughly blended.

3. Spoon the pudding into a serving bowl. Cover and refrigerate until completely cooled. Serve cold or warmed briefly in a microwave.

Making Dulce de Leche

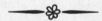

THE PROCESS OF MAKING DULCE DE LECHE sounds scary, but it really is safe. Put an unopened can of sweetened condensed milk on a steamer or other metal holder and immerse it in a tall pot of water. Boil it for 2 hours, making sure the water level covers the can at all times. Let the can cool completely before opening. One might think that the can would explode, but it doesn't. Really. If you boil it for 3 hours, it will turn into candy that you can cut into pieces, but the can still won't explode.

Honey-Vanilla Rice Pudding

This is the easiest possible version of rice pudding, but that doesn't make it any less wonderful. After simmering the rice in milk, all that is left to do is stir in the yogurt and flavorings. Use a high-quality vanilla yogurt. If you like, replace the honey with maple syrup or brown sugar. Fruit makes a terrific addition. In the winter, simmer ½ cup of raisins with the rice, or stir frozen berries into the still-warm cooked rice. In the summer, fresh berries or chopped nectarines or peaches are a delicious option.

Serves 4 to 6

....

    ½ *cup uncooked Arborio rice*
    2 *cups whole milk*
    2 *cups vanilla yogurt*
    ¼ *cup honey*
    ¼ *teaspoon freshly grated nutmeg*

....

1. In the top of a double boiler set over simmering water, simmer the rice in the milk for 1 hour, until the grains are completely tender and the milk is mostly absorbed. Spoon into a bowl and set aside to cool.

2. When the rice has cooled, mix in the yogurt, honey, and nutmeg. Chill well before serving.

Pudding is poison when it is too much boiled.

— Jonathan Swift

Caramel Custard

Caramel custard appears on menus in France, Spain, and Mexico as *flan* or *crème caramel*. It is a sweet custard baked in a mold that has been coated with a caramel syrup. It is surprisingly easy to prepare at home and is an elegant dessert for special occasions. You will need eight (4-ounce) custard cups or ramekins and a shallow roasting pan (or 9-by 13-inch pan) to hold them while they bake.

Serves 8

CARAMELIZED SYRUP

¾ cup sugar
1 teaspoon fresh lemon juice

CUSTARD

4 large eggs
1 (14-ounce) can sweetened
   condensed milk
1 (14-ounce) can evaporated milk

1 cup whole milk or low-fat milk
2 teaspoons vanilla extract
   Pinch of salt

1. Preheat the oven to 325°F.

2. To prepare the caramelized syrup, combine the sugar and lemon juice in a small, heavy saucepan. Cook over medium-high heat, swirling the pan from side to side and back and forth, until the sugar dissolves. Continue cooking for about 4 minutes, until the syrup turns a golden color. Immediately pour a little syrup into the bottom of each custard cup or ramekin, carefully tipping the syrup around until the caramelized sugar coats the bottom. Set aside.

3. To prepare the custard, break the eggs into a blender or food processor. Add the sweetened condensed milk, evaporated milk, whole milk, vanilla, and salt. Process until thoroughly combined. Pour the mixture into the prepared custard cups. Place the cups in a baking pan and add hot water to the pan, to a depth of 1 inch.

4. Bake for 45 to 50 minutes, until a knife inserted near the center of one of the cups comes out clean. The center of the custard should jiggle, but it will firm up as it cools.

5. Remove the custards from the hot water and place in 1 inch of cool water to stop the cooking. When cool, cover each cup with plastic wrap and chill for at least 3 hours.

6. To serve, run a dinner knife around the outside edge of each custard to loosen. Place the custard cup on a dessert plate upside down. Allow the syrup to run down over the custard. After 2 to 3 minutes, lift off the cup. Serve immediately.

Baker's Tip

✳ If you find you have trouble unmolding the custards, place the cups in a skillet filled with about ½ inch of very hot water. Let them sit for a few minutes to loose the caramel syrup. Then invert the cups onto the dessert plates.

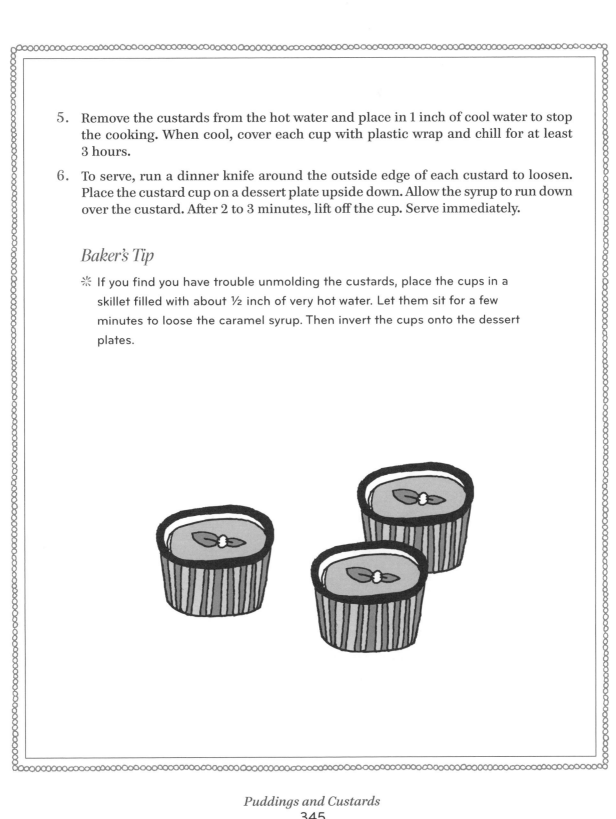

Bread Pudding

This recipe is a boon to the thrifty cook. Vary the flavor with different breads, including quick breads, such as banana bread.

Serves 6

4 slices firm white bread	½ teaspoon ground cinnamon
1–2 tablespoons butter, at room temperature	⅛ teaspoon freshly grated nutmeg
½ cup raisins	Pinch of salt
2¼ cups whole milk, warmed	1 teaspoon vanilla extract
2 large eggs	1 teaspoon granulated sugar
⅓ cup firmly packed light brown sugar	Whipped cream, to serve
	Berries, to serve

1. Thoroughly grease an 8-inch square or round baking pan.

2. Toast the bread on both sides until lightly colored. The bread should remain soft inside. Spread butter on both sides of each slice, then cut each slice into 1-inch cubes. You should have 2½ to 3 cups of bread cubes. Arrange the cubes in the baking pan and sprinkle with the raisins.

3. Heat the milk in a microwave or in a saucepan over low heat, just until warm.

4. Lightly beat the eggs in a medium bowl with a whisk. Add the brown sugar, cinnamon, nutmeg, and salt. Gradually add the warm milk and vanilla, whisking until combined. Pour the mixture over the bread cubes. Let stand for 30 minutes, pressing down the bread occasionally to absorb the mixture.

5. Preheat the oven to 325°F. Sprinkle the granulated sugar over the top of the mixture.

6. Bake for 50 to 60 minutes, until a knife inserted between the center and edge of the pan comes out clean. The pudding should be golden brown and puffed.

7. Cool on a wire rack. Serve warm or cold with whipped cream and fresh berries.

Noodle Kugel

A kugel is an Old World pudding, brought to this country by Jewish immigrants. It can be savory or sweet. A sweetened noodle kugel is traditionally served at the end of Yom Kippur, when Jews who have fasted all day are looking for comfort food and cooks are happy to serve a dish that is easy to make in advance and reheat. In this version, the noodles soak in a custard mixture overnight and don't require precooking.

Serves 10 to 12

- 4 large eggs
- 1 (16-ounce) carton small-curd cottage cheese
- 3 ounces cream cheese, at room temperature
- ¾ cup plus 3 tablespoons sugar
- 1 teaspoon minced orange zest
- 1 teaspoon salt
- 1½ teaspoons ground cinnamon
- ¼ teaspoon freshly grated nutmeg
- 3 cups milk
- 1 (12-ounce) package wide egg noodles
- ½ cup chopped dried apricots
- ½ cup golden raisins

1. Grease a 9- by 13-inch baking pan.

2. Combine the eggs, cottage cheese, cream cheese, the ¾ cup sugar, and the orange zest, salt, ½ teaspoon of the cinnamon, and the nutmeg in a food processor and process until smooth. Transfer to a large bowl and stir in the milk. Add the uncooked noodles, apricots, and golden raisins and stir gently to mix.

3. Spoon the noodle mixture into the prepared baking dish, cover with plastic wrap, and refrigerate overnight. Check every so often to make sure all the noodles are immersed in the liquid.

4. Preheat the oven to 350°F.

5. Uncover the kugel. Mix together the 3 tablespoons sugar and the remaining 1 teaspoon cinnamon in a small bowl, then sprinkle over the top of the kugel. Cover with aluminum foil.

6. Bake for 35 minutes. Uncover and bake for 40 minutes longer, until the kugel is firm in the center, puffed, and golden on top.

7. Cut into squares and serve hot or at room temperature.

Persimmon Pudding

Alas, you will have to go to southern Indiana to taste this pudding made with the authentic American persimmon, a small oval fruit that is burnt sienna in color. (Indianans call the color "persimmon color.") The persimmons sold in the supermarket are two different Japanese varieties that grow well on the West Coast: Hachiya and Fuyu. Choose the Hachiya variety for this pudding, which is reminiscent of plum pudding. It looks like a rich chocolate pudding with a chewy crust but tastes light, fruity, and spicy.

Serves 6 to 8

....

1½ cups puréed ripe persimmons
    (3–4 large persimmons)
1½ teaspoons fresh lemon juice
1½ cups sifted unbleached all-
    purpose flour
1½ teaspoons ground cinnamon
1 teaspoon baking powder
1 teaspoon baking soda
1 teaspoon ground ginger
½ teaspoon freshly grated nutmeg
½ teaspoon salt
2 large eggs

½ cup lightly packed dark brown
    sugar
½ cup granulated sugar
3 tablespoons butter, melted
1 teaspoon vanilla extract
¾ cup milk or half-and-half
½ cup raisins
½ cup chopped walnuts
    Hard Sauce (recipe follows) or
    whipped cream flavored with
    brandy, to serve

....

1. To prepare the persimmon purée, cut the fruit in half and scoop out the pulp with a spoon. Discard the skin, stem, and seeds. Purée the pulp in a blender or food processor or strain through a food mill. Measure out 1½ cups and mix with the lemon juice. Set aside.

2. Preheat the oven to 350°F. Thoroughly grease and flour a 9-inch baking dish.

3. Sift the flour, cinnamon, baking powder, baking soda, ginger, nutmeg, and salt into a medium bowl.

4. Beat the eggs in a large bowl until light. Beat in the brown sugar, granulated sugar, persimmon purée, butter, and vanilla. Add the flour mixture alternately with the milk, mixing just until the batter is smooth and blended. Fold in the raisins and walnuts. Spoon into the prepared pan.

5. Bake for 60 to 70 minutes, until the pudding pulls away from the sides of the pan and a knife inserted 1 inch from the edge comes out clean. The center will be a little bit soft.

6. Cool on a wire rack for 5 minutes. To serve, cut into squares. Serve with the refrigerated hard sauce or whipped cream.

HARD SAUCE

4 tablespoons butter, at room temperature
1¼ cups sifted confectioners' sugar

1–2 tablespoons brandy
1 teaspoon fresh lemon juice
Freshly grated nutmeg

1. Beat the butter in a small bowl until creamy. Gradually add the sugar. Add 1 tablespoon of the brandy and the the lemon juice and mix until thoroughly blended and fluffy. Add more brandy, if desired.

2. Spoon the sauce into a sauce dish and sprinkle with the nutmeg. Refrigerate before serving.

Makes about 1½ cups

Palatable Persimmons

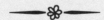

WHAT A TIME THE EARLY COLONISTS MUST HAVE HAD, tasting the new foods they encountered! Take persimmons, which are plentiful in the Midwest, the Carolinas, and Virginia. In Virginia, during the early 1700s, John Smith called the persimmon "one of the most palatable fruits of this land." The taste of a ripe persimmon is said to be something like a cross among a guava, mango, apricot, and tomato — very tasty in puddings and cakes. But the unripe persimmon is so acidic that it could, as one early diarist recorded, "drawe a man's mouth awrie with much torment." One must pity the poor explorer who had not yet learned the difference between the ripe and the unripe fruit.

Indian Pudding

This is one of the very oldest American desserts, taught to the colonists by the Native Americans, who called this dish *sagamite*. This version tastes faintly reminiscent of pumpkin pie, with its soft creamy texture under a glossy chestnut brown skin. The pudding will be soft when it comes out of the oven but will firm up when refrigerated.

Serves 6

4 cups whole milk	¼ teaspoon salt
⅓ cup yellow cornmeal	½ cup dark molasses
¼ cup sugar	2 tablespoons butter
½ teaspoon ground cinnamon	1 cup light cream
½ teaspoon ground ginger	Vanilla ice cream, to serve
¼ teaspoon freshly grated nutmeg	

1. Lightly grease a 1½-quart baking dish. Set it into a slightly larger pan that is at least 2 inches deep.

2. In a heavy saucepan, heat 3 cups of the milk just to the boiling point. Mix the cornmeal with the remaining 1 cup cold milk. With a whisk, gradually stir the cornmeal mixture into the hot milk. Cook over medium heat for 20 minutes, stirring frequently. The mixture will be slightly thickened. Remove from the heat.

3. Preheat the oven to 300°F.

4. Combine the sugar, cinnamon, ginger, nutmeg, and salt. Add to the cornmeal mixture, along with the molasses and butter, stirring until blended.

5. Pour the mixture into the baking dish. Pour 1 inch of hot water around dish. Place on an oven rack. Carefully spoon the light cream over the top of the mixture; do not stir it in. The cream will form a skin as it cooks. Bake for 3 hours.

6. Transfer the baking dish to a wire rack for 15 minutes to allow the pudding to set.

7. Serve warm with the vanilla ice cream.

Baked Custard

This is the ultimate in comfort food: soft, smooth, and sweet. Baked custard certainly didn't originate in America, but it has been enjoyed here as much as in the Old World.

Serves 6

- 3 cups whole milk
- 4 large eggs
- 6 tablespoons sugar
- ¼ teaspoon salt
- 1 teaspoon vanilla extract
  Freshly grated nutmeg
  Maple syrup or sliced fresh fruit,
    to serve

1. Preheat the oven to 325°F.

2. Heat the milk until hot, not boiling.

3. Lightly beat the eggs in a medium bowl with a whisk. Stir in the sugar and salt. Add the hot milk gradually, stirring constantly. Add the vanilla. Strain.

4. Pour the filling into six custard cups or a 1-quart baking dish. Set the cups or baking dish into a shallow pan at least 2 inches deep. Sprinkle the custards with nutmeg. Pour 1 inch of hot water around the custard cups or baking dish.

5. Bake individual cups for 45 to 50 minutes; bake a large baking dish for 60 to 75 minutes. The custard is done when a knife inserted near the center comes out clean. The center will still be soft.

6. Remove the custard from the hot water and place in 1 inch of cool water to stop the cooking. Serve cold or at room temperature. Custard is delicious served with maple syrup or fresh fruit.

Chocolate Mousse

Mousses originated in France but have become quite popular since the 1960s. This mousse has intense chocolate flavor.

Serves 6

4 ounces semisweet chocolate, coarsely chopped
2 ounces unsweetened chocolate, coarsely chopped
¼ cup strong brewed coffee
¼ cup plus 3 tablespoons sugar
4 large eggs, separated

⅛ teaspoon cream of tartar
Pinch of salt
1 cup whipping cream
1 tablespoon brandy or 1 teaspoon vanilla extract
Whipped cream, to serve
Shaved chocolate, to garnish

1. In the top of a double boiler, combine the semisweet chocolate, unsweetened chocolate, coffee, and the ¼ cup sugar. Place the top of the double boiler over simmering water. Stir until the chocolate is melted. Remove the pan from the heat and let cool for 3 minutes. Add the egg yolks, one at a time, beating thoroughly after each addition. Set aside until cool, 10 to 15 minutes.

2. Beat the egg whites until foamy. Add the cream of tartar and salt and beat until soft peaks form. Gradually add the 3 tablespoons sugar and continue beating until the egg whites are stiff but not dry. The egg whites should hold their shape. Mix one-quarter of the beaten egg whites into the chocolate mixture, just enough to lighten it. Gently fold in the remaining egg whites.

3. Beat the cream until stiff. Beat in the brandy and then gently fold into the chocolate mixture. Spoon into six soufflé or dessert dishes, and refrigerate until firm.

4. Serve the mousse cold with additional whipped cream and a sprinkling of chocolate shavings.

Baker's Tip

❊ The eggs in this recipe are not cooked. Please see "Egg Information" on page 388.

Lemon Mousse

Columbus brought the first lemon seeds to the Americas. Spanish missionaries planted them in California, where lemon trees flourished.

Serves 8

---

1 (¼-ounce) envelope unflavored gelatin
¼ cup cold water
3 large eggs, separated
¾ cup sugar
1 tablespoon finely grated lemon zest

⅔ cup fresh lemon juice
⅛ teaspoon cream of tartar
Pinch of salt
1 cup whipping cream
1 lemon, thinly sliced

---

1. Sprinkle the gelatin over the cold water in a small bowl. Set aside to soften.

2. In the top of a double boiler, beat the egg yolks with a wire whisk until thick and lemon-colored. Gradually add ½ cup of the sugar, beating until thoroughly blended. Mix in the lemon zest and lemon juice. Place the top of the double boiler over simmering water. Cook, stirring constantly, until the mixture coats a metal spoon, about 8 minutes. Add the softened gelatin, stirring until dissolved. Place the pan in a bowl of ice water, stirring until the mixture mounds slightly when dropped from a spoon. It should be cold but not set.

3. Beat the egg whites until foamy. Add the cream of tartar and salt and beat until soft peaks form. Gradually add the remaining ¼ cup sugar and continue beating until the egg whites are stiff but not dry. The egg whites should hold their shape. Gently fold into the mousse mixture.

4. Whip the cream until stiff. Fold half of it into the mousse mixture. Spoon the mousse into a 1½-quart soufflé dish or eight custard cups or dessert dishes. Refrigerate until firm.

5. Garnish each portion with dollops of the remaining cream and the lemon slices.

Baker's Tip

❊ The eggs in this recipe are not cooked. Please see "Egg Information" on page 388.

Ice Cream and Frozen Desserts

Making ice cream and frozen yogurt at home is surprisingly fast and easy. And the flavor is incomparable. You can mix in or flavor your ice cream any way you choose. And by making it at home, you avoid the stabilizers and artificial flavors and colors that are added to most commercial ice creams.

But even if you don't choose to make ice cream from scratch, there are plenty of wonderful desserts that start with purchased ice cream. Ice cream desserts always taste greater than the sum of their parts. So, who cares if you start with a trip to the supermarket for the ice cream? The dessert will taste as though you worked for hours just to please your family and friends.

Ingredients

○ **Ice cream, whether purchased or home-made, picks up flavors from the freezer, so enjoy it within a week of making or buying.**

○ **Ice cream is best stored in an airtight container in the freezer.** Wrap opened cardboard cartons in plastic bags to avoid picking up other flavors.

○ **For best results, use whole milk and whipping cream when making ice cream from scratch.**

○ **When mixing fruit into an ice cream, consider roasting the fruit first to concentrate flavors and reduce the water content of the fruit.**

○ **You can improve on commercial vanilla or chocolate ice cream by mixing in crushed cookies, chopped nuts, chopped fresh fruit, chopped chocolate-covered candies, or nuts.** Use ½ cup of mix-ins for every pint of ice cream. Spoon the pint into a large bowl and let it soften until it can be stirred. Mix in your extra ingredient(s), spoon into an airtight container, and refreeze for at least 2 hours.

○ **Cookies for ice cream sandwiches should be soft and chewy, rather than crisp.**

○ **Whipped cream on an ice cream cake or pie will freeze well, if leftovers need to go back into the freezer.**

Techniques

○ **When making a custard for the ice cream mixture, cook the egg and cream mixture slowly over low heat, stirring constantly until the mixture reaches 170°F on an instant-read thermometer.** The mixture should coat the back of a spoon.

○ **For best results, the ice cream base should be chilled overnight before freezing in an ice cream maker.**

○ **The faster the freezing process, the smoother the texture of the finished ice cream.**

○ **For best flavor, allow homemade ice cream to "ripen" in the freezer for at least 4 hours before serving.**

○ **Ease frozen ice cream pies from the pan by dipping the pie pan in hot water for just a few seconds before slicing and serving.**

Vanilla Ice Cream

We take vanilla for granted — it is a common, everyday flavoring. In truth, it is quite remarkable, made from the only one of some 20,000 orchid species that produces an edible pod. The orchid (*Vanilla planifolia*) flowers for just a few hours on one day of the year and is pollinated by only one type of bee. So, for a commercial crop, the flower is hand-pollinated to guarantee the development of a pod, which must be picked green and then cured for 3 to 6 months. Then the pods are boiled, baked in the sun, and fermented under blankets. All for a flavor we hardly consider special — until it is featured in something as simple and luxurious as homemade ice cream.

Makes 1½ quarts

2 cups whipping cream	8 large egg yolks
2 cups whole milk	¾ cup sugar
3 vanilla beans	Pinch of salt

1. Combine the cream and milk in a large heavy saucepan. With a paring knife, split the vanilla beans lengthwise. Scrape the pulp inside the beans into the milk and add the beans as well. Bring almost to a boil, then reduce the heat and simmer over low heat for 1 minute.

2. Remove the saucepan from the heat, cover, and let the mixture steep for 30 minutes.

3. Beat the egg yolks with a whisk in a medium bowl. Gradually add the sugar and salt, whisking until the sugar is dissolved and the mixture is thick and lemon-colored. Gradually whisk one-quarter of the warm milk mixture into the egg yolks. Then slowly stir the egg yolks into the remaining milk mixture in the saucepan.

4. Cook over low heat, stirring with a metal spoon, until the mixture thickens slightly and coats the back of a spoon. Do not let the mixture come to a boil. Remove the vanilla beans.

5. Strain the mixture into a bowl and then stir a few times. Cover with plastic wrap and refrigerate. The flavors are enhanced if the mixture is refrigerated overnight.

6. Freeze in an ice cream maker according to the manufacturer's directions.

Chocolate Ice Cream

There is something beautifully restrained about chocolate ice cream. But mix-ins are always fun. About 10 minutes before the ice cream machine has finished its work, consider incorporating ½ to 1 cup of chopped chocolate brownies, candies, marshmallows, canned cherries, or raspberries.

Makes 1½ quarts

2 cups whipping cream
2 cups whole milk
3 vanilla beans
8 large egg yolks
¾ cup sugar

Pinch of salt
2 ounces unsweetened chocolate, melted
2 ounces semisweet, dark, or bittersweet chocolate, melted

1. Combine the cream and milk in a large heavy saucepan. With a paring knife, split the vanilla beans lengthwise. Scrape the pulp inside the beans into the milk and add the beans as well. Bring almost to a boil, then reduce the heat and simmer over low heat for 1 minute.

2. Remove the saucepan from the heat, cover, and let the mixture steep for 30 minutes.

3. Beat the egg yolks in a medium bowl with a whisk. Gradually add the sugar and salt, whisking until the sugar is dissolved and the mixture is thick and lemon-colored. Gradually whisk one-quarter of the warm milk mixture into the egg yolks. Then slowly stir the egg yolks into the remaining milk mixture in the saucepan.

4. Cook over low heat, stirring with a metal spoon, until the mixture thickens slightly and coats the back of a spoon. Do not let the mixture come to a boil. Remove the vanilla beans. Stir in the melted chocolates until combined.

5. Strain the mixture into a bowl and then stir a few times. Cover with plastic wrap and refrigerate. The flavors are enhanced if the mixture is refrigerated overnight.

6. Freeze in an ice cream maker according to the manufacturer's directions.

Strawberry Ice Cream

A durable classic, strawberry ice cream never falters as one of America's top three ice cream flavors.

Makes 1½ quarts

2 cups whipping cream	1¼ cups sugar
2 cups whole milk	Pinch of salt
3 vanilla beans	2 cups coarsely chopped
8 large egg yolks	strawberries

1. Combine the cream and milk in a large heavy saucepan. With a paring knife, split the vanilla beans lengthwise. Scrape the pulp inside the beans into the milk and add the beans as well. Bring almost to a boil, then reduce the heat and simmer over low heat for 1 minute.

2. Remove the saucepan from the heat, cover, and let the mixture steep for 30 minutes.

3. Beat the egg yolks in a medium bowl with a whisk. Gradually add ¾ cup of the sugar and the salt, whisking until the sugar is dissolved and the mixture is thick and lemon-colored. Gradually whisk one-quarter of the warm milk mixture into the egg yolks. Then slowly stir the egg yolks into the remaining milk mixture in the saucepan.

4. Cook over low heat, stirring with a metal spoon, until the mixture thickens slightly and coats the back of a spoon. Do not let the mixture come to a boil. Remove the vanilla beans.

5. Strain the mixture into a bowl and then stir a few times. Cover with plastic wrap and refrigerate. The flavors are enhanced if the mixture is refrigerated overnight.

6. Combine the strawberries and the remaining ½ cup sugar and let stand for 30 minutes. Stir into the refrigerated cream base.

7. Freeze in an ice cream maker according to the manufacturer's directions.

Butter Pecan Ice Cream

Texans claim to have invented butter pecan ice cream, and that claim seems reasonable, given that the pecan tree has it origins in the area that is now Texas and northern Mexico. The name *pecan* comes from the Algonquin word *pacane*, meaning "nut to be cracked with a rock." Wild pecans were a major food source for various Native American tribes, whose activities and settlements in the fall and winter followed the maturing harvest of the wild trees.

Spanish explorers noted an abundance of wild pecan trees in their early explorations of the New World. Thomas Jefferson transplanted some pecan trees from the Mississippi River Valley to his home, Monticello, and presented some of the trees to George Washington, who planted them at Mount Vernon. Washington referred to pecans as "Mississippi nuts." Three of those original trees still thrive at Mount Vernon. The pecan was a favorite nut of both presidents. In fact, George Washington was said to walk around carrying pecans in his pocket for handy snacking. Pecans, of course, are easier to carry in the pocket than ice cream.

Makes 1½ quarts

1¼ cups pecan halves, coarsely chopped	¾ cup firmly packed dark brown sugar
2 cups whole milk	6 large egg yolks
2 cups whipping cream	⅛ teaspoon salt
4 tablespoons butter	1 teaspoon vanilla extract

1. Preheat the oven to 300°F.

2. Spread out the pecans in a shallow pan and toast for 6 to 8 minutes, stirring once or twice, until lightly colored and fragrant. Remove from the oven and set aside.

3. Combine the milk and cream in a large heavy saucepan. Warm the mixture over low to medium heat until bubbles begin to appear around the edge of the pan. The mixture should be hot but not boiling. Reduce the heat to low and simmer, stirring, for 1 minute. Remove the pan from the heat.

4. Melt the butter in a medium, deep skillet, just until it begins to brown. Add the brown sugar and stir over medium heat until the sugar completely melts. Spoon the mixture gradually into the hot milk and cream (be careful: the mixture may bubble up rapidly and create steam) and stir until they are combined. Some of the syrupy brown sugar may harden, but it will dissolve as you continue to stir.

5. Beat the egg yolks and salt in a medium bowl with a whisk until the yolks are thick and lemon-colored. Gradually whisk one-quarter of the warm milk mixture into the egg yolks. Then slowly stir the egg yolks into the remaining milk mixture in the saucepan.

6. Cook over low heat, stirring, until the custard thickens slightly and coats the back of a spoon, 6 to 7 minutes. Do not let it boil or it will curdle. Remove the pan from the heat.

7. Strain the custard into a bowl, then stir a few times and let cool.

8. Stir in the vanilla, cover with plastic wrap, and refrigerate. The flavors are enhanced if the mixture is refrigerated overnight.

9. Stir in the pecans and freeze in an ice cream maker according to the manufacturer's directions.

Peach Ice Cream

More than any other flavor, peach ice cream seems to stir memories of lazy summer afternoons spent with extended family, where dozens of cousins provided the elbow grease to make old-fashioned, hand-churned ice cream.

Makes 2 quarts

....

6–7 *fresh ripe peaches, peeled and coarsely chopped (about 6 cups)*
1¼ *cups sugar*
½ *teaspoon freshly grated nutmeg*
Finely grated zest of ½ lemon

2 *tablespoons fresh lemon juice*
2 *cups whole milk*
2 *cups whipping cream*
8 *egg yolks*
⅛ *teaspoon salt*

....

1. Purée half the peaches in a food processor. Transfer the purée to a bowl, add ¼ cup of the sugar, and the nutmeg, lemon zest, and lemon juice. Let stand for 30 minutes while you prepare the custard.

2. Combine the milk and cream in a large heavy saucepan over medium heat. Cook until bubbles begin to appear around the edge of pan and it just begins to simmer. Do not let the mixture boil. Remove the pan from the heat and set aside.

3. Beat the egg yolks with a whisk in a medium bowl until the yolks are thick and lemon-colored. Gradually add the remaining 1 cup sugar and the salt, whisking until the sugar is dissolved. Slowly whisk in one-quarter of the hot cream mixture. Then very slowly stir the egg yolks into the remaining milk mixture in the saucepan.

4. Cook over low heat, stirring, until the mixture thickens slightly and coats the back of a spoon. Do not let the mixture come to a boil or it will curdle. Remove the pan from the heat.

5. Strain the mixture into a bowl and then stir a few times. Cover with plastic wrap and chill until cold.

6. Combine the peach purée and remaining chopped peaches with the custard. The flavors will be enhanced if the custard can remain in the refrigerator overnight.

7. Freeze in an ice cream maker according to the manufacturer's directions.

Honey-Vanilla Frozen Yogurt

Frozen yogurt has the consistency of soft-serve ice cream and is lower in fat than ice cream, even when made with whole-milk yogurt. This version couldn't be simpler to make. Start with your favorite vanilla-flavored yogurt (there are some very good, organic versions out there). Sweetener is added because you can't taste the sweetness as fully in frozen foods.

Makes about 1½ quarts

2　quarts high-quality whole-milk
　　vanilla yogurt
3　tablespoons honey

1. Put the yogurt in a fine-mesh strainer or a colander lined with cheesecloth or paper coffee filters. Allow the yogurt to drain until thick, about 2 hours.

2. Transfer the thickened yogurt to a bowl and stir in the honey.

3. Freeze in an ice cream maker according to the manufacturer's directions.

I shall remember that sundae all my life. In a sumptuous confectioner's shop, light, airy, full of fragrance, we were served with a mountain of coffee ice cream, sprinkled with cream and scattered with walnuts, honey, peanuts, and various fruits. When I carried the first spoonful to my mouth . . . my taste buds experienced a violent ecstasy. A whole opera of sensation rolled off my tongue.

— Henri Troyat, French writer (1911–2007)

Maple Frozen Yogurt

Real maple syrup — not maple-flavored pancake syrup — is a must for this dessert. It is delicious on its own, and it also makes a great topping for apple crisps and pies.

Makes about 1¾ quarts

....

 2 quarts whole-milk plain yogurt
 1¼ cups maple syrup
 ½ cup firmly packed brown sugar

 1 teaspoon vanilla extract
 ¼ teaspoon freshly grated nutmeg

....

1. Put the yogurt in fine-mesh strainer or colander lined with cheesecloth or paper coffee filters. Allow the yogurt to drain until thick, about 2 hours.

2. Transfer the thickened yogurt to a bowl and stir in the maple syrup, brown sugar, vanilla, and nutmeg.

3. Freeze in an ice cream maker according to the manufacturer's directions.

In Case of Emergency, Eat This

ICE CREAM AND U.S. WAR EFFORTS are apparently linked. During the Civil War, Jacob Fussell, considered the father of the commercial wholesale ice cream industry, supplied Union soldiers with ice cream from his ice cream factory. During World War I, although food rationing was instituted in the United States, ice cream was declared an "essential foodstuff," so its ingredients were not rationed. During World War II, sugar was rationed, which cut back on civilian ice cream consumption. However, the Navy spent a million dollars to build a floating ice cream parlor capable of producing 10 gallons of ice cream per second. Ice cream, it turns out, was a more effective morale booster than beer. To American soldiers, ice cream represented all that was good in the United States and all that they were fighting to preserve.

Strawberry Sorbet

Call it strawberry ice and delight the kids. Call it strawberry sorbet and serve it as either a palate cleanser or a dessert. For the grown-ups, you might want to punch up the flavor by infusing the sugar syrup with a sprig of basil, which you remove before freezing.

Makes about 1 quart

....

    1 *pound fresh strawberries, rinsed
        and stemmed*
    1 *tablespoon fresh lemon juice*
    1 *cup sugar*
    1 *cup water*
      Mint leaves, to garnish

....

1. Reserve a few strawberries for the garnish and then purée the remaining strawberries in a food processor. (You should have 2 cups.) Transfer to a large bowl and add the lemon juice. Refrigerate until cold.

2. Combine the sugar and water in a saucepan. Bring to a boil over medium heat, stirring until the sugar is dissolved, 3 to 5 minutes. Boil for 2 to 3 minutes, until the mixture is syrupy. Chill in the refrigerator until cold.

3. Combine the strawberry purée and syrup. Pour into a shallow, nonreactive 8-inch square baking dish and set in the freezer. Freeze until frozen, 3 to 4 hours.

4. Remove from the freezer and let stand at room temperature until partially defrosted, 10 to 20 minutes. Spoon into a food processor and process just long enough to break up the ice crystals. It will look like a smooth slush.

5. Return the mixture to the baking dish, cover, and refreeze for about 3 hours before serving.

6. Serve in wine goblets, garnished with slices of fresh strawberries and mint.

Lime Sorbet

When the dog days of summer come around, light sorbets make the perfect dessert. It's not a bad idea to stock some in your freezer for nights when you want something special but don't want to turn on the oven.

Makes about 1 quart

½ cup water
¼ cup sugar
1 tablespoon honey
1 (12-ounce) can frozen limeade, partially thawed

1¼ cups ice water
Finely grated zest of 1 lime
1 lime, thinly sliced, sprigs of fresh mint or rose geranium leaf, to garnish

1. Combine the ½ cup water, sugar, and honey in a small saucepan and bring to a boil. Boil for 1 minute, stirring until the sugar is dissolved and the honey is melted. Remove from the heat and pour into a food processor. Add the limeade, the 1¼ cups ice water, and the lime zest. Process until smooth. Pour into a shallow, 8-inch square, nonreactive baking dish. Cover with plastic wrap and set in the freezer. Freeze until frozen, about 4 hours.

2. Remove the pan from the freezer and let stand at room temperature until partially defrosted and easy to break up with a fork, 10 to 20 minutes. Spoon into the food processor and process just long enough to break up the ice crystals. It will look like a smooth slush.

3. Return the sorbet to the baking dish, cover, and freeze for about 3 hours.

4. Serve in goblets with a thin slice of lime and a mint leaf or rose geranium leaf.

Baker's Tip

❊ If all the sorbet isn't eaten, it can be stored for 2 to 3 weeks in a covered container and reprocessed in a food processor before serving.

Variation

Lemon Sorbet. Substitute frozen lemonade concentrate for the limeade. Substitute grated lemon zest for the lime zest and garnish with a thinly sliced lemon.

Mint Chocolate Chip Ice Cream Pie

Mint chocolate chip ice cream served in a chocolate cookie crust becomes a special dessert with very little effort. Make sure you soften the ice cream enough to make a smooth filling, but don't let it turn into soup. The final topping will make a smooth coating, as long as it is poured on very hard, very cold ice cream.

Serves 8 to 10

Chocolate Crumb Crust (page 265)	2 tablespoons dark corn syrup
3 pints mint chocolate chip ice cream, softened slightly	4 ounces semisweet chocolate, chopped
⅓ cup whole milk	¼ teaspoon peppermint extract

1. Prepare the crust according to the recipe directions and let cool.

2. Spoon the ice cream into the crust. Use a palette knife or an offset spatula to smooth the top. Freeze until the ice cream is firm, about 3 hours.

3. Combine the milk and corn syrup in a small heavy saucepan. Bring to a simmer over medium heat, whisking constantly. Remove the pan from the heat. Add the chocolate and peppermint and whisk until melted and smooth. Cool until barely lukewarm, whisking occasionally, about 10 minutes. Pour over the center of the pie. The glaze will harden quickly, so spread with a palette knife or an offset spatula over the entire top. Transfer to the freezer and freeze until completely firm, at least 4 hours.

4. To serve, let the pie soften slightly at room temperature, 5 to 10 minutes. Cut into wedges and serve.

Peach Melba Ice Cream Sundaes

In the old days, opera stars were treated like pop stars are today. The famous French chef Auguste Escoffier dedicated quite a few of his dishes to opera stars and royalty. This luscious dish of ice cream, topped with peaches in raspberry sauce, was dedicated to the Australian opera diva Dame Nellie Melba.

Serves 6

POACHED PEACHES

½ cup granulated sugar
¾ cup cold water
1 tablespoon fresh lemon juice
4 whole cloves

2 cinnamon sticks
3 large firm ripe fresh peaches, peeled, halved, and pitted

RASPBERRY SAUCE

3 cups fresh or frozen, thawed, unsweetened raspberries
½ cup freshly squeezed orange juice

¼–½ cup superfine sugar
2 tablespoons Grand Marnier or other orange liqueur

ASSEMBLY

1 cup whipping cream
1 tablespoon confectioners' sugar
2 teaspoons raspberry or orange liqueur

1½ pints vanilla ice cream
1 cup fresh raspberries

1. Combine the granulated sugar, water, lemon juice, cloves, and cinnamon sticks in a medium saucepan and bring to a boil over medium heat. Lower the heat and simmer, stirring until the sugar is dissolved. Add the peach halves to the hot syrup. Cover the pan and simmer the peaches until barely tender, 4 to 5 minutes. Let the peaches cool in the syrup.

2. To make the raspberry sauce, combine the raspberries with the orange juice in a blender or food processor and process until puréed. Add ¼ cup of the superfine sugar and the orange liqueur and blend for 20 to 25 seconds. Taste for sweetness,

adding superfine sugar as needed, 1 tablespoon at a time. Pass the raspberry mixture through a fine-mesh sieve into a bowl and discard the seeds. Cover and chill for several hours.

3. To assemble, beat the cream until soft peaks form. Add the confectioners' sugar and liqueur and beat just until almost but not quite stiff.

4. Place a peach half, cut-side up, in the bottom of a dessert dish or a wide goblet. Top each peach half with a scoop of ice cream. Spoon some of the raspberry sauce over the ice cream. Garnish with a spoonful of whipped cream and a few fresh raspberries.

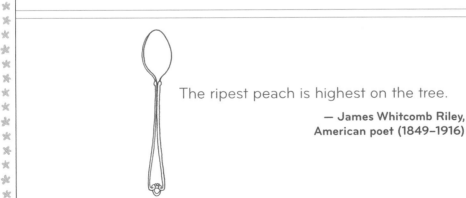

The ripest peach is highest on the tree.

— James Whitcomb Riley,
American poet (1849–1916)

Three-Flavor Ice Cream Bombe

A timeless classic, the ice cream bombe was a particular favorite in Victorian times, when ice cream (and other desserts) served at fancy parties was often molded into festive shapes. This dessert is more craft project than baker's challenge. The recipe can be made successfully by anyone with patience; no baking skills required.

Serves 16 to 20

3½ pints chocolate ice cream
1 quart strawberry ice cream
1 pint coffee ice cream
½ cup medium-size pieces chopped chocolate-coated toffee or use two (1.4-ounce) Heath Bars, chopped or hammered into small pieces

½ cup grated dark or bittersweet chocolate
1 cup whipping cream, whipped, to garnish
Fresh strawberries, sliced in half vertically, to garnish
Hot Fudge Sauce (page 385), warmed

1. Line a 2-quart bombe mold or stainless steel bowl (8 or 9 inches in diameter) with plastic wrap, allowing a 2-inch overhang. The overhang will be used as handles to lift the finished bombe out of the bowl. Chill the bowl for 15 minutes.

2. Soften the chocolate ice cream to a spreading consistency. Using a large spoon, quickly spread the chocolate ice cream in the bowl, pressing it firmly over the bottom and up the sides of the bowl. Make the layer about 1 inch thick and bring the layer to within ½ to 1 inch of the top of the bowl. Freeze for 1 hour, until set.

3. Soften the strawberry ice cream and spread it over the chocolate layer. Return the mold to the freezer to harden, 1 to 2 hours.

4. Soften the coffee ice cream and mix with the toffee candy. Fill the center of the mold with the coffee mixture, smoothing the top. Cover with aluminum foil and freeze for at least 4 hours or overnight.

5. Chill a large serving plate. Remove the bombe from the freezer and let it soften slightly. Remove the foil. Lift up the plastic wrap to help release the bombe from the bowl. Place the platter, right-side down, over the bombe and then, holding the two together, invert them. Lift off the bowl and pull off the plastic wrap. Sprinkle the outside of the bombe with the grated chocolate. The bombe can be served now or covered loosely with foil and returned to the freezer for several hours.

6. To serve, let the bombe soften at room temperature for 10 minutes. Surround the bottom with piped or spooned whipped cream and strawberry halves. Use a sturdy, sharp knife to cut the bombe into wedges. Serve with fudge sauce.

Baker's Tip

❋ Molds and bowls vary in size and shape, so the amount of ice cream may have to be adjusted.

The Ice Cream Cone

SOMETIMES, MANY PEOPLE have the same good idea at the same time. The ice cream cone was one such idea. It was effectively introduced to the world at the St. Louis World's Fair in 1904, where 50 vendors sold at least 5,000 gallons of ice cream a day, some of it in edible containers.

Who first thought to sell ice cream in an edible container? It might have been Italo Marchiony, who sold his homemade ice cream from a pushcart on Wall Street. To reduce losses caused by customers breaking or wandering off with his serving glasses, he decided to bake edible waffle cups with sloping sides and a flat bottom. He patented his idea in 1903 but was making them as early as 1896.

However, many others take credit for the ice cream cone, including a Syrian immigrant named Ernest A. Hamwi, who rolled up a Persian pastry for an ice cream vendor who ran out of dishes at the St. Louis Fair of 1904. Another possible inventor was a Turkish immigrant, David Avayo, also a vendor at the fair, who rolled up wafer cookies in the style of paper cones he saw in France. Then there is still another vendor, Abe Doumar, who sold waffle cones he called "cornucopias."

Brownie Cupcake Ice Cream Sundaes

Here's a festive way to prepare brownies á la mode, using brownies made in a muffin tin and premade balls of ice cream. When you want to serve cake and ice cream at a birthday party, this recipe makes it fun and easy. Go wild with the ice cream flavor!

Serves 12

BROWNIES

- 2 ounces unsweetened chocolate, coarsely chopped
- 4 tablespoons butter
- 1 cup sugar
- 2 large eggs
- 1 teaspoon vanilla extract
- ⅔ cup unbleached all-purpose flour
- 1 teaspoon baking powder
- ⅛ teaspoon salt

TOPPING

- 1 quart ice cream
  Hot Fudge Sauce (page 385)
  Whipped cream
- ½ cup toasted sliced almonds
- 12 maraschino cherries (optional)

1. Preheat the oven to 350°F. Line a 12-cup muffin tin with paper or foil baking cups.

2. To prepare the brownies, melt the chocolate and butter in a heavy saucepan over low to medium heat, stirring until smooth. Remove the pan from the heat and add the sugar, stirring until combined.

3. Mix in the eggs, one at a time, beating until light and smooth. Mix in the vanilla.

4. Whisk the flour, baking powder, and salt until thoroughly mixed. Fold the flour mixture into the chocolate mixture in the saucepan, stirring until combined. Spoon the batter into the baking cups.

5. Bake for 20 to 22 minutes, until the tops are just becoming firm to the touch. Place on a wire rack to cool for 5 minutes. Remove the cupcakes from the pan and cool completely on the rack.

6. Line a baking sheet with parchment paper. Using a large spoon or a standard, trigger-style ice cream scoop, make balls about the size of the cupcake tops, using about ⅓ cup ice cream for each ball. Make one side of the ball flat; the flat side will

sit on the flat top of the cupcake. Put the balls on the prepared baking sheet and freeze until serving.

7. Prepare the Hot Fudge Sauce. Spoon into a small heatproof pitcher. Warm before serving.

8. To serve, remove and discard paper liners from the brownie cupcakes. Place each brownie in a deep serving dish or bowl. Arrange an ice cream ball on top of each brownie and top with dollops of whipped cream. Drizzle a little sauce over the top and garnish with a few sprinkles of almonds and a cherry, if using. Serve extra chocolate sauce at the table.

Ice Cream Around the World

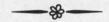

- Italy is widely regarded as producing the very best ice cream, known as *gelato*. It is denser than American-style ice cream, and the flavor is usually more intense.

- In India, ice cream made from reduced and concentrated milk is called *kulfi*. Pistachio is a favorite flavor there.

- In the Philippines, ice cream was introduced by the Spanish but adapted to use native ingredients. Among favorite flavors are coconut, corn, and purple yam.

- In the Middle East, ice cream is often made with *salep*, a starchy root that is virtually flavorless but contributes an elastic quality. The ice cream may be flavored with rosewater and sprinkled with pistachios.

- In Argentina, the ice cream is similar in style to Italian gelato. The most popular flavor there is dulce de leche.

- In Japan, the four most popular ice cream flavors are vanilla, chocolate, *matcha* (powdered green tea), and strawberry. Other notable popular flavors are milk, caramel, and *azuki* (red bean).

Toffee Ice Cream Pie

An ice cream pie is one of the simplest desserts to make. When you want a dessert that seems as though you have slaved for hours (but you didn't really), this is the way to go. Just allow plenty of time for the pie to harden after it is made — or you will be serving ice cream soup rather than pie.

Serves 8 to 10

PIE

Nut Crust (page 266)
3 pints vanilla or coffee ice cream
1½ cups chopped chocolate-coated toffee or use 4 (1.4-ounce) Heath Bars, chopped or hammered into small pieces

CHOCOLATE GLAZE

4 ounces semisweet, dark, or bittersweet chocolate, coarsely chopped
3 tablespoons butter
2 teaspoons light corn syrup
½ cup whipping cream
½ teaspoon vanilla extract
1 tablespoon finely chopped almonds, to garnish

1. Prepare and bake the piecrust according to the recipe directions. Cool completely. (The crust can be prepared several days ahead and refrigerated or frozen.)

2. Put the ice cream in a large bowl and allow it to soften. When the ice cream is soft enough to stir but not melted, mix in the toffee and spoon it into the piecrust. Smooth the top of the ice cream with an offset spatula or palette knife and then cover it with plastic wrap. Freeze until firm, 4 to 6 hours.

3. When the ice cream has hardened, remove the plastic wrap and use a wet spatula to once again smooth the top of the ice cream. Return the pie to the freezer.

4. To prepare the chocolate glaze, combine the chocolate, butter, and corn syrup in the top of a double boiler over simmering water. Cook, stirring, until the mixture is melted and smooth. Remove the pan from the double boiler and cool for 10 to 15 minutes, stirring occasionally, until the glaze is cool but still liquid. Pour over the center of the pie. The glaze will harden quickly, so spread with a palette knife or offset spatula over the entire top. Transfer to the freezer.

5. Whip the cream until it holds soft peaks. Fold in the vanilla. Refrigerate until you are ready to serve the pie.

6. To serve, let the pie soften at room temperature for about 10 minutes. Using a spoon, put dollops of whipped cream around the edge of the pie. Sprinkle nuts over the whipped cream. Use a very sharp knife to cut through the crunchy, hardened chocolate glaze and cut into wedges.

Looking at Ice Cream Machines

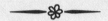

THE OLD-FASHIONED HAND-CHURNED ICE CREAM MAKERS require rock salt (to lower the melting temperature of the ice) and ice in the tub surrounding the freezing container. They also require a certain amount of work. The wonderful thing about these old-fashioned machines is that they can become a centerpiece of a party, with everyone pitching in and burning off some calories. Also, you can make fairly large quantities at once, and the machines are relatively inexpensive to boot.

Electric ice cream makers take all the work out of the freezing process. The refrigerated units are like mini freezers; just plug one in, allow cooling to occur, place the ingredients in a bowl, and the ice cream is ready within 20 minutes. Some electric ice cream makers contain a freezing liner. This liner, or freezing container, must go in the freezer the night before. Then you place it in the ice cream maker, add the ingredients, and the stirring is done for you. Some machines are quite noisy and others are relatively quiet; it is something you might want to investigate before purchasing.

There are manual ice cream makers that contain a freezing liner and operate just like the similar electric ones — except that you have to stir by rotating a crank every few minutes. This continuously scrapes off the ice crystals that form along the metal container and incorporates air into the mixture to achieve the proper texture.

Easy No-Bake Ice Cream Cake

Something this easy shouldn't be this good, but it is. The only requirements are patience, a springform pan, and a freezer that holds food at around 0°F. (Older refrigerators with inefficient freezers will not be powerful enough to freeze this cake.) I recommend using two contrasting colors of ice cream (chocolate and vanilla, for example), but that isn't necessary. The candy garnish can range from chocolate-covered coffee beans to colorful M&Ms.

Serves 10

- 1 (7-ounce) package ladyfingers (you will not need the entire package)
- 2 pints ice cream
  About 12 chocolate wafer cookies
- 1 cup whipping cream
- 2 tablespoons superfine sugar
  Candy or shaved chocolate, to garnish

1. Remove 1 pint of the ice cream from the freezer and allow it to soften at room temperature for about 15 minutes.

2. Very lightly oil an 8-inch springform pan. Separate the ladyfingers and line the bottom and sides of the pan with them, rounded side facing down and out; ladyfingers along the sides should be standing upright. You may have to cut some of the ladyfingers to cover the bottom of the pan. Scoop out the ice cream and evenly distribute it in the pan. Use a palette knife or offset spatula to smooth the ice cream into an even layer.

3. Freeze for at least 1 hour, until solid.

4. Remove the remaining pint of ice cream from the freezer and allow it to soften at room temperature for about 15 minutes.

5. Remove the cake from the freezer. Cover the bottom layer of ice cream with a generous layer of wafer cookies. Top with the softened ice cream, smoothed into an even layer. Return to the freezer for at least 4 hours. Place a bowl for whipped cream and beaters in the freezer.

6. About 10 minutes before serving, remove the ice cream, bowl, and beaters from the freezer. Pour the cream and sugar into the bowl and beat until stiff. Pipe or spoon onto the top of the ice cream cake. Garnish with candy, remove the sides of the pan, and serve.

Frozen Tiramisù

Tiramisù, which translates literally as "pick me up" from the Italian, is a dessert that was invented in the 1960s and became an instant classic. It is usually made as a layered dessert of ladyfingers, mascarpone cheese, espresso, and chocolate. This adaptation contains all the right flavors in a delicious, frozen version.

Serves 10

- 1 pint coffee ice cream
- 1 (7-ounce) package ladyfingers (you will not need the entire package)
- ⅓ cup coffee liqueur

- 8 ounces mascarpone cheese
- 1 cup whipping cream
- 2 tablespoons superfine sugar
- 2 ounces bittersweet or dark chocolate, grated

1. Very lightly oil an 8-inch springform pan. Remove the ice cream from the freezer and allow to soften at room temperature for about 15 minutes.

2. Separate the ladyfingers and arrange on a large tray, curved-side down. Brush the coffee liqueur on the surface facing up.

3. Combine the mascarpone, cream, and sugar in a medium bowl and beat until soft peaks form.

4. To assemble the dessert, line the bottom and sides of the prepared pan with the ladyfingers, rounded side facing down and out; ladyfingers along the sides should be standing upright. You may have to cut some of the ladyfingers to cover the bottom of the pan. Scoop out the ice cream and evenly distribute it in the pan. Use a palette knife or offset spatula to smooth the ice cream into an even layer. Sprinkle the ice cream with half of the grated chocolate.

5. Top with the mascarpone mixture. Use the back of the spoon to create decorative swirls on the surface. Sprinkle with the remaining grated chocolate. Freeze for at least 4 hours, until solid.

6. Let the dessert soften at room temperature for about 20 minutes before serving. Leftovers can be covered in plastic wrap and stored in the freezer for about 1 week.

Ice Cream–Filled Cream Puffs

Is this a complicated recipe? No. Does the dessert look complicated? Yes, enough to win you extravagant praise. This classic dessert is most often made with vanilla ice cream and chocolate sauce, but any combination works: for example, butter pecan ice cream and caramel sauce, mint ice cream and chocolate sauce, chocolate ice cream and butterscotch sauce . . . the possibilities are endless.

Serves 10

CREAM PUFFS

- 1 cup cold water
- ½ cup (1 stick) butter, cut into small pieces
- 1 teaspoon sugar
- ¼ teaspoon salt
- 1 cup unbleached all-purpose flour
- 4 large eggs

ASSEMBLY

- 2 pints vanilla or coffee ice cream, slightly softened
- Warm Chocolate Sauce (page 387) or other ice cream topping

1. Preheat the oven to 400°F. Cover two baking sheets with parchment paper.

2. To make the cream puffs, combine the water, butter, sugar, and salt in a heavy saucepan and bring to a boil. When the butter is melted, remove the pan from the heat, add the flour all at once, and stir rapidly. When the dough is well blended, return the pan to medium heat and beat the mixture with a wooden spoon for 2 to 3 minutes, until the dough forms a ball and pulls away from the sides of the pan. Remove the saucepan from the stove.

3. Blend in the eggs, one at a time, beating well after each addition, until the egg is absorbed and the mixture is smooth and glossy. You want to beat in as much air as possible.

4. To form the cream puffs, dip two large tablespoons in cold water. Using the wet spoons, scoop up some dough and form rounded balls about 2 inches in diameter, mounding them slightly higher in the center. Place the rounded balls of dough 2 to 3 inches apart on the parchment paper. Using wet fingers, smooth out any lumpy points on top.

5. Bake for 20 to 25 minutes, until the cream puffs are puffed and pale gold. Rotate the pans from front to back. Lower the oven temperature to 350°F. Bake for 15 to 20 minutes longer, until the puffs are well browned and crusty. (If you want a crispier cream puff, pierce the sides of each two or three times with a sharp knife after baking. Return the pan to the oven, turn off the oven, and leave the oven door ajar for 10 minutes.)

6. Remove the cream puffs from the oven and cool on wire racks.

7. To fill the cream puffs, partially slice off the bottom of each. Don't worry if the slices becomes detached; the ice cream will glue them back together. Pull out and discard any of the uncooked soft dough. Using a tablespoon, fill the tops with ice cream. Replace the bottom slice. Place the filled cream puffs upside down in a baking pan with sides, separating layers of cream puffs with plastic wrap. Cover with plastic wrap and freeze until serving time. (The cream puffs can be kept in the freezer for 1 week. When the ice cream has frozen, it is a good idea to wrap the cream puffs individually in aluminum foil.)

8. To serve, place the cream puffs on serving plates. Drizzle a little sauce over the cream puffs and around the plates.

More About Cream Puffs
—❄—

YOU CAN FILL CREAM PUFFS with any sort of filling, including puddings and custards. The unfilled cream puffs can be completely baked, wrapped well, and frozen. When you're ready to eat them, take them from the freezer, remove the wrapping, and reheat in a 375°F oven for 8 to 10 minutes. Then cool and fill spoon in a filling of your choice.

Baked Alaska

This dessert dates back to American scientist Benjamin Thompson, later awarded the name Count Rumford for his studies on the resistance of stiffly beaten egg whites to heat. Rumford's "omelette surprise" (or *omelette à la norvégienne*, Norwegian omelette, *omelette norvegienne*, and *glace au four*) eventually became the baked Alaska we know today — a brick of ice cream atop a cake layer and covered in meringue. The recipe gets high marks for its simplicity, despite the appearance of complexity.

Serves 10 to 12

ICE CREAM CAKE LAYERS

9-inch round sponge cake (see Baker's Tips opposite)
1 *quart chocolate ice cream*
1 *quart coffee ice cream*

MERINGUE

6 *large egg whites, at room temperature*
½ *teaspoon cream of tartar*
Pinch of salt
¾ *cup sugar*
1 *teaspoon vanilla extract*
Warm Chocolate Sauce (page 387) (optional)

1. The cake should be about 1 inch tall. If it is any taller, cut it horizontally to make a 1-inch layer. Save the leftover cake for another use. Place the 1-inch cake layer on an aluminum foil-covered board or on an ovenproof serving platter.

2. Let the chocolate ice cream stand at room temperature until it is soft enough to mold, but do not allow it to melt. Spread a layer of the ice cream on the cake, leaving a border of about 1 inch all the way around the outer edge. Freeze until firm.

3. Let the coffee ice cream stand at room temperature until it is soft enough to mold, but do not allow it to melt. Mound the coffee ice cream on top of the chocolate layer. Freeze until firm.

4. Cover the cake and ice cream with plastic wrap and freeze thoroughly, about 4 hours.

5. Preheat the oven to 475°F with a rack in the lower third of the oven.

6. To make the meringue, beat the egg whites with an electric mixer until foamy. Add the cream of tartar and salt and beat until soft peaks form. Gradually add the sugar, 2 tablespoons at a time, beating until the egg whites are stiff but not dry. The egg whites should hold their shape. Beat in the vanilla.

7. Remove the cake and ice cream from the freezer. Peel off the plastic wrap. Quickly spread the meringue over the ice cream and cake, covering completely. Seal the meringue to the serving board or platter. (If desired, the dessert can be returned to the freezer at this point, but only up to 2 hours.)

8. Bake the dessert for 3 to 5 minutes, until the meringue is lightly browned.

9. Serve immediately, passing the sauce on the side.

Baker's Tips

※ You can use a purchased sponge cake or the thin sponge cake used for the Jelly Roll on page 120, prepared as described in the Baker's Tip on page 121.

※ The egg whites in this recipe are not completely cooked. Please see "Egg Information" on page 388.

Homemade Ice Cream Drumsticks

This dessert is more about engineering than cooking. It is about assembling a treat that is greater than the sum of its parts. It is hard to explain how wonderful a freshly made ice cream drumstick is, but after one taste, you'll never buy one from a convenience store freezer chest again.

Serves 8

6 sugar cones
4 ounces semisweet, dark, or bitter-
    sweet chocolate, coarsely chopped
1 pint ice cream (any flavor, but make
    sure the mix-ins are small)

4 tablespoons butter
¼ cup finely chopped roasted and
    salted nuts (any kind)

1. Turn an empty egg carton upside down. Make a hole in every other egg cup. Insert a cone in the holes you made. Make room in the freezer for the egg carton.

2. Melt the chocolate in the top of a double boiler set over barely simmering water. Stir until completely smooth and glossy. Remove the top of the double boiler from the heat. Spoon about 1 teaspoon of chocolate into each cone — don't bother measuring — and return the cones to the egg carton. Place the carton in the freezer.

3. Remove the ice cream from the freezer and allow it to soften on the counter while the chocolate plug in the bottom of each cone hardens, about 15 minutes. You want the ice cream quite soft. Fill each cone with the softened ice cream, again using a teaspoon. You will get about three spoonfuls into each cone. Return the filled cones, still in the carton, to the freezer to firm up, about 15 minutes.

4. Working quickly, add a scoop of ice cream to each cone. A small, trigger-style ice cream scoop works best, but you can fashion a round scoop with two soup spoons. Return the carton to the freezer and freeze for at least 3 hours.

5. Reheat the chocolate until melted. Stir in the butter until the mixture is thin and smooth. Pour into a small bowl and let cool for about 5 minutes, so the chocolate is liquid but not hot. Put the chopped nuts in a second bowl. Working with one ice cream cone at a time, dip the exposed ice cream in the chocolate, turning to coat completely, and then dip in the nuts, again turning to coat. Return the cones to the freezer and freeze for 1 to 2 hours before serving. If you like, you can store the frozen cones in an airtight bag in the freezer for up to 1 week.

Butterscotch Sauce

Although there is butter in the recipe, there is definitely no scotch in this sauce. So why the name? There are many theories, but the definitive answer lies buried in the past. The "scotch" part of its name may be derived from a connection to Scotland, or it may come from the word *scorch*, which is easy to do when you are working with sugar and cream but not at all desirable. Butterscotch is easy enough to make, but if you overcook it, you will end up with toffee, which isn't a bad thing to mix into ice cream, if you are so inclined.

Makes 1½ cups

1 cup firmly packed light brown sugar	½ cup heavy cream
⅓ cup light corn syrup	1 teaspoon vanilla extract
3 tablespoons butter, cut into chunks	Pinch of salt

1. Combine the brown sugar, corn syrup, and butter in a heavy saucepan. Bring to a boil over medium heat, stirring with a wooden spoon until the sugar is dissolved and the butter is melted.

2. Increase the heat to medium-high and bring to a full boil. Boil for 1 minute without stirring, swirling the pan from side to side and rotating it back and forth to keep the sugar from scorching.

3. Remove the pan from the heat. Carefully add the cream, vanilla, and salt, stirring until smooth. Decrease the heat to medium and heat the sauce for about 30 seconds, until cream is just heated through; do not boil. Remove from the heat.

4. Serve at once or cool completely, cover, and refrigerate for up to 1 week. The sauce will thicken as it cools, and it will need to be warmed before using.

Caramel Sauce

Caramel sauce is similar to butterscotch sauce, but the sugar is more fully caramelized, giving the sauce a distinctive flavor. Before starting to prepare the recipe, have all utensils and ingredients ready to use at the stove. You don't want to be distracted because the sugar can burn, which will ruin the sauce. Serve the sauce hot or cold.

Makes 1 cup

1 cup sugar
⅓ cup water
1 teaspoon apple cider vinegar
½ cup heavy cream, warmed
1 teaspoon vanilla extract

Pinch of salt
2 tablespoons butter, at room temperature and cut into chunks

1. Combine the sugar, water, and vinegar in a tall heavy saucepan over medium-high heat. Bring the mixture to a boil, swirling and tipping the pan occasionally or stirring with a wooden spoon until the sugar dissolves. Using a pastry brush dipped in a cup of water, brush down any sugar crystals that form on the inner walls of the pan. Once the sugar mixture boils, decrease the heat to medium and cook, tipping and swirling the pan occasionally, until the sugar mixture turns a rich golden brown; this should take 8 to 10 minutes. Watch carefully so the sugar doesn't burn.

2. Remove the pan from the heat and carefully pour in the warm cream, all at once. Be very careful because the hot sugar mixture will bubble up and foam as you stir. Add the vanilla and salt. Stir until the caramel sauce is smooth and has stopped bubbling. Sprinkle the butter pieces over the sauce and stir until melted and combined. Cool for 5 to 10 minutes.

3. Pour the caramel sauce into a glass or ceramic bowl. Cover and refrigerate for 25 to 30 minutes to cool. It will keep well in the refrigerator. If the sauce thickens too much, microwave it for a minute, or set the bowl in a pan of simmering water until it is warm.

Hot Fudge Sauce

If you are making sundaes with this sauce, figure that 1½ cups will be enough for six sundaes, or ¼ cup each. This sauce is the perfect topping for a brownie sundae, made with warm brownies, vanilla or chocolate ice cream, and whipped cream. Oh, and don't forget the cherry.

Makes 1½ cups

6 ounces dark or bittersweet chocolate, cut into chunks	6 tablespoons heavy cream or half-and-half
4 tablespoons butter	¼ cup light corn syrup
½ cup sugar	Pinch of salt
¼ cup boiling water	1 teaspoon vanilla extract

1. Melt the chocolate and butter in a small heavy saucepan. Stir in the sugar, boiling water, cream, corn syrup, and salt. Using a wooden spoon, stir over medium-low heat until smooth. Continue heating slowly and stirring, until the mixture starts to boil. Reduce the heat so that the sauce cooks at a low boil. Stir occasionally for about 5 minutes, until the sauce thickens and becomes glossy. Do not overcook; if you leave the sauce over the heat for too long, it will become fudge.

2. Remove from the heat and add the vanilla. Pour into a small heatproof bowl or pitcher. Serve hot or warm. The sauce will become chewy when spooned over ice cream. To reheat the sauce, put it in a heatproof bowl and set the bowl in a pan of hot water; stir until heated through. Or microwave for a few seconds. Leftovers can be covered and stored in the refrigerator for up to a 1 week.

Strawberry Sauce

Strawberry sauce is wonderful on ice cream, waffles, or crepes. Folded into whipped cream, it becomes an instant dessert: Strawberry Fool. The sugar draws the juices out of the fruit and creates the sauce.

Makes a scant 4 cups

1 *pound fresh strawberries, hulled and finely chopped*
¼ *cup sugar*

Combine the strawberries and sugar in a bowl and let stand for at least 30 minutes, up to 2 hours. Refrigerate for up to 3 days.

A Little Ice Cream History

SOME SCHOLARS CREDIT THE first frozen dessert to Emperor Nero of Rome. Nero sent slaves into the mountains to retrieve snow, which he had mixed with nectar, fruit pulp, and honey. Other scholars believe Marco Polo brought back to Europe recipes for water ices that were said to be used in Asia for thousands of years.

Ice cream has been popular in America since the creation of the country. George Washington spent about $200 — a princely sum in those days — on ice cream in the summer of 1790, and Thomas Jefferson is credited with bringing "French-style" ice cream made with egg yolks to the United States. Dolley Madison, wife of James, popularized ice cream by serving it frequently at the White House. The ready availability of ice and the invention, in 1846, of a home-size, hand-cranked ice cream maker turned ice cream into a summer tradition.

Warm Chocolate Sauce

Simpler to make than Hot Fudge Sauce (page 385), it serves the same purpose when spooned over ice cream.

Makes about 1½ cups

....

    8 *ounces semisweet chocolate,*
         chopped
    1 *cup whipping cream*
    ½ *teaspoon instant coffee powder or*
         powdered espresso (optional)

....

1. In a heavy saucepan over low heat or in a double boiler set over simmering water, combine the chocolate, cream, and instant coffee (if using). Stir until the chocolate is melted and the sauce is smooth.

2. Remove from the heat and serve at once, or hold in the refrigerator for up to 1 week and reheat before serving. If the sauce is too stiff, stir in a little milk or brewed coffee to thin it.

METRIC CONVERSIONS

— ❀ —

Unless you have finely calibrated measuring equipment, conversions between U.S. and metric measurements will be somewhat inexact. It's important to convert the measurements for all of the ingredients in a recipe to maintain the same proportions as the original.

GENERAL FORMULA FOR METRIC CONVERSION

Ounces to grams	multiply ounces by 28.35
Grams to ounces	multiply grams by 0.035
Pounds to grams	multiply pounds by 453.5
Pounds to kilograms	multiply pounds by 0.45
Cups to liters	multiply cups by 0.24
Fahrenheit to Celsius	subtract 32 from Fahrenheit temperature, multiply by 5, then divide by 9
Celsius to Fahrenheit	multiply Celsius temperature by 9, divide by 5, then add 32

APPROXIMATE EQUIVALENTS BY VOLUME

U.S.	Metric
1 teaspoon	5 millileters
1 tablespoon	15 millileters
¼ cup	60 milliliters
½ cup	120 milliliters
1 cup	230 milliliters
1¼ cups	300 milliliters
1½ cups	360 milliliters
2 cups	460 milliliters
2½ cups	600 milliliters
3 cups	700 milliliters
4 cups (1 quart)	0.95 liter
1.06 quarts	1 liter
4 quarts (1 gallon)	3.8 liters

APPROXIMATE EQUIVALENTS BY WEIGHT

U.S.	Metric	U.S.	Metric
¼ ounce	7 grams	0.035 ounce	1 gram
½ ounce	14 grams	1.75 ounces	50 grams
1 ounce	28 grams	3.5 ounces	100 grams
1¼ ounces	35 grams	8.75 ounces	250 grams
1½ ounces	40 grams	1.1 pounds	500 grams
2½ ounces	70 grams	2.2 pounds	1 kilogram
4 ounces	112 grams		
5 ounces	140 grams		
8 ounces	228 grams		
10 ounces	280 grams		
15 ounces	425 grams		
16 ounces (1 pound)	454 grams		

Egg Information

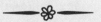

EATING EGGS or egg whites that are not completely cooked poses the possibility of salmonella food poisoning. The risk is greater for pregnant women, the elderly and the very young, and people with impaired immune systems. If you are concerned about salmonella, you can use reconstituted powdered egg whites, such as Just Whites. Pasteurized eggs, such as Davidson's, reduce the risk of salmonella food poisoning and are now available in some areas.

INDEX

Other Storey Titles You Will Enjoy

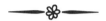

101 Perfect Chocolate Chip Cookies, by Gwen Steege.
The best melt-in-your-mouth variations of the classic favorite,
selected from thousands of contest entries.
144 pages. Paper. ISBN 978-1-58017-312-4.

500 Treasured Country Recipes, by Martha Storey & Friends.
Hundreds of recipes to stock your pantry and put together great meals,
each one with country soul.
544 pages. Paper. ISBN 978-1-58017-291-2.

The Baking Answer Book, by Lauren Chattman.
Answers every question about common and specialty ingredients,
the best equipment, and the science behind the magic of baking.
384 pages. Flexibind. ISBN 978-1-60342-439-4.

Cookie Craft, by Valerie Peterson & Janice Fryer.
Clear instruction, practical methods, and all the tips and
tricks for beautifully decorated special occasion cookies.
168 pages. Hardcover. ISBN 978-1-58017-694-1.

Ghoulish Goodies, by Sharon Bowers.
A colorful collection of creepy treats for celebrating
Halloween or any frightful occasion.
160 pages. Paper. ISBN 978-1-60342-146-1.

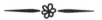

These and other books from Storey Publishing are available
wherever quality books are sold or by calling 1-800-441-5700.
Visit us at *www.storey.com*.